THE
A-E-I-O-U
OF
LEADERSHIP
AND Y IT MATTERS

A PRACTICAL GUIDE FOR
PRACTITIONERS, *NOT POSERS!*

JAMES R. DELUNG, PH.D.

ISBN: 979-8-89079-439-0 (hardcover)
ISBN: 979-8-89079-440-6 (paperback)
ISBN: 979-8-89079-441-3 (ebook)

Editor - Laura Fry, Ph.D.
Title Credit - Laura Fry, Ph.D. and James R. DeLung, Ph.D.

Table of Contents

Foreword by Dr. Stephen M. Hennessy. vii

Preface: A Message to Practitioners - Must Read!. ix

PART I:
THE FOUNDATION

Chapter 1:   Why This Book Was Written. 3

Chapter 2:   The A-E-I-O-U Framework 13

Chapter 3:   The Leadership Development Crisis 26

PART II:
INTRAPERSONAL LEADERSHIP —
LEADING YOURSELF

Chapter 4:   Self-Awareness - What To Learn About
             Knowing Yourself 43

Chapter 5:   Self-Regulation - How To Master Your Reactions. . .53

Chapter 6:   Values Clarity - The North Star We Follow 61

Chapter 7:   Purpose-Driven Leadership - Why We Lead. 67

Chapter 8:   Reflection - The Practice We Can't Skip. 72

PART III:
INTERPERSONAL LEADERSHIP —
LEADING INDIVIDUALS

Chapter 9:   One-on-One Influence - How We Connect
             and Inspire 79
Chapter 10: Coaching vs. Managing - When We Use Which. . .86
Chapter 11: Difficult Conversations - A Framework for
             Hard Conversations .93
Chapter 12: Motivation - Discover What Really
             Drives People 101
Chapter 13: Feedback That Works - An Approach to Growth
             Conversations. 108

PART IV:
TEAM LEADERSHIP — LEADING GROUPS

Chapter 14: Team Dynamics - What Is Observed in
             High-Performing Teams 119
Chapter 15: Psychological Safety - How We Create Trust 127
Chapter 16: Productive Conflict - Why We Embrace
             Disagreement 134
Chapter 17: Delegation Done Right - Your System for
             Empowerment 146
Chapter 18: Performance Culture - How We
             Build Excellence. 157

PART V:
ORGANIZATIONAL LEADERSHIP —
LEADING SYSTEMS

Chapter 19: Vision and Strategy - Your Approach to
             Direction Setting 171
Chapter 20: Culture Change - How We Transform
             Organizations. 183

Chapter 21: Systems Thinking - The Lens We Use for
Complex Problems 196

Chapter 22: Change Management - A Methodology
That Actually Works. 208

Chapter 23: Ethical Leadership - The Standards You
Won't Compromise. 220

PART VI: EXTERNAL LEADERSHIP — LEADING STAKEHOLDERS

Chapter 24: Customer Leadership - How We Create Value . . .235

Chapter 25: Stakeholder Management - A Relationship
Strategy 246

Chapter 26: Crisis Leadership - What We Do When
Everything Falls Apart. 259

PART VII: LEGACY LEADERSHIP — WHAT YOU LEAVE BEHIND

Chapter 27: Developing Others - How To Multiply
Your Impact 275

Chapter 28: Building Leadership Systems - Your Approach
to Scale 287

Chapter 29: Leadership Legacy - The Story You Want
to Leave 300

APPENDICES

Appendix A: A-E-I-O-U Assessment Tools To Use. 315

Appendix B: A 90-Day Implementation Guide 325

Appendix C: Recommended Resources 336

About the Author. 347

References 349

Foreword by
Dr. Stephen M. Hennessy

In my professional life of 55 years of combined private, public, and University experience, I have had countless opportunities not only to exercise leadership in small and large organizations but to develop and teach many leadership courses in my career. During this time, I had the opportunity to meet and work for years with the author, Dr. Jim DeLung, and watched as his abilities and career experience developed and grew in the 4,000 person Southwestern public safety organization in which we both worked. He became a highly respected and competent leader in that organization. He later went on to bring his vast and continuing leadership experience to a state licensing bureau that worked with various organizations throughout the entire United States. As his reputation grew, he became highly sought after for his organizational development, teaching and mentoring skills throughout North America.

During these past years, I closely followed the author's research and career accomplishments and was more than pleased that he chose to put his vast experience and knowledge into this pragmatic, easy to understand book. He takes the countless theories of leadership and leadership development to a whole new level. His clear and direct conversational writing style enables the reader to move easily from theory to proactive actions that increase one's ability to lead. He strikes an important balance between the theories and practical leadership skills.

For years, many leadership writing styles seemed to be predominately academic or relatively complex or even mundane. Dr. DeLung, however, combines the many theories of leadership and moves them from the theory phase into the "hands-on" phase which involves exercising daily leadership skills. It is fascinating and important to note that no matter what mission and skill set required of any profession, effective leadership involves working with people and organizations to accomplish whatever their mission may be.

The author brings with him countless years of leadership experience, not only in exercising effective leadership but how to combine a leaders knowledge base of leadership theory into the "how to make it happen" phase. He moves the reader step by step through the science of leadership and then how to apply those theories to the art of leading people. He writes in a very easy to understand, pragmatic style. Of the numerous books on leadership I have read over the years, I truly believe this book should be on the top of every leader's desk. As executives and leaders, we all need every tool we can lay our hands on in exercising the role of leadership, especially as this complex world we live in becomes more challenging.

I wish you an extremely successful leadership career. Follow the journey that Dr. DeLung takes you on and it will happen.

Stephen M. Hennessy, Ed.D.
Professor Emeritus St. Cloud State University, Minnesota
Former Special Agent FBI
Assistant Superintendent,
Minnesota Bureau of Criminal Apprehension
Training Advisor, Phoenix, Arizona Police Department

Preface: A Message to Practitioners - Must Read!

From frontline supervisors to CEOs, military and police commanders to nonprofit directors, startup founders to academic institution executives ... I've worked with and for leaders at every level during twenty-plus years of service. I've seen what works and what doesn't, watched brilliant people fail as leaders and average people become extraordinary leaders. I've studied the research, obtained the degrees, tested the theories, and refined the practices in the real world. And this book represents everything I've learned about what actually makes leaders effective.

I didn't write this for people who want to feel good about leadership. I wrote it for people who want to get good and be good at leadership. The difference matters more than most people realize.

Why This Book Exists

I decided to write a book that I wished I had when I started my leadership journey. Bookstores are filled with inspiring stories about transformational leaders and profound insights into authentic leadership. Conference stages feature charismatic speakers sharing breakthrough moments and motivational messages. Yet, over the years, I've been consistently frustrated by the gap between leadership theory and leadership practice.

When I worked with real leaders facing real challenges in real organizations, I discovered that:

1. Inspiration without instruction is useless.
2. Good intentions without practical tools create frustration, not results.
3. Awareness without application changes nothing.

This book is a comprehensive guide that combines rigorous research with practical application. It addresses the full scope of leadership challenges, and provides specific tools we - you and I as leaders - can use immediately to improve our leadership effectiveness.

I can't make you a better leader by writing about leadership any more than I can make you a better athlete by writing about sports. But, like a good coach, I can provide guidance, structure, and accountability to help you think better and get your progress to be actionable.

A Commitment to You

By the time you finish this book and complete the included exercises, you will have:

- A clear understanding of your current leadership strengths and development priorities.
- Specific tools for leading yourself, individuals, teams, organizations, and external customers, clients, and stakeholders.
- A systematic approach to continuous leadership improvement.
- Practical strategies for handling the most common leadership challenges.
- A personal leadership philosophy that guides your decisions and actions.

What remains? You must do the work.

Leadership is a practice, not a theory. It's developed through application, not just understanding.

How To Best Use This Book

This book is organized as a complete leadership development program spanning seven parts and twenty-nine chapters:

- Each part addresses a different domain of leadership responsibility.
- Each chapter includes research-based insights, practical tools, list, acronyms, and specific exercises.
- Use of acronyms, rhymes, and poetic alliteration are employed to assist you - the leader reader - with remembering the material. If you cannot recall the concepts, you will not use them!

The concepts build on each other, and the exercises are cumulative. I recommend:

- reading this book sequentially rather than jumping around.
- treating this as a six-month development program rather than a weekend read.
- scheduling dedicated time for the exercises.
- seeking feedback from others or a partner and reading with a colleague for accountability.
- tracking your progress and adjusting your approach based on feedback and results.

A Note About This Approach

Leadership is both an art and a science, and leadership development never ends… that's my belief.

❖ The science and research provide frameworks, tools, and evidence-based practices.
❖ The art involves adapting these approaches to your unique personality, context, and challenges. I've tried to provide both the science and guidance for the art.

The challenges you face will evolve. The people you lead will change. The context in which you operate will shift. Your leadership must continue growing throughout your lifetime. This book provides a foundation, not the final destination.

My Challenge to You

Before you continue, before you turn to the next page - I encourage you to evaluate your next step. If you are:

- Interested in learning about leadership ... this may not be the book for you. If you're merely interested in leadership, I respect that choice, but I recommend finding a different book.
- Wanting to develop leadership capabilities ... keep reading. The next question will determine whether this book assists you or just takes up more space on your shelf with your other leadership books.
- Committed to the process ... let's get going! If you're committed to doing the hard work of leadership development, I am excited to help guide you through that process.

This is a book for leadership practitioners, not posers!

Do I have your attention now? Let's begin........

PART I
THE FOUNDATION

CHAPTER 1

Why This Book Was Written

The Crisis

Over my twenty-plus years of working with leaders across every industry and organizational level, I've observed a troubling pattern. Despite enormous investments in leadership development, companies spend billions of dollars annually on leadership training. According to recent estimates, organizational performance remains stubbornly mediocre, employee engagement continues to hover around 30%, and leadership failures dominate business headlines.

I've watched brilliant executives derail their careers through preventable mistakes. I've seen well-intentioned managers destroy team morale through poor communication. I've observed organizations with excellent strategies fail due to inadequate execution. I've witnessed leaders with strong technical skills struggle to inspire and motivate others. I have also seen many leaders thrive. For the rare that succeed, what makes the difference?

The problem isn't lack of good intentions or intelligence. Most of the leaders I've worked with are smart, hardworking people who genuinely want to be effective. The problem is that leadership development has become disconnected from leadership practice. This book was created as a guide focused on inspiration rather than instruction, on awareness rather than behavior change, and on application rather than theory.

The Knowing-Doing Gap

In my consulting, I regularly encounter what Pfeffer and Sutton (2000) called the "knowing-doing gap" - the chasm between what people know about leadership and what they do as leaders. Countless executives can articulate sophisticated leadership philosophies, but struggle to give effective feedback to their direct reports. Managers understand the importance of delegation, but micromanage their teams. Leaders preach the value of mental diversity and preventing groupthink, but suppress dissent and hire people who act like themselves.

This gap isn't due to lack of knowledge. Most leaders have read extensively about leadership. They've attended multiple training programs and classes. They can quote research about emotional intelligence, psychological safety, and transformational leadership. But they haven't translated this knowledge into applied/changed behavior. There are several factors that contribute to this problem:

The Inspiration Trap: Much leadership development focuses on inspiring people to want to be better leaders rather than teaching them how to become better leaders. Inspiration feels good but fades quickly. Skill development is harder but lasts longer.

The Complexity Curse: Many leadership models are so complex that they're impossible to remember and apply in real situations. When you're dealing with a performance problem or managing a conflict, you need simple, practical tools, not elaborate theoretical frameworks.

The Context Problem: Most leadership development uses generic approaches that don't account for the specific challenges leaders face in their unique roles, industries, and organizational cultures. What works for a tech startup CEO may not work for a hospital administrator or military officer.

The Practice Gap: Leadership development often occurs in classroom settings that bear little resemblance to the messy, ambiguous, high-pressure situations where leadership is required. People learn concepts in artificial environments and struggle to apply them in real-world contexts.

My Definition of Leadership

"Leadership is the ability to adapt your approach to meet the development needs of each individual while achieving team and organizational objectives in ways that sustain and enhance both job satisfaction and performance over time."

In simpler terms: The most effective leaders have the ability to change their style to meet the needs of the follower while completing the mission and increasing job satisfaction and performance. Leadership is about **them**, not you!

My definition of leadership is best explained by the following key elements:

Adaptive Approach

- *Idea:* Effective leaders modify their communication style, decision-making processes, and development strategies based on each person's competence, commitment, and growth needs rather than using one-size-fits-all methods.
- *Application:* Change your style to meet the person, mission, AND (not or) context.

Individual Development Focus

- *Idea:* A leader recognizes that sustainable results come through, rather than despite, people.
- *Application:* True leadership prioritizes developing each person's capabilities and potential.

Mission Achievement

- *Idea:* Good intentions, without results, are not leadership.
- *Application:* Leadership must deliver results and accomplish organizational objectives.

Dual Outcome Responsibility

- *Idea:* Leaders are accountable for both immediate performance outcomes and the long-term satisfaction and engagement of the people who produce those outcomes.
- *Application:* Performance and satisfaction is measured over time, by evaluating the sustainability of what changed.

Fundamentally, leadership requires four things:

- **Adaptability** - changing your approach to meet each person's needs
- **Mission completion** - achieving the results your organization requires
- **People satisfaction** - keeping employees engaged and productive
- **Performance enhancement** - continuously improving individual and team effectiveness

Great leaders excel at all four simultaneously rather than sacrificing one for the others.

Leadership Philosophy

Through my years of research and practice, I've developed several core beliefs about leadership that inform everything in this book:

Leadership is Learnable: While people have different starting points based on personality and experience, the skills that make leaders effective can be developed through deliberate practice. I've seen introverts become inspiring communicators, analytical thinkers develop strong emotional intelligence, and conflict-averse people learn to manage difficult conversations effectively.

Leadership is Contextual: There's no one-size-fits-all approach to leadership. Effective leaders adapt their style to the situation, the people they're leading, and the challenges they're facing. My framework provides principles that apply across contexts while allowing for individual adaptation.

Leadership is About Results: Ultimately, leadership is judged by outcomes, not intentions. Good leaders create positive results for their organizations, their teams, and the people they serve. Everything else is secondary.

Leadership is a Practice: Like medicine, law, or engineering, leadership is a professional practice that requires continuous learning, skill development, and ethical behavior. It's not just about natural talent or personality; it's about competence developed through study and application.

Leadership is Personal: While leadership involves working with others, it starts with self-leadership. You can't effectively lead others if you can't lead yourself. Personal development isn't separate from leadership development; it's the foundation of it.

The A-E-I-O-U Solution

The framework presented in this book emerged from my frustration with existing leadership development approaches. I wanted to create something that was:

- Comprehensive enough to address the full scope of leadership challenges
- Simple enough to remember and apply under pressure
- Practical enough to use in real situations with real people
- Flexible enough to adapt to different contexts and leadership styles
- Evidence-based enough to be credible and effective

The A-E-I-O-U framework meets all these criteria. Each letter represents a critical leadership capability:

Application: The ability to translate knowledge into action, insights into behaviors, and intentions into results. This addresses the knowing-doing gap that prevents most leadership development from creating lasting change.

Execution: The discipline to complete important initiatives despite competing priorities, resource constraints, and changing circumstances. This addresses the completion gap that prevents leaders from delivering consistent results.

Implementation: The skill to create systems, processes, and structures that enable sustainable performance beyond individual effort. This addresses the scalability gap that prevents leadership effectiveness from spreading throughout organizations.

Ownership: The courage to take full responsibility for outcomes, both positive and negative. This addresses the accountability gap that prevents leaders from learning from failures and building trust with others.

Unity: The ability to create alignment among diverse stakeholders toward shared objectives. This addresses the coordination gap that prevents teams and organizations from working effectively together.

I've formally taught and informally tested this framework with leaders across multiple industries and organizational levels. I've refined it based on feedback, results, and ongoing research. I am confident it can work for you because I've seen it work repeatedly in the most challenging leadership situations.

Organized Leadership Thinking

This book reflects my belief that leadership operates across five interconnected domains using multiple areas of scholarship (as shown in the graphic at the end of this chapter):

Intrapersonal Leadership – Leading Yourself (Psychology): The foundation of all leadership effectiveness is the ability to lead yourself. This includes self-awareness, emotional regulation, values clarity, and personal development. Without these capabilities, attempts to lead others will be inconsistent and ineffective.

Interpersonal Leadership – Leading Individuals (Social Psychology): Most leadership happens in one-on-one relationships. The ability to influence, coach, motivate, and collaborate with individuals is essential for leadership success at any level.

Group and Team Leadership (Sociology): Leading groups requires different skills than leading individuals. Team dynamics, conflict management, and collective performance create unique challenges that require specific capabilities.

Organizational Leadership (Anthropology): Leading at scale requires understanding systems, culture, and change processes.

Organizational leaders must work through others to create alignment and achieve results across multiple levels and functions.

External Leadership – Leading Customers, Clients, and Stakeholders (Business/Public Administration and Political Science): Increasingly, leaders must influence people outside their direct authority, including customers, partners, tax-paying communities, and other stakeholders. This requires different approaches than internal leadership.

Each domain builds on the previous ones, but all five are interconnected and utilized differently throughout your career and authority level. A weakness in any domain can limit overall leadership effectiveness, regardless of your strengths in other areas.

Commitment to Evidence

I want to help develop researchers as well as practitioners. Every concept in this book is supported by peer-reviewed research, and I've included extensive references for readers who want to explore the academic foundations of my recommendations. But I've also tested every concept in real-world situations with real leaders facing genuine challenges.

I believe the best leadership development combines rigorous research with practical application. Theory without practice is academic. Practice without theory is random. Both together create systematic approaches to leadership development and improvement.

Expectations of You

I can't make you a better leader by writing about leadership. I can provide frameworks, tools, and guidance, but you must do the actual work of behavior change and skill development. This requires several commitments from you:

Honest Self-Assessment/Efficacy: You must be willing to look objectively at your current leadership effectiveness, including areas where you're not performing well. Self-deception is the enemy of development.

Sustained Effort: Leadership development takes time and practice. You must be willing to work on these skills consistently over months and years, not just days and weeks.

Feedback Seeking: You must actively solicit input from others about your leadership effectiveness. Your self-perception may not match others' experiences of your leadership.

Experimentation: You must be willing to try new approaches, even when they feel uncomfortable or unnatural. Growth requires stepping outside your comfort zone.

Patience: Leadership development is a long-term process. You must be willing to invest effort now for results that may not be apparent for weeks or months.

If you're not willing to make these commitments, this book won't help you. But if you are, I believe it can significantly accelerate your leadership development and effectiveness.

What Is Promised in Return

If you do the work outlined in this book, I believe you can:

- Develop greater self-awareness and emotional regulation
- Improve your ability to influence and motivate others
- Build stronger, more effective teams
- Create positive organizational change
- Lead with greater confidence and authenticity
- Achieve better results through others
- Build a leadership legacy you're proud of for generations

These aren't just my opinions; they're outcomes I've observed repeat-edly when leaders systematically apply the principles and practices I describe.

I am excited to share this journey with you. Leadership development is challenging work, but it's also some of the most rewarding work you can do. The impact you have on others, the results you create, and the legacy you build will extend far beyond your individual career.

Now, let's get started!

THE LEADERSHIP TARGET

Leading Customers, Clients, & Stakeholders

Leading Organizations

Leading Groups & Teams

Leading Individuals

YOU

Psychology

Social Psychology

Sociology

Anthropology

Business/Public Administration & Political Science

CHAPTER 2

The A-E-I-O-U Framework

Beyond a Simple Acronym

When I first developed the A-E-I-O-U framework, colleagues warned me that it might seem silly or gimmicky. "Leadership is complex. You can't reduce it to five letters." I understood their concern, but I had learned something important from my years of working with leaders: complexity kills application, implementation, and execution.

I have seen brilliant executives struggle to remember and apply elaborate leadership models under pressure. I had seen comprehensive frameworks collect dust on bookshelves because they were too cumbersome to use in real situations. I had observed that the most effective leaders often relied on simple principles that they could access quickly and apply consistently.

The A-E-I-O-U framework isn't simple because leadership is simple; it's simple because simplicity works. Each letter represents a complex set of capabilities, but the framework itself is designed to be memorable and usable when you're in the middle of challenging leadership situations.

I've informally and formally used this framework with leaders across every industry and organizational level, and now I am releasing it in this book. I've tested it in crisis situations, growth phases, transformation efforts, and steady-state operations. I've adapted it to different cultures, leadership styles, and organizational contexts. The framework has proven to be both robust and flexible yet sophisticated enough to guide complex leadership challenges while simple enough to remember and apply under pressure.

A - Application: The Bridge Between Knowing and Doing

The first element of my framework addresses what I consider the most fundamental challenge in leadership development: the gap between knowledge and action. I've worked with countless leaders who could articulate sophisticated theories about emotional intelligence, strategic thinking, and change management but struggled to demonstrate these capabilities in their daily leadership practice.

Application is the systematic process of translating insights into actions, concepts into behaviors, and intentions into results. It's the difference between being a student of leadership and being a practitioner of leadership.

I've identified four components of strong application capability:

Behavioral Commitment: Effective application requires translating abstract concepts into specific, observable behaviors. For example, "emotional intelligence" must become "when I feel myself getting defensive in a meeting, I take a deep breath, ask a clarifying question, and listen to the response before reacting." Vague concepts don't drive behavior change; your specific behavioral commitments do.

Practice: New behaviors require deliberate practice opportunities. I've learned that leaders who simply intend to apply new concepts rarely follow through consistently. Leaders who create specific plans for when, where, and how they'll practice new behaviors are significantly more likely to develop lasting capabilities.

Implementation Intentions: Research by Gollwitzer (1999) demonstrated that people who create "if-then" plans are much more likely to follow through on behavioral commitments than those who rely on general intentions. I help leaders create implementation intentions like "If I find myself interrupting someone in a meeting, then I will immediately apologize and ask them to continue."

Progress Tracking: Application requires feedback about whether new behaviors are producing better results. I've found that leaders who systematically track their application of new concepts develop capabilities much faster than those who rely on general impressions of their progress.

The leaders I work with who excel at application share several characteristics: they're willing to start small and build gradually, they actively seek opportunities to practice new skills, they're comfortable with initial awkwardness as they develop new capabilities, and they systematically seek feedback about their progress.

E - Execution: The Discipline of Completion

Execution is the most undervalued leadership capability. Organizations are filled with people who can create compelling visions, develop sophisticated strategies, and inspire others with their ideas. But they struggle to consistently deliver results over time. They start strong but finish weak. They excel at launching initiatives but struggle to complete them successfully.

I've studied numerous failed projects, stalled initiatives, and abandoned transformations. In most cases, the original ideas were sound, the plans were reasonable, and the resources were adequate. What was missing was disciplined execution, as a systematic follow-through was required to turn intentions into results.

Execution involves several key capabilities:

Goal Clarity: Effective execution requires crystal-clear objectives that specify not just what will be accomplished but when, by whom, and to what standard. I've learned that vague goals produce vague results, while specific goals drive specific actions.

Milestone Management: Large initiatives must be broken down into smaller, manageable milestones with clear deliverables and deadlines. I help leaders create milestone schedules that provide regular opportunities to assess progress, identify problems, and make adjustments.

Obstacle Anticipation: Effective execution requires anticipating potential barriers and developing contingency plans before problems occur. I've found that leaders who proactively identify and address obstacles are much more likely to complete initiatives successfully than those who simply react to problems as they arise.

Progress Monitoring: Execution requires systematic tracking of progress against plans, with regular reviews and adjustments as needed. I help leaders establish monitoring systems that provide early warning of problems while they can still be addressed effectively.

Accountability Systems: Sustainable execution requires clear accountability for results, not just activities. I've learned that what gets measured and reviewed gets completed, while what gets ignored gets abandoned.

The leaders I work with who excel at execution are relentlessly focused on results, comfortable with repetitive tasks, willing to address problems quickly, and skilled at maintaining momentum over extended periods.

I - Implementation: Building Systems That Scale

Implementation is perhaps the most sophisticated element of my framework. It's the difference between solving problems through individual heroics and solving them through systematic approaches that work regardless of who's involved. I've observed many leaders who are excellent at handling crises personally but poor at creating systems that prevent crises from recurring.

Implementation involves creating processes, structures, and capabilities that enable consistent performance beyond individual effort. It's about building organizational muscle memory that persists regardless of personnel changes.

I've identified several levels of implementation sophistication:

Process Documentation: The first level involves capturing tribal knowledge, which is critical information that currently exists only in certain people's heads and making it accessible to others through procedures, checklists, and guidelines.

System Integration: The second level involves connecting individual processes into seamless workflows that eliminate gaps, redundancies, and handoff problems. This requires understanding how different parts of the organization interact and designing interfaces that support smooth coordination.

Capability Building: The third level involves developing people's skills and knowledge systematically so they can execute processes effectively. This goes beyond training to include coaching, mentoring, and continuous development.

Cultural Embedding: The highest level involves making systematic approaches part of "how we do things around here" as cultural norms that guide behavior even when no one is watching.

Implementation requires several specific skills:

- Systems thinking - the ability to see how parts connect to wholes
- Process design - the ability to create efficient workflows
- Change management - the ability to help people adopt new approaches
- Patience - the willingness to invest upfront effort for long-term benefits

O - Ownership: Taking Full Responsibility

I've observed that ownership is what most clearly distinguishes leaders from managers. Managers tend to focus on their specific responsibilities and assume someone else will handle everything else. Leaders take responsibility for overall outcomes, even when they don't have direct control over all the factors that influence those outcomes.

Ownership involves both psychological and behavioral components:

Psychological Ownership: This is the internal commitment to taking responsibility for results, not just activities. Leaders with a strong ownership mentality focus on outcomes rather than outputs, results rather than efforts, and solutions rather than excuses.

Behavioral Ownership: This involves specific actions that demonstrate responsibility: admitting mistakes quickly, seeking solutions rather than assigning blame, taking initiative to address problems even when they're not technically your responsibility, and holding others accountable for their commitments.

I've identified several levels of ownership:

Task Ownership: Taking responsibility for completing assigned work to acceptable standards and timelines.

Process Ownership: Taking responsibility for entire workflows and outcomes, not just individual tasks.

Relationship Ownership: Taking responsibility for the quality of working relationships and addressing conflicts constructively.

Organizational Ownership: Taking responsibility for overall organizational success, even beyond your specific area of authority.

Stakeholder Ownership: Taking responsibility for creating value for all stakeholders, including employees, customers, and communities.

Leaders who demonstrate strong ownership create cultures of accountability, build trust through their reliability, solve problems rather than escalate them, and inspire others to take responsibility for their own performance.

U - Unity: Creating Alignment That Works

The final element of my framework addresses one of the most complex challenges leaders face: creating alignment among diverse stakeholders who may have different priorities, perspectives, and interests. I've worked with many organizations where people were working hard but not working together, where individual excellence didn't translate into collective effectiveness.

Unity isn't about eliminating disagreement or forcing consensus. It's about creating alignment around shared objectives while respecting different viewpoints and approaches. Effective unity balances individual autonomy with collective coordination.

I've identified four dimensions of unity:

Directional Unity: Everyone understands and commits to shared objectives, even if they have different ideas about how to achieve them.

Operational Unity: People understand how their work connects to others' work and coordinate their efforts accordingly.

Cultural Unity: Shared values and norms guide behavior and decision-making across the organization.

Temporal Unity: Activities are properly sequenced and timed to support rather than interfere with each other.

Creating unity requires several specific capabilities:

- Communication - the ability to share information clearly and persuasively
- Facilitation - the ability to help groups work through differences constructively
- Negotiation (the ability to find mutually acceptable solutions to competing interests
- Systems thinking (the ability to understand how individual actions affect overall performance

Y - You: The Center of Leadership

In my leadership work, one truth emerges again and again: the most overlooked, yet most decisive, factor in any leadership equation is YOU. Your beliefs, your behaviors, your blind spots. Your emotional state, energy, habits, and presence. You are not outside the system you lead; you are its gravitational center.

Leadership is deeply personal before it is organizational. Initiatives succeed or stall not just because of strategy or execution, but because of the person driving them. When leaders grow, their teams grow. When leaders stagnate, their organizations follow.

I often remind my clients: you can't scale what you haven't internalized. If you don't embody the very principles you're asking others to commit to (application, execution, implementation, ownership, and unity), your credibility suffers, and alignment erodes.

I've identified four core elements of You-centered leadership:

Self-Awareness/Efficacy: Great leaders begin by understanding how they see the world, because that lens shapes every decision, interaction, and reaction. I've found that leaders who cultivate ongoing self-awareness are far better equipped to handle complexity and conflict than those who operate on assumption and autopilot.
This involves identifying personal biases, recognizing emotional triggers, understanding strengths and limitations, and accepting feedback not as criticism but as calibration. Leaders who know themselves lead themselves and others with far greater integrity.

Emotional Intelligence: Pressure doesn't create character; it reveals and amplifies it. Leaders who cannot regulate their internal state will inadvertently leak that state into the team culture.
I coach leaders to develop the ability to notice and shift their emotional state in real time. That includes stress management, breath control, mental framing, and the ability to pause before reacting. In environments where stakes are high, the most powerful signal a leader can send is a calm, focused presence.

Intentional Identity: Based on a belief that true leaders stand up and stand out when times are difficult, I ask leaders, "Who do you intend to be when it's hard to lead?" Without a clearly defined leadership identity, especially one rooted in values and vision, leaders default to old patterns under pressure. If leadership were easy, everyone would do it!

I help clients articulate and internalize a personal leadership identity: a conscious declaration of the kind of leader they aspire to be, anchored in specific behaviors. This becomes their internal compass when circumstances get messy and clarity gets clouded.

Inner Alignment: Leadership isn't about performing externally; it's about aligning internally. Leaders must live what they preach. If you demand ownership from others but avoid hard conversations yourself, the culture sees the contradiction. If you ask for execution but overcommit and under-deliver, trust erodes.

I've seen that when leaders integrate the other vowels (Application, Execution, Implementation, Ownership, Unity) into their daily life, they don't need to "drive culture." They become the culture, and others naturally follow.

Leaders who embody "you" as a core leadership discipline are not just technically competent; they are personally congruent. They model integrity, signal trustworthiness, and build followership through authenticity and consistency. The most powerful leadership tool you will ever have is YOU!

The Integration Challenge

While I've described each element of the framework separately, they're highly interconnected in practice. Strong application capabilities enable better execution by ensuring that plans are translated into action. Effective execution creates the foundation for successful implementation by demonstrating that initiatives can be completed successfully. Solid implementation provides the systems and processes that make ownership possible by clarifying roles and accountabilities. Clear ownership creates the foundation for unity by ensuring that someone is responsible for coordinating different efforts.

The leaders I work with who are most effective have developed capabilities in all five areas. They can translate insights into actions (application), complete important initiatives (execution), build sustainable systems (implementation), take full responsibility for results (ownership), and create alignment among diverse stakeholders (unity).

Adapting the Framework to Your Context

One of the strengths of the A-E-I-O-U framework is its adaptability. While the core elements remain constant, how you apply them will depend on your specific role, organization, and challenges. A startup founder will emphasize different aspects than a corporate executive. A military leader will apply the framework differently from a nonprofit director.

I encourage you to use the framework as a diagnostic tool for assessing your current capabilities and identifying development priorities. You may be strong in some areas and weak in others. Focus your development efforts on the areas that will have the greatest impact on your leadership effectiveness.

I also encourage you to adapt the specific tools and techniques I provide to fit your leadership style and organizational culture. The principles are universal, but the applications should be personal.

Your Framework Assessment

Before moving forward, complete this assessment to identify your current strengths and development opportunities within the A-E-I-O-U framework. For greater self-awareness/efficacy development, you can have a co-worker score as well:

Application Assessment (Rate yourself 1-10 on each):

- I consistently translate leadership concepts I learn into specific behavioral changes
- I create deliberate practice opportunities for developing new leadership skills

- I track my progress in applying new leadership behaviors
- Others would say I "walk the talk" when it comes to leadership principles

Execution Assessment (Rate yourself 1-10 on each):

- I consistently complete important initiatives on time and within budget
- I break large projects into manageable milestones with clear deadlines
- I proactively identify and address obstacles before they derail projects
- I maintain momentum and focus even when projects become difficult or tedious

Implementation Assessment (Rate yourself 1-10 on each):

- I create systems and processes that prevent problems from recurring
- I build capabilities in others rather than solving everything myself
- I think systematically about how to scale successful approaches
- I invest time in creating sustainable solutions rather than quick fixes

Ownership Assessment (Rate yourself 1-10 on each):

- I take full responsibility for outcomes in my area of leadership
- I admit mistakes quickly and focus on learning from them
- I hold myself and others accountable for commitments and results
- I take the initiative to address problems even when they're not technically my responsibility

Unity Assessment (Rate yourself 1-10 on each):

- I effectively align diverse stakeholders around shared objectives
- I help groups work through disagreements constructively
- I create clear communication and coordination across different functions
- I build consensus while respecting different perspectives and approaches

Your lowest scores indicate your highest development priorities. These are the areas where focused improvement will have the greatest impact on your overall leadership effectiveness.

In the following chapters, I'll provide detailed guidance for developing capabilities in each of these areas. But first, I need to address why so much leadership development fails to create lasting change.

CHAPTER 3

The Leadership Development Crisis

The Billion Dollar Problem

Every year, organizations around the world invest billions of dollars in leadership development. They send people to prestigious programs, hire expensive consultants, and create elaborate internal training systems. Despite this massive investment, research consistently shows that most leadership development efforts fail to produce lasting improvement in leadership effectiveness.

I've had a front-row seat to this crisis. Over my combined careers, I've been involved in a myriad of leadership development initiatives across every type of organization. I've seen well-designed programs with excellent content fail to change behavior. I've watched inspiring speakers motivate audiences who return to work and continue their old patterns. I've observed expensive assessments and coaching engagements that increase self-awareness but don't improve performance.

The problem isn't a lack of good content or well-intentioned effort. The problem is that most leadership development is based on flawed assumptions that adults will change their behavior and develop new capabilities.

The Five Fatal Flaws

Through my research and experience, I've identified five fundamental flaws that prevent most leadership development from creating lasting change:

Flaw #1: The Inspiration Addiction

Most leadership development focuses on inspiring people to want to be better leaders rather than teaching them how to become better leaders. Conferences feature charismatic speakers sharing transformational stories. Books promise breakthrough insights that will change everything. Programs emphasize motivation over education.

Inspiration feels good, but it doesn't last. Research by Klayman and Ha (1987) found that inspiration-based learning creates temporary enthusiasm but rarely produces sustained behavior change. People leave development programs feeling energized and committed, but within weeks, they've reverted to their previous patterns.

I've learned that effective leadership development must go beyond inspiration to provide specific tools, systematic practice opportunities, and ongoing support for behavior change. Motivation gets you started, but skill development keeps you going.

Flaw #2: The Complexity Trap

Many leadership models are so elaborate that they're impossible to remember and apply under pressure. I've seen 360-degree assessments with forty-seven different competencies, leadership frameworks with twelve dimensions and sixty-four sub-categories, and development programs that introduce seventeen different tools and techniques.

When you're dealing with a crisis, managing a conflict, or making a difficult decision, you need simple principles you can access quickly, not comprehensive models you have to think through carefully. Complexity kills the application.

Research by Miller (1956) on cognitive processing found that people can effectively manage about seven pieces of information simultaneously. Leadership models that exceed this limit become academic exercises rather than practical tools.

I've deliberately designed the A-E-I-O-U framework to be simple enough to remember and apply under pressure while still being comprehensive enough to address the full scope of leadership challenges.

Flaw #3: The Generic Approach Problem

Most leadership development uses one-size-fits-all approaches that don't account for differences in roles, industries, organizational cultures, or individual learning styles. A program designed for corporate executives gets delivered to nonprofit managers. A framework developed for large organizations is applied to small businesses. A model created for extroverts gets used with introverts.

Effective leadership development must be adapted to specific contexts and individual needs. What works for a technology startup CEO won't work for a hospital administrator or military commander. What works for someone who's naturally outgoing won't work for someone who's more reserved.

I've learned to start with universal principles but always adapt the applications to specific situations and individual preferences.

Flaw #4: The Practice Gap

Most leadership development occurs in classroom settings that bear little resemblance to the complex, ambiguous, high-pressure situations where leadership is required. People learn concepts in artificial environments and struggle to apply them in real-world contexts.

Research by Ericsson and Pool (2016) on expert performance found that skill development requires deliberate practice in realistic conditions, not just conceptual understanding in safe environments.

Professional athletes don't just study plays; they practice them repeatedly under game-like conditions. Professional musicians don't just learn theory; they practice scales and pieces until they become automatic.

Professional leaders need the same kind of deliberate practice opportunities, but most leadership development doesn't provide them.

Flaw #5: The Follow-Through Failure

Most leadership development is front-loaded. Organizations invest heavily in initial training but provide little ongoing support for application and behavior change. People attend a program, receive some coaching, and then are expected to implement everything they've learned on their own.

Research by Goldsmith (2007) on executive development found that behavior change requires sustained effort over months and years, not days and weeks. Without ongoing support, accountability, and reinforcement, most development efforts fade quickly.

I've learned that effective leadership development must include systematic follow-through support, not just initial education.

The Research on What Actually Works

While most leadership development fails, some approaches do produce lasting improvement in leadership effectiveness. I've studied these successful programs to understand what makes them different.

Research by Avolio et al. (2009) analyzed the effectiveness of different leadership development approaches and found several factors that distinguish successful programs from unsuccessful ones:

Behavior-Focused Rather Than Awareness-Focused: Successful programs emphasize changing specific behaviors rather than just increasing self-awareness. They help people identify particular actions they need to start, stop, or modify, rather than just helping them understand their personality type or leadership style.

Practice-Based Rather Than Theory-Based: Successful programs provide multiple opportunities to practice new skills in realistic situations with feedback and coaching. They use simulations, role-playing, action learning projects, and on-the-job assignments rather than just lectures and discussions.

Sustained Rather Than Event-Based: Successful programs extend over months rather than days and include ongoing support, accountability, and reinforcement. They treat leadership development as a process rather than an event.

Customized Rather Than Generic: Successful programs adapt content and methods to specific participants, roles, and organizational contexts rather than using standard approaches for everyone.

Measurement-Based Rather Than Activity-Based: Successful programs track actual behavior change and business results rather than just participation and satisfaction. They measure outcomes, not just outputs.

An Alternative Approach

Based on this research and my own experience, I've developed an approach to leadership development that addresses the five fatal flaws:

Instruction Over Inspiration: While I want people to be motivated to improve their leadership, the primary focus is on teaching specific skills and providing practical tools. I believe competence creates confidence more reliably than inspiration creates competence.

Simplicity Over Complexity: I've designed this framework to be memorable and usable under pressure while still being comprehensive enough to address real leadership challenges. Five elements are manageable; fifty are overwhelming.

Customization Over Standardization: While these core principles are universal, I help leaders adapt the applications to their specific roles, organizations, and leadership styles. The framework provides structure, but the implementation is personal.

Practice Over Theory: Every concept I present includes specific exercises for developing the associated skills. I believe leadership is learned through doing, not just thinking or discussing.

Process Over Event: I've designed this book as a comprehensive development program that extends over months, not a quick read that you complete in a weekend. Leadership development is a marathon, not a sprint.

The Adult Learning Challenge

One of the reasons leadership development is so difficult is that it requires adult behavior change, which is inherently challenging. Unlike children, who are constantly learning new skills and forming new habits, adults have well-established patterns of behavior that have been reinforced over years or decades.

Research by Kegan and Lahey (2009) on adult development found that behavior change is particularly difficult when it conflicts with your existing identity or requires you to admit that your current approaches aren't working. Many leaders resist development because it implies criticism of their current effectiveness.

I've learned that effective adult leadership development must address several psychological factors:

Identity Protection: Adults need to feel that development enhances rather than threatens their professional identity. I frame development as building on existing strengths rather than fixing fundamental flaws.

Autonomy Preservation: Adults need to feel they have choice and control over their development process. I provide frameworks and tools, but encourage people to adapt them to their own style and situation.

Relevance Connection: Adults need to see clear connections between development activities and their real-world challenges. I use practical examples and applications rather than abstract concepts.

Progress Recognition: Adults need to see evidence that their efforts are producing results. I help people track their progress and celebrate improvements, even small ones.

Social Support: Adults learn more effectively in supportive environments where they can share experiences and learn from others. I encourage people to work through development with colleagues, mentors, or coaches.

Recent advances in neuroscience have provided important insights into how adults change their behavior patterns. Research by Duhigg (2012) on habit formation found that most adult behavior is driven by unconscious routines rather than conscious decisions.

This has important implications for leadership development. Simply deciding to be a better leader isn't enough to change deeply ingrained behavioral patterns. You must systematically work to:

Identify Current Patterns: Most people aren't aware of their automatic behaviors until they consciously observe them. Leadership development must begin with honest self-assessment of current patterns.

Understand Triggers: Every habit has a trigger that initiates the behavioral sequence. Understanding what situations, emotions, or thoughts trigger your current leadership behaviors is essential for changing them.

Practice New Responses: Developing new behavioral patterns requires deliberate practice of new responses to familiar triggers. This takes time and repetition.

Create Environmental Support: Changing habits is easier when your environment supports new behaviors rather than reinforcing old ones. This might mean changing how you structure meetings, interact with colleagues, or organize your workspace.

Build Social Accountability: Behavioral change is more likely when others are aware of your commitments and can provide feedback on your progress.

The Expertise Development Model

Another important insight from research is that developing leadership expertise follows the same patterns as developing expertise in other complex domains. Studies by Ericsson et al. (1993) found that expert performance in any field requires approximately 10,000 hours of deliberate practice over a period of at least ten years.

Deliberate practice has several characteristics that distinguish it from regular practice:

Focused Attention: Deliberate practice requires complete concentration on the specific skill being developed, not just going through the motions.

Immediate Feedback: Deliberate practice includes systematic feedback about performance, allowing for rapid correction of errors and refinement of techniques.

Progressive Challenge: Deliberate practice involves gradually increasing the difficulty of challenges to continuously stretch capabilities.

Error Correction: Deliberate practice focuses on identifying and correcting mistakes rather than just reinforcing existing capabilities.

Mental Models: Deliberate practice develops sophisticated mental models that enable expert-level performance in complex, ambiguous situations.

This research suggests that leadership development should be treated as a long-term capability-building process rather than a short-term training event. The most effective leaders I work with approach their development with the same systematic dedication that professional athletes or musicians bring to their craft.

Development Philosophy

I've developed several principles that guide this approach to leadership development:

Start Where You Are: Effective development begins with an honest assessment of current capabilities rather than wishful thinking about desired capabilities. You can't improve what you don't acknowledge. Self-awareness/efficacy is paramount to identifying your leadership baseline.

Focus on Behavior: Leadership is ultimately about behavior, not knowledge or intentions. Development must focus on changing what you actually do, not just what you know or believe.

Practice Deliberately: Random experience doesn't create expertise, but deliberate practice does. Development requires systematic work on specific skills with feedback and adjustment.

Embrace Discomfort: Growth requires stepping outside your comfort zone and trying approaches that initially feel awkward or unnatural. Comfort is the enemy of development.

Seek Feedback: Development requires an external perspective on your progress. Your self-perception may not match others' experience of your leadership. Have the courage to ask for honest and open feedback from your colleagues and employees.

Be Patient: Leadership development takes time. Sustainable change happens gradually through consistent effort over months and years, not through dramatic transformations overnight.

Stay Curious: The best leaders are continuous learners who remain open to new ideas, feedback, and approaches throughout their careers. Commit to a lifetime of learning the art and science of leadership.

The Individual vs. Organizational Challenge

One of the complexities I've observed in leadership development is the tension between individual growth and organizational systems. Many leaders develop new capabilities but struggle to apply them in organizational cultures that don't support or reward those behaviors. For example, a leader might develop better listening skills but work in an organization that rewards quick decision-making over careful consultation. Or a leader might learn to delegate more effectively but be evaluated based on personal productivity rather than team development. This creates what I call the "system trap." Individual leaders can't be fully effective without supportive organizational systems, but organizational systems can't change without effective individual leaders.

I've learned that successful leadership development must address both individual capabilities and organizational context. Sometimes this means helping leaders adapt their approaches to existing organizational realities. Sometimes it means helping leaders change organizational systems to support more effective leadership. Often it means both.

The Role of Failure in Development

One of the most important insights I've gained about leadership development is the critical role of failure in the learning process. The most effective leaders I work with have typically experienced significant failures that forced them to confront their limitations and develop new capabilities.

Research by Bennis and Thomas (2002) on executive development found that crucible experiences, such as challenging situations that require leaders to stretch beyond their current capabilities, are essential for developing leadership expertise. These experiences force leaders to:

- Question their assumptions about what works and what does not
- Develop new skills under pressure
- Build resilience and confidence through adversity
- Gain empathy for others facing similar challenges – You're not alone
- Learn to recover from setbacks quickly

I encourage the leaders I work with to seek challenging assignments that will stretch their capabilities, even if those assignments carry the risk of failure. Playing it safe may preserve your reputation in the short term, but it limits your development in the long term.

The Measurement Challenge

One of the persistent challenges in leadership development is measurement. How do you know if development efforts are improving leadership effectiveness? Traditional metrics like training hours completed, satisfaction scores, and self-assessments often don't correlate with actual behavior change or improved results.

I've learned that effective measurement of leadership development requires multiple approaches:

Behavioral Indicators: Track specific changes in observable behaviors rather than general impressions of improvement. For example, measure the frequency of one-on-one meetings, the quality of feedback given to direct reports, or the speed of decision-making.

360-Degree Feedback: Gather input from supervisors, peers, and subordinates about changes in leadership effectiveness over time. Others often observe changes that leaders themselves don't notice.

Business Results: Track metrics that reflect leadership effectiveness, such as employee engagement, retention rates, team performance, and customer satisfaction.

Self-Reflection: While self-assessment has limitations, it's still valuable for understanding internal changes in confidence, clarity, and commitment.

Longitudinal Tracking: Measure changes over months and years rather than days and weeks. Sustainable development takes time to become apparent.

Your Development Readiness Assessment

Before I move into the specific content of leadership development, I want you to assess your readiness for the development process. Research shows that readiness is one of the strongest predictors of development success.

Rate yourself honestly on each of the following factors (1 = strongly disagree, 5 = strongly agree):

Motivation for Development:

- I genuinely want to improve my leadership effectiveness
- I'm willing to invest significant time and effort in development
- I see leadership development as essential for my career success
- I'm motivated by intrinsic satisfaction, not just external rewards

Openness to Feedback:

- I actively seek feedback about my leadership effectiveness
- I can hear criticism without becoming defensive
- I'm curious about how others experience my leadership
- I view feedback as a gift, even when it's difficult to hear

Commitment to Practice:

- I'm willing to practice new skills even when they feel uncomfortable
- I understand that development requires sustained effort over time
- I'm prepared to make mistakes as I learn new approaches
- I'm committed to systematic skill development, not just random experience

Support System:

- I have relationships with people who can provide honest feedback
- I have access to mentors, coaches, or colleagues who can support my development
- My organization values and supports leadership development
- I can create or access opportunities to practice new skills

Growth Mindset:

- I believe my leadership capabilities can be developed through effort
- I view challenges as opportunities to learn rather than threats to my competence
- I'm willing to admit when I don't know something
- I see failure as a learning opportunity rather than a reflection of my worth

If you scored below four on any of these factors, spend some time addressing those areas before proceeding with intensive development work. Development is most effective when you're truly ready for the challenge.

The Journey Ahead

In the following chapters, I'll guide you through a comprehensive approach to developing each element of the A-E-I-O-U framework. I'll start with intrapersonal leadership (leading yourself), which is the foundation of all leadership effectiveness and progress through interpersonal, team, organizational, and external leadership domains.

Each chapter includes:

- Research-based insights into specific leadership capabilities
- Practical tools and techniques you can apply immediately
- Specific exercises for developing the associated skills
- Assessment tools for tracking your progress

I encourage you to work through this material systematically rather than jumping around. The concepts build on each other, and the exercises are cumulative. Treat this as a comprehensive development program, not casual reading.

Most importantly, remember that reading about leadership won't make you a better leader any more than reading about sports will make you a better athlete. Leadership is developed through practice, not just study. The concepts I share are only valuable if you apply them consistently in your daily leadership challenges.

I am very excited to guide you through this development journey. The work isn't easy, but the results are worth the effort. Let's begin with the foundation of all leadership effectiveness: learning to lead yourself.

PART II

INTRAPERSONAL LEADERSHIP — LEADING YOURSELF

CHAPTER 4

Self-Awareness - What To Learn About Knowing Yourself

The Foundation

Working with leaders, I've consistently found that self-awareness is the foundation of all leadership effectiveness. Leaders who understand themselves clearly make better decisions, build stronger relationships, and create more positive organizational cultures. Leaders who lack self-awareness consistently underperform, regardless of their intelligence, experience, or technical skills.

Yet self-awareness is also the most overestimated leadership capability. Research by Eurich (2017) found that while 95% of leaders believe they're self-aware, only 10-15% actually are. This creates a massive blind spot that limits leadership effectiveness across organizations worldwide.

I've learned that true self-awareness is much more complex and challenging than most people realize. It's not just about understanding your personality type or knowing your strengths and weaknesses. It's about developing real-time awareness of your thoughts, emotions, behaviors, and impact on others, and using that awareness to make more effective choices moment by moment.

The Two Types of Self-Awareness

Through my research and consulting work, I've identified two distinct types of self-awareness that leaders must develop:

> **Internal Self-Awareness**: This is your understanding of your own values, passions, aspirations, fit with your environment, reactions to situations, and impact on others. It's the clarity you have about what drives you, what triggers you, what energizes you, and what drains you.

> **External Self-Awareness**: This is your understanding of how others view you in terms of those same factors. It's the accuracy of your perception of how others experience your leadership, communication style, decision-making, and overall effectiveness.

I've found that these two types of awareness are surprisingly independent. Some leaders are excellent at understanding their own internal experience but completely clueless about how others perceive them. Other leaders are skilled at reading others' reactions but lack insight into their own motivations and patterns.

The most effective leaders I work with have developed both types of awareness. They understand themselves clearly, and they understand how others experience them. This dual awareness enables them to make conscious choices about how to show up in different situations rather than just reacting automatically based on their default patterns.

The Four Pillars of Leadership Self-Awareness

Through extensive work with leaders, I've identified four critical areas where self-awareness most impacts leadership effectiveness:

Pillar 1: Emotional Patterns

Most leaders operate on emotional autopilot. They react to situations without understanding what's driving their reactions. They feel frustrated, excited, anxious, or confident but don't recognize the specific triggers that create these emotional states.

I've learned that emotional self-awareness requires understanding several components:

Emotional Vocabulary: Most people use vague terms like "stressed" or "upset" to describe their emotional states. Effective leaders develop more precise emotional vocabulary that helps them understand and communicate their experience more clearly.

Physical Awareness: Emotions create physical sensations that provide early warning signals before full emotional reactions occur. Leaders who tune into these physical cues can often choose their responses rather than just reacting automatically.

Recovery Patterns: How long does it take you to recover from strong emotional reactions? What helps you regain emotional equilibrium? Understanding your recovery patterns helps you manage your emotional state more effectively.

Pillar 2: Behavioral Impact

There's often a significant gap between how leaders intend their behavior to be perceived and how others experience it. I've worked with countless leaders who were shocked to learn that their attempts to be helpful were experienced as micromanaging, their efforts to be thorough were seen as indecisive, or their direct communication style was perceived as harsh or dismissive.

Behavioral impact awareness requires understanding:

Communication Style: How do others experience your verbal and nonverbal communication? What messages do you send beyond the words you use? I've found that leaders often focus on content while others react more strongly to tone, body language, and energy.

Decision-Making Approach: How do others experience your decision-making process? Do they see you as collaborative or controlling, decisive or impulsive, thorough or slow? Understanding how your decision-making style affects others helps you adapt your approach when needed.

Feedback Delivery: How do others experience your feedback and coaching? Do they find it helpful or threatening, clear or confusing, supportive or critical? I've observed many leaders who think they're giving constructive feedback but are creating anxiety and defensiveness.

Meeting Leadership: How do others experience your meeting facilitation? Do they feel heard or ignored, engaged or bored, productive or frustrated? Meeting leadership is where many behavioral impact gaps become apparent.

Pillar 3: Strength Overuse

One of the most important discoveries is that leaders' greatest strengths often become their greatest weaknesses when overused or misapplied. I've seen confident leaders become arrogant, detail-oriented leaders become micromanagers, results-focused leaders become people-insensitive, and collaborative leaders become indecisive.

Strength overuse happens because leaders continue using approaches that worked in previous situations even when they're not appropriate for current challenges. What got you promoted to your current role might limit your effectiveness in that role.

Understanding strength overuse requires:

Strength Identification: What are your core strengths? What capabilities have contributed most to your success? I help leaders identify their key strengths through multiple assessment methods.

Overuse Recognition: When do your strengths become liabilities? In what situations might your natural approaches be counter-productive? I've found that strength overuse often occurs under stress or in unfamiliar situations.

Situational Adaptation: How can you modify your approach when your natural strengths aren't appropriate? This requires developing flexibility in your leadership style rather than just relying on your comfort zone.

Pillar 4: Values Alignment

I've consistently found that leaders are most effective when their daily behaviors align with their stated values. But I've also observed significant values-behavior gaps in many leaders I work with. They say they value collaboration but make decisions unilaterally. They claim to prioritize development but rarely invest time in coaching others. They espouse work-life balance but send emails at all hours.

Values alignment awareness requires:

Values Clarification: What do you value, not just what you think you should value? I help leaders identify their authentic values through examining their peak experiences, frustrations, and difficult decisions.

Behavior Audit: How do your daily behaviors reflect your stated values? I encourage leaders to track their time, decisions, and actions to identify alignment or gaps.

Priority Setting: When your values conflict with each other or with external pressures, how do you make choices? Understanding your value hierarchy helps you make consistent decisions.

Integrity Monitoring: How do you recognize when you're compromising your values? What systems do you have for maintaining alignment between your beliefs and your actions?

The Self-Awareness Development Process

Based on experience, I believe a systematic approach is best when helping leaders develop greater self-awareness:

Phase 1: Data Gathering

Self-awareness development begins with collecting accurate information about your current patterns, behaviors, and impact. This requires multiple data sources because self-perception is often inaccurate.

Self-Assessment Tools: Use validated instruments to help leaders understand their personality, strengths, values, and leadership style preferences (MBTI, DiSC, etc.). While these tools have limitations, they provide useful starting points for self-exploration.

360-Degree Feedback: I gather input from supervisors, peers, and direct reports about the leader's effectiveness in different areas. This external perspective often reveals blind spots that aren't apparent through self-assessment alone.

Behavioral Observation: I encourage leaders to track their own behavior systematically, noting patterns in their reactions, decisions, and interactions. Many leaders are surprised by what they discover when they start paying attention consciously.

Phase 2: Pattern Recognition

Once I've gathered sufficient data, I help leaders identify patterns in their behavior, reactions, and impact. This requires moving beyond individual incidents to see systemic themes.

Strength-Weakness Patterns: How do your strengths show up across different situations? When do they serve you well, and when do they create problems? Most leaders discover that their patterns are more predictable than they initially realized.

Themes: What consistent feedback do you receive from others? What themes appear across different relationships and situations? External feedback often reveals patterns that aren't apparent from your internal experience.

Values-Behavior Gaps: Where do you see the largest incongruence between what you say you value and how you behave? These gaps often indicate areas where development is needed.

Phase 3: Choice Points

Self-awareness is only valuable if it leads to better choices. I help leaders identify specific moments where increased awareness can lead to more effective behavior.

Decision Points: What recurring decisions could you handle more effectively with greater self-awareness? This might include hiring decisions, conflict resolution, or strategic planning.

Interaction: What types of interpersonal interactions could you navigate more skillfully? This might include feedback conversations, team meetings, or one-on-one discussions.

Stress Situations: When do you most need to override your automatic reactions and choose more effective responses? Understanding your stress patterns helps you prepare for challenging situations.

Communication Opportunities: When do you most need to adapt your communication style to be more effective with different audiences? This requires understanding both your natural style and others' preferences.

Phase 4: Skill Development

The final phase involves building specific skills for increasing self-awareness in real-time and using that awareness to make better choices.

Mindfulness Practices: I teach leaders simple mindfulness techniques for increasing moment-to-moment awareness of their thoughts, emotions, and reactions. Even basic practices can significantly improve self-awareness over time.

Reflection Disciplines: I help leaders establish regular reflection practices that enable them to learn from their experiences systematically rather than just moving from one situation to the next.

Feedback Seeking: I teach leaders how to actively seek feedback from others in ways that provide useful information for improvement. Most leaders are poor at soliciting helpful feedback.

Self-Monitoring Systems: I help leaders create personal systems for tracking their behavior and progress over time. What gets measured gets managed, and self-awareness is no exception.

The Self-Awareness Challenges

I've identified several common challenges that prevent leaders from developing greater self-awareness:

The Competence Assumption

Many successful leaders assume they must already be self-aware because they've achieved career success. They resist feedback that suggests they have blind spots because it threatens their professional identity. I've learned that success can inhibit self-awareness development by reducing the perceived need for improvement.

The Busy Excuse

Self-awareness development requires time for reflection, feedback gathering, and pattern recognition. Many leaders claim they're too busy with these activities, but I've found that investing time in self-awareness makes them more efficient by helping them avoid repeated mistakes and interpersonal problems. You're never too busy to develop your leadership competencies; it's just not your priority.

The Discomfort Avoidance

Developing self-awareness often involves confronting uncomfortable truths about your behavior and impact. Many leaders prefer comfortable delusions to uncomfortable realities. I've learned that sustainable development requires a willingness to sit with discomfort temporarily in service of long-term improvement.

The Change Resistance

Some leaders develop self-awareness but resist changing their behavior because their current approaches feel natural and comfortable. Awareness without action is just an intellectual exercise. I've found that behavioral change requires both understanding and commitment to practice new approaches.

Your Self-Awareness Development Plan

Here's the recommended development approach:

Week 1-2: Baseline Assessment Complete a comprehensive self-assessment using validated tools and gather 360-degree feedback from at least five people who work with you regularly. Focus on identifying patterns rather than just collecting data.

Week 3-4: Pattern Analysis Review all assessment data to identify themes, surprises, and gaps between self-perception and others' perceptions. Look particularly for strength overuse patterns and values-behavior misalignments.

Week 5-6: Choice Point Identification Identify specific situations where greater self-awareness could lead to more effective behavior. Focus on recurring challenges rather than one-time events.

Week 7-8: Skill Practice Begin practicing self-awareness skills in low-stakes situations. Start with simple mindfulness techniques and basic reflection practices. Build the habit before tackling difficult situations.

Week 9-10: Real-World Application Apply self-awareness skills in more challenging situations. Practice recognizing your patterns and choosing different responses in real-time.

Week 11-12: Progress Review Gather feedback on changes others have observed and assess your own progress. Identify what's working and what needs adjustment in your approach.

Self-awareness is the foundation of all other leadership capabilities. Without it, you're flying blind. With it, you can navigate even the most challenging leadership situations with greater skill and effectiveness.

The leaders I most admire aren't those who started with perfect self-awareness, yet they are those who committed to developing it continuously throughout their careers. That development starts with honest assessment and continues with deliberate practice. I'll guide you through both.

CHAPTER 5

Self-Regulation - How To Master Your Reactions

The Leadership Moment That Changes Everything

We have all been there. You're in an important meeting when someone challenges your decision publicly. You feel your face flush, your heart rate increases, and your jaw tightens. In that moment, you have a choice: react from your emotional state or respond from your leadership principles. How you handle this moment, and thousands of others like it, determines your leadership effectiveness more than your strategy, vision, or technical skills.

I call these "leadership moments." These are situations where your automatic reactions conflict with your leadership intentions. How you navigate these moments reveals your capacity for self-regulation, which I've identified as the most critical factor distinguishing excellent leaders from average ones.

In my work with leaders, I've observed that self-regulation is what separates those who inspire confidence from those who create anxiety, those who build trust from those who generate fear, and those who solve problems from those who create drama. It's the difference between leadership and management, between influence and authority, between long-term effectiveness and short-term results.

Emotional Hijacking

Neuroscience research has revealed that emotional reactions can literally hijack rational thinking in milliseconds. When your brain perceives a threat, whether physical, psychological, or social, the amygdala triggers fight-or-flight responses before your prefrontal cortex (your thinking brain) can evaluate the situation objectively.

This creates what I call the "leadership paradox": the situations that most require thoughtful leadership are exactly the situations most likely to trigger emotional reactions that interfere with thoughtful leadership. Crisis moments, conflict situations, high-stakes decisions, and public challenges all activate my threat-detection systems at precisely the moments when I most need my rational capabilities.

I've identified several factors that make leaders particularly vulnerable to emotional hijacking:

Ego Threats: Challenges to your competence, authority, or reputation trigger particularly strong reactions because they threaten your professional identity.

Time Pressure: When you feel rushed, your brain defaults to automatic reactions rather than thoughtful responses.

Ambiguity: Unclear situations activate anxiety, which narrows your thinking and pushes you toward premature closure.

High Stakes: When outcomes matter greatly, the pressure can overwhelm your rational thinking processes.

Fatigue: When you're tired, your self-regulation capacity is diminished, making emotional hijacking more likely.

Multiple Stressors: When several challenges occur simultaneously, your coping capacity can become overwhelmed.

The Four Components of Self-Regulation

Through my research and consulting experience, I've identified four essential components of leadership self-regulation:

Component 1: Trigger Recognition

The first step in self-regulation is recognizing your emotional triggers before they overwhelm your thinking. I've found that most leaders have predictable patterns, but they're often unaware of them until they start paying attention systematically.

I help leaders identify their triggers through several approaches:

Situation Analysis: What types of situations consistently create strong reactions? Public disagreement? Resource constraints? Performance problems? Organizational politics? Understanding your situational triggers helps you prepare for challenging circumstances.

People Patterns: What types of people or behaviors tend to trigger your strongest reactions? Disrespectful behavior? Micromanaging? Indecisiveness? Poor preparation? Recognizing your triggers helps you manage your reactions to difficult relationships.

Internal States: What internal conditions make you more vulnerable to triggering? Tiredness? Hunger? Stress? Time pressure? Being aware of your internal state helps you adjust your approach when you're not at your best.

Physical Signals: What physical sensations occur before you become emotionally hijacked? Changes in breathing? Muscle tension? Temperature changes? Heart rate increases? Learning to recognize these early warning signals gives you more time to choose your response.

Your Self-Regulation Challenge #1: Keep a trigger log for one week. When you feel a strong emotional reaction, write down: What happened? What emotion did I feel? How did I respond? What patterns do you notice?

Component 2: Pause Creation

Once you recognize that you're being triggered, the next step is creating space between the trigger and your response. This pause allows your rational brain to engage before your emotional brain takes over completely.

There are several techniques for creating effective pauses:

The Six-Second Rule: Neurochemical research shows that the initial flood of emotion typically lasts about six seconds. If you can avoid reacting for six seconds, you can access your rational thinking. I teach leaders to count slowly to six, take three deep breaths, or use other brief delay tactics.

The Question Pause: Instead of responding immediately, ask a clarifying question. This buys you time to think while appearing engaged and curious rather than defensive or aggressive.

The Physical Reset: Change your physical position, take a drink of water, or suggest a brief break. Physical movement helps reset your nervous system and gives you time to gather your thoughts.

The Reframe Request: Ask for time to consider the situation: "Let me think about that and get back to you," or "Can I schedule time to discuss this properly?" This gives you time to respond thoughtfully rather than react emotionally.

Your Self-Regulation Challenge #2: Practice the body scan technique. Several times per day, quickly assess your physical state. Notice areas of tension, your breathing pattern, and your energy level. This builds awareness of your physiological responses.

Component 3: Perspective Taking

During your pause, the next step is consciously choosing a more effective perspective on the situation. The stories you tell yourself about what's happening determine your emotional reactions and behavioral responses.

I recommend several reframing techniques:

Assume Positive Intent: Instead of assuming people are trying to undermine you, consider that they might have legitimate concerns or different information. Most workplace conflicts stem from misunderstandings rather than malicious intent.

Zoom Out: Consider the broader context and long-term implications rather than just the immediate situation. Will this matter in a year? What outcome do you really want to achieve?

Flip the Perspective: Try to understand the situation from the other person's point of view. What pressures might they be facing? What information might they have that you don't?

Focus on Learning: Instead of viewing challenges as threats, frame them as learning opportunities. What can this situation teach you about leadership, relationships, or problem-solving?

Your Self-Regulation Challenge #3: When you notice a strong emotional reaction, ask yourself: "What story am I telling myself about this situation? What other interpretations are possible?" Practice generating at least three alternative explanations for challenging situations.

Component 4: Response Choice

The final component is consciously choosing your response based on your leadership principles rather than your emotional state. This requires having a repertoire of response options and the discipline to choose the most effective one rather than the most satisfying one.

I help leaders develop response repertoires for common challenging situations:

Receiving Criticism: Instead of defending or attacking, you might thank the person for their feedback, ask clarifying questions, acknowledge valid points, or request time to consider their concerns.

Managing Conflict: Instead of taking sides or avoiding the issue, you might facilitate discussion between the parties, clarify different perspectives, look for common ground, or establish ground rules for productive dialogue.

Handling Pressure: Instead of rushing to decisions or becoming overwhelmed, you might clarify priorities, request additional resources, delegate appropriately, or communicate constraints clearly.

Dealing with Poor Performance: Instead of ignoring problems or reacting angrily, you might gather specific examples, schedule private conversations, focus on improvement rather than blame, or provide additional support and coaching.

Your Self-Regulation Development Plan

Helping leaders improve their self-regulation capacity, here's the development approach I recommend:

Week 1-2: Assessment and Awareness

- Complete a comprehensive assessment of your current self-regulation patterns
- Gather feedback from colleagues about your emotional impact
- Begin tracking your emotional reactions and triggers systematically
- Identify your highest-priority development areas

Week 3-4: Basic Skill Development

- Learn and practice basic mindfulness techniques
- Develop your personal repertoire of pause and reflect techniques
- Practice cognitive reframing in low-stakes situations
- Begin working on stress management and energy management

Week 5-6: Communication Enhancement

- Practice non-violent communication techniques
- Work on active listening skills, especially in challenging conversations
- Learn de-escalation techniques for heated discussions
- Practice assertive communication without aggression

Week 7-8: Real-World Application

- Apply your new skills in increasingly challenging situations
- Practice situational preparation before difficult meetings or conversations

- Develop your personal recovery protocols for when you make mistakes
- Seek feedback on the changes others are observing in you

Self-regulation is a skill that requires deliberate practice. The leaders who master it have a significant advantage in every situation they encounter. Stop being a victim of your emotional reactions. Start choosing your responses consciously. Your leadership effectiveness depends on it.

CHAPTER 6

Values Clarity - The North Star We Follow

The Values Confusion Crisis

In my years of consulting with leaders across every industry, I believe some leaders can't clearly articulate what they value, as opposed to what they think they should value. They recite generic corporate values like "integrity," "excellence," and "teamwork," but these words provide no real guidance when facing difficult decisions or competing priorities.

I've watched leaders make decisions that directly contradict their stated values because those values were never truly their own. These values were borrowed from others or chosen because they sounded impressive or were read in a book somewhere. I've seen organizations with beautiful values statements on their walls while their actual culture rewards behaviors that violate every principle they claim to embrace.

This value confusion creates several serious problems: inconsistent decision-making that confuses teams, ethical compromises that damage trust, and leadership that feels inauthentic because it's not grounded in genuine beliefs. Most importantly, it prevents leaders from accessing the clarity, confidence, and courage that come from knowing exactly what you stand for.

Values Clarity

When I talk about value clarity, I am not referring to the ability to recite a list of admirable qualities. I mean the deep understanding of the principles that guide your decisions when you're under pressure, facing uncertainty, or choosing between competing goods.

Real values clarity has several characteristics:

Authentic: Your values emerge from your genuine beliefs and experiences, not from what others expect or what sounds impressive.

Specific: Your values are defined clearly enough to guide behavior in ambiguous situations, not so vague that they can justify any action.

Tested: Your values have been proven through difficult decisions where following them required sacrifice or courage.

Integrated: Your values are woven into your daily decision-making processes, not just referenced during annual planning sessions.

Hierarchical: You understand how your values prioritize when they conflict with each other, which they inevitably will.

Through my consulting with leaders, I've learned that value clarity is both simpler and more complex than most people realize. It's simpler because most people have clear values; they just haven't taken the time to identify and articulate them. It's more complex because living your values consistently requires courage, discipline, and the willingness to accept the costs that sometimes come with principled leadership.

The Values Discovery Process

Most approaches to values clarification ask people to choose from lists of admirable qualities or to rank abstract concepts in order of importance. I've found these methods produce intellectually correct but emotionally disconnected results. People choose values that sound good rather than values that drive their behavior.

My approach is different. I help leaders discover their authentic values by examining their actual experiences, decisions, and reactions. Values aren't chosen; they're discovered through honest self-examination.

Step 1: Peak Experience Analysis

I start by asking leaders to identify three to five times when they felt most proud of their leadership, most aligned with their authentic selves, and most energized by their work. These peak experiences reveal what values were being honored when they were at their best.

For each peak experience, I explore several questions:

- What exactly were you doing in this situation?
- What principles were you demonstrating through your actions?
- What beliefs guided your decisions during this experience?
- What would have felt like a betrayal of yourself in this situation?
- What aspects of this experience do you most want to replicate?

Step 2: Values Violation Analysis

Next, I ask leaders to identify three to five times when they felt most frustrated, disappointed, or angry about workplace situations. These negative experiences often reveal what values were being violated when they felt worse.

For each difficult experience, I explore:

- What exactly happened that created such a strong reaction?
- What principles were being violated in this situation?
- What would have needed to be different for you to feel better about the situation?
- What did this experience teach you about what you won't tolerate?
- How did this experience clarify what you value?

Step 3: Difficult Decision Review

I then ask leaders to examine three to five difficult decisions they've made where they had to choose between competing alternatives, each of which had merit. These decision points reveal what values take priority when they conflict with each other.

For each difficult decision, I will explore:

- What made this decision so challenging?
- What competing values or interests were at stake?
- What principle ultimately guided your choice?
- What were you willing to sacrifice to honor your primary value?
- How did you feel about the decision afterward?
- What would you do differently if you faced a similar situation again?

Step 4: Role Model (Coach or Mentor) Analysis

Finally, I ask leaders to identify three to five leaders they most admire and respect. These role models often embody values that resonate with my own authentic beliefs.

For each role model, explore:

- What specifically do you admire about this person's leadership?
- What principles do they demonstrate that you want to emulate?

- What behaviors do they exhibit that you find inspiring?
- What would it look like for you to demonstrate similar values in your context?
- How are these values already present in your own leadership?

Your Values Clarification Challenge

Week 1: Peak Experience Analysis Identify and analyze three to five peak leadership experiences. Extract the values that were being honored during these experiences. Look for patterns across different situations.

Week 2: Values Violation Analysis Identify and analyze three to five frustrating leadership experiences. Identify what values were being violated. Notice which violations created the strongest reactions.

Week 3: Difficult Decision Review Examine three to five difficult decisions you've made. Identify what principles guided your choices when you couldn't honor all your values simultaneously.

Week 4: Role Model Analysis Identify three to five leaders you admire. Analyze what values they embody that resonate with you. Consider how you might strengthen these values in yourself.

Week 5: Values Integration Based on your analysis, identify your top five core values. Define each value specifically enough to guide behavior. Create a personal values statement.

Week 6: Decision Framework Development Create a decision-making framework that incorporates your values. Practice applying this framework to current decisions and priorities.

Values clarity is not a destination; it's an ongoing practice. Your values may evolve as you grow and face new challenges. What's important is that you remain conscious of what drives your decisions and committed to living those principles consistently, especially when it's difficult.

The leaders I most respect are not those who never face value conflicts; they're those who handle those conflicts with integrity, courage, and clarity about what matters most. That clarity starts with knowing what you truly value and continues with the discipline to live those values even when it's costly.

Your values are your leadership compass. When you're clear about what you stand for, you can navigate even the most challenging situations with confidence and authenticity.

CHAPTER 7

Purpose-Driven Leadership - Why We Lead

The Purpose Crisis

The majority of leaders I encounter can't clearly articulate why they lead beyond advancing their careers or meeting organizational expectations. They can describe what they do and how they do it, but they struggle to explain why it matters to them personally or why others should care.

This deficit creates several serious problems. Leaders without a clear purpose make decisions based on short-term pressures rather than long-term principles. They struggle to inspire others because they're not genuinely inspired themselves. They burn out more quickly because their work feels like an obligation rather than a calling. Most importantly, they miss the opportunity to create the kind of meaningful impact that makes leadership truly satisfying.

I've learned that purpose isn't just a nice-to-have for leaders, but it's a fundamental requirement for sustained effectiveness. Research consistently shows that purpose-driven leaders are more resilient, more inspiring, more creative, and more successful over the long term. They also create more engaged teams and more sustainable organizations.

But purpose can't be manufactured through mission statement exercises or borrowed from other leaders. It must be discovered through honest self-examination and developed through deliberate practice. It's deeply personal work that many leaders avoid because it requires confronting fundamental questions about meaning, contribution, and legacy.

The Purpose Discovery Process

Most approaches to purpose discovery ask people to think abstractly about what they want to accomplish or what the world needs. I've found these methods often produce intellectually correct but emotionally disconnected results. My approach is more practical, experiential, and personal.

Step 1: Peak Impact Analysis

I ask leaders to identify three to five times when they felt their leadership had the most positive impact on others. These might be times when they helped someone develop a new capability, solved a problem that others had struggled with, or created an opportunity that benefited many people.

For each peak impact experience, I explore:

- What exactly did you do that created a positive impact?
- How did you know your leadership made a difference?
- What aspects of creating this impact were most satisfying to you?
- What would you have felt like if you hadn't been able to create this impact?
- What kind of difference do you most want to make?

Step 2: Legacy Visioning

I ask leaders to imagine their retirement celebration, and someone is giving a speech about their leadership impact. What would they most want that person to say? What difference would they want to have made? What would they want to be remembered for?

This exercise helps leaders think beyond immediate goals to consider the long-term impact they want to create. It often reveals aspirations that they haven't been conscious of or haven't prioritized in their current leadership approach.

Step 3: Energy Analysis

I ask leaders to identify what aspects of their leadership work give them the most energy and what aspects drain them most. This isn't about what they're good at or what they're expected to do; it's about what genuinely energizes them.

Energy patterns reveal purpose because purpose-aligned activities feel energizing even when they're difficult, while purpose-misaligned activities feel draining even when they're easy.

Step 4: Problem Passion Assessment

I ask leaders to identify problems in the world that genuinely frustrate or concern them, such as issues they would work on even if they weren't paid to do so. These might be organizational problems, societal challenges, or human needs that they feel strongly about addressing.

Problems that evoke genuine passion often point toward purpose. The issues you can't ignore, the challenges that keep you up at night, the inequities that make you angry - these reveal what you feel called to address through your leadership.

Step 5: Values-Purpose Integration

Finally, I help leaders connect their identified purpose with their core values. Authentic purpose is always grounded in deeply held values.

If your purpose feels disconnected from your values, it's probably not your authentic purpose.

Your Purpose Development Plan

Helping leaders clarify and live their purpose, here's the development approach I recommend:

Week 1: Peak Impact Analysis Identify and analyze three to five times when your leadership created the most positive impact. Look for patterns in the type of impact that most energizes you.

Week 2: Legacy Visioning Complete the retirement speech exercise and other legacy-focused reflections. Consider what you most want to be remembered for as a leader.

Week 3: Energy and Problem Assessment Track what aspects of your leadership work give you energy versus drain you. Identify problems in the world that genuinely concern you.

Week 4: Values-Purpose Integration Connect your emerging sense of purpose with your core values. Ensure that your purpose feels authentic and sustainable.

Week 5: Purpose Articulation: Develop a clear, concise statement of your leadership purpose. Practice communicating it in different contexts.

Week 6: Decision Framework Integration Begin using your purpose as a filter for decisions and priorities. Notice how this changes your approach to leadership challenges.

Week 7: Team Purpose Development Begin conversations with your team about individual and collective purpose. Help others connect their work to meaningful impact.

Week 8: Purpose-Driven Planning Review your current goals and initiatives through your purpose lens. Adjust priorities to better align with your deeper calling.

Purpose-driven leadership isn't about perfection; it's about direction. It's about choosing to lead from your deepest values and highest aspirations rather than just responding to immediate pressures and external expectations.

Your purpose is your gift to the world. Do not keep it hidden.

CHAPTER 8

Reflection - The Practice We Can't Skip

The Reflection Crisis in Leadership

In my fast-paced, always-connected business environment, I've observed that reflection has become a lost art among leaders. Most of the leaders I work with are addicted to action, moving from one meeting to the next, one crisis to the next, one decision to the next, without ever pausing to learn from their experiences.

This creates what I call "experience without learning." This is when leaders accumulate years of experience but don't develop wisdom. They repeat the same mistakes because they never pause to understand why those mistakes happened. They miss important patterns because they're always focused on the next challenge rather than learning from the current one.

Research consistently shows that reflection is one of the most powerful tools for leadership development. Studies by Gioia and Thomas (1996) found that executives who practice regular reflection develop better judgment, make more creative decisions, and learn from experiences more effectively than those who don't. Yet reflection is often the first thing leaders abandon when they get busy.

The Four Types of Leadership Reflection

Based on my research and experience, I've identified four distinct types of reflection that leaders need to practice regularly:

Type 1: Daily Reflection

This is a brief, focused reflection on immediate experiences and their lessons. Daily reflection helps you learn from experiences while they're still fresh and make small adjustments before patterns become entrenched.

I recommend spending 10-15 minutes each evening answering these questions:

- What went well in my leadership today? What made it go well?
- What didn't go as well as I hoped? What contributed to the problems?
- What did I learn about myself, others, or the situation?
- What will I do differently tomorrow based on what I learned today?

Type 2: Weekly/Monthly Reflection

This is a deeper reflection on patterns, trends, and progress toward longer-term goals. Weekly/monthly reflection helps you see themes that aren't apparent in daily experiences and make strategic adjustments to your leadership approach.

I recommend spending 30-45 minutes each week/month answering these questions:

- What patterns do I notice in my leadership effectiveness this week?
- How did I demonstrate my values and purpose through my actions?
- What progress did I make toward my development goals?

- What relationships need attention or improvement?
- What adjustments do I need to make in my approach?

Type 3: Project Reflection

This is a comprehensive reflection on completed initiatives, major decisions, or significant experiences. Project reflection helps you extract maximum learning from important experiences and improve your approach to similar challenges in the future.

Use a structured after-action review process:

- What was I trying to accomplish?
- What actually happened?
- Why were there differences between intent and results?
- What worked well that I want to replicate?
- What didn't work well that I want to change?
- What did I learn that will help us in future similar situations?

Type 4: Annual Reflection

This is a strategic reflection on your overall leadership development, career direction, and life priorities. Annual reflection helps you make major adjustments and set direction for continued growth. Get feedback from mentors, colleagues, and followers.

I recommend spending a half-day annually examining these questions:

- How have I grown as a leader this year?
- What were my most significant successes and failures?
- How have my values and purpose evolved?
- What relationships have I strengthened or neglected?
- What do I want to focus on developing next year?
- How do I need to adjust my leadership approach for future challenges?

Your Reflection Development Plan

Here's the approach I recommend for developing a sustainable reflection practice by asking, "What can I do more, better, and/or differently?"

Week 1: Daily Reflection Establishment Begin a daily reflection practice using the four basic questions I provided. Start with just 5-10 minutes to build the habit.

Week 2: Weekly Reflection Integration Add weekly reflection sessions focusing on patterns and progress toward goals. Schedule this time in your calendar like any other important commitment. If you can't get to it every week, make it monthly. The point is to be consistent and make this plan work for you!

Week 3: Reflection Tool Development Experiment with different reflection tools, such as journaling, voice recording, and structured templates, to find what works best for you.

Week 4: Social Reflection Addition Identify someone who could serve as a reflection partner and begin regular reflection conversations with them.

Ongoing: Reflection Habit Maintenance Continue developing your reflection practice. Adjust the process based on what you learn about your own learning style and what generates the most useful insights.

Don't let another day of leadership experience go unexamined. Start reflecting systematically and watch how it accelerates your development and effectiveness.

PART III

INTERPERSONAL LEADERSHIP — LEADING INDIVIDUALS

CHAPTER 9

One-on-One Influence - How We Connect and Inspire

The Individual Relationship Crisis

Most leaders are so focused on managing teams, processes, and systems that they've forgotten how to lead individuals effectively. They conduct efficient meetings, send clear emails, and deliver polished presentations, but they struggle to create genuine connections with the people they're supposed to be leading.

This creates what I call "leadership at a distance." This is when leaders influence groups but can't inspire individuals, who can manage performance but can't motivate growth, who can direct activities but can't develop people. The result is organizations full of employees who comply with directives but aren't truly engaged, who complete tasks but don't contribute discretionary effort, who show up physically but not emotionally.

Research consistently shows that the quality of the relationship between a leader and each individual team member is the strongest predictor of that person's engagement, performance, and retention.

Studies by Gallup (2020) found that managers account for 70% of the variance in employee engagement scores. Yet most leaders receive little training in one-on-one influence and relationship building.

One-on-One Influence

When I talk about one-on-one influence, I am not referring to manipulation, coercion, or political maneuvering. I mean the ability to create genuine connections with individuals that inspire them to commit their best efforts to shared objectives. This kind of influence is based on trust, respect, and mutual benefit rather than position, power, or pressure.

Authentic one-on-one influence has several characteristics I've identified:

Relationship-Based: It's built on genuine care for the individual as a person, not just as a resource to accomplish tasks.

Value-Creating: It helps individuals grow, develop, and achieve their own goals while contributing to organizational objectives.

Voluntary: People choose to follow because they want to, not because they have to. The influence persists even when formal authority is absent.

Sustainable: It deepens over time through consistent behavior and builds resilience through challenges and setbacks.

Mutual: It involves genuine two-way interaction where the leader learns from and is influenced by others, not just one-way direction.

Authentic: It reflects the leader's genuine personality and values rather than artificial techniques or manipulative strategies.

The Psychology of Individual Influence

To influence individuals effectively, you must understand what drives human behavior, motivation, and decision-making. Through my research and consulting experience, I've identified several key psychological principles that govern one-on-one influence:

Principle 1: People Follow People They Trust

Trust is the foundation of all influence. Without trust, your interactions become transactions, because people do what you ask because they have to, not because they want to. With trust, your influence extends beyond your formal authority to include voluntary commitment and discretionary effort.

Trust has four components I've identified:

- *Competence*: People need to believe you know what you're doing and can help them be successful
- *Character*: People need to believe you have good intentions and will act in their best interests
- *Care*: People need to believe you genuinely care about them as individuals, not just as performers
- *Consistency*: People need to see reliable patterns in your behavior over time

Principle 2: People Are Motivated by Their Own Interests

WIIFM "What's in it for me?" This isn't cynical, it's realistic. People are most motivated when they see clear connections between what you're asking them to do and what they want to achieve for themselves. This might include career advancement, skill development, recognition, meaningful work, or personal satisfaction.

Effective influence requires understanding what each individual values most and helping them see how contributing to organizational goals also serves their personal interests.

Principle 3: People Need to Feel Valued and Understood

Everyone wants to feel like their contributions matter and their perspectives are valued. People are more likely to be influenced by leaders who take time to understand their viewpoints, acknowledge their contributions, and treat them as individuals rather than interchangeable resources.

The One-on-One Influence Process

Use this systematic process for building influence with individuals over time:

Phase 1: Foundation Building

Before you can influence someone effectively, you must establish a foundation of trust and understanding.

Get to Know the Person: Invest time in understanding each individual as a complete person, not just an employee. Learn about their background, interests, goals, concerns, and motivations. Remembering birthdays, spouses, and kids' names is incredibly influential.

Demonstrate Competence: Show that you can help them be successful through your knowledge, skills, and judgment.

Show Genuine Care: Demonstrate through your actions that you care about their success and well-being.

Be Consistent: Behave reliably over time so they can predict how you'll respond in different situations.

Phase 2: Understanding and Alignment

Once you've built a foundation of trust, the next phase involves understanding their perspective and finding areas of mutual interest.

Listen Actively: Spend more time listening than talking. Ask questions to understand their viewpoints, concerns, and ideas.

Identify Shared Interests: Look for areas where their personal goals align with organizational needs.

Understand Their Motivations: Learn what energizes them, what concerns them, and what they're trying to achieve.

Acknowledge Their Contributions: Recognize their strengths, skills, and contributions regularly.

Phase 3: Collaborative Direction

Once you understand their perspective and they trust your intentions, you can begin influencing their choices and actions through collaborative approaches.

Involve Them in Problem-Solving: Rather than just telling them what to do, involve them in figuring out how to address challenges and opportunities.

Frame Requests as Opportunities: Present tasks and responsibilities as opportunities for them to grow, contribute, or advance their goals.

Provide Context and Rationale: Help them understand why something needs to be done and how it fits into larger objectives.

Offer Choices When Possible: Give them options about how to accomplish objectives when feasible.

Phase 4: Support and Development

The final phase involves ongoing support that strengthens the relationship and increases their capability and commitment over time.

Provide Resources and Support: Help them be successful by providing the resources, information, and support they need.

Offer Development Opportunities: Look for ways to help them grow and develop their capabilities.

Give Credit and Recognition: Acknowledge their contributions publicly and give them credit for successes.

Learn from Them: Be open to their ideas, feedback, and suggestions.

Your One-on-One Influence Development Plan

Here's the approach I recommend for developing stronger one-on-one influence capabilities:

Week 1: Relationship Assessment Evaluate the quality of your relationships with key individuals you need to influence. Identify your strongest and weakest relationships and the factors that contribute to each.

Week 2: Individual Understanding Choose three important relationships and invest significant time in understanding each person better, such as their motivations, communication style, goals, and concerns.

Week 3: Trust Building Focus Identify specific actions you can take to build trust with each person, for example, demonstrating competence, showing care, increasing consistency, or improving character perceptions.

Week 4: Communication Skills Practice Focus on improving your active listening, empathetic communication, and persuasive communication skills in your daily interactions.

Week 5: Influence Flexibility Development Practice adapting your communication and influence approach based on each individual's personality and preferences.

Week 6: Difficult Conversation Practice Identify and engage in at least one difficult conversation that you've been avoiding, using frameworks that preserve relationships while addressing issues.

Week 7: Mutual Benefit Focus Look for opportunities to help others achieve their goals while advancing organizational objectives. Practice win-win thinking and solution development.

Week 8: Feedback and Adjustment Seek feedback on how others experience your influence attempts. Adjust your approach based on what you learn.

Start building that influence one relationship at a time.

CHAPTER 10

Coaching vs. Managing - When We Use Which

The Development Dilemma

I've observed a persistent confusion between managing and coaching that significantly limits leadership effectiveness. Most leaders default to management approaches in almost every situation by telling people what to do, how to do it, and when to get it done. While this approach can produce short-term compliance, it fails to develop people's capabilities, engagement, or ownership.

I've watched brilliant technical experts get promoted to leadership roles and struggle because they try to solve every problem themselves rather than develop others' problem-solving capabilities. I've seen experienced managers become frustrated because their team members keep coming to them with the same types of problems instead of learning to handle challenges independently. I've observed organizations where innovation stagnates because people wait for direction rather than taking initiative.

The root of this problem is that most leaders don't understand the difference between managing and coaching, when to use each approach, or how to transition between them effectively. They use management techniques when coaching is more effective, and they attempt coaching when management is needed.

Managing vs. Coaching

The distinction between managing and coaching isn't about good versus bad leadership. Both approaches are essential for effective leadership. The key is understanding when each approach is most appropriate and how to execute each one skillfully.

Managing is about directing, coordinating, and controlling work to ensure that tasks are completed efficiently and effectively. It focuses on immediate results, compliance with standards, and operational efficiency. Management is necessary when:

- People lack the knowledge or skills to complete tasks independently.
- Time pressure requires immediate action without lengthy development conversations.
- Safety or quality standards must be maintained precisely.
- New team members need clear direction and structure.
- Crisis situations require quick, coordinated responses.

Coaching is about developing people's capabilities, thinking, and ownership so they can handle challenges more independently and effectively. It focuses on long-term development, enhanced thinking, and increased autonomy. Coaching is most effective when:

- People have basic competence but need to develop better judgment or problem-solving skills.
- You want to increase engagement and ownership of outcomes.
- Development of capabilities is as important as immediate results.
- People are facing new challenges that require them to stretch and grow.

- You want to build organizational capacity for handling future challenges.

The Situational Leadership Model

One of the most useful frameworks I've found for determining when to manage versus coach is Ken Blanchard's Situational Leadership II Model, which suggests that your approach should be based on the person's competence and commitment to the specific task or challenge they're facing.

Directing (High Direction, Low Support)

- **When to use**: Person has low competence and high commitment.
- **Approach**: Clear instructions, close supervision, frequent feedback.
- **Communication style**: "Here's what needs to be done and how to do it."
- **Example**: Training a new employee in company procedures.

Coaching (High Direction, High Support)

- **When to use**: A Person has some competence but low commitment or confidence.
- **Approach**: Explain decisions, solicit suggestions, and provide support.
- **Communication style**: "Let me show you why this works and get your input."
- **Example**: Helping an experienced employee tackle a new type of challenge.

Supporting (Low Direction, High Support)

- **When to use**: Person has moderate to high competence but variable commitment.

- **Approach**: Facilitate problem-solving, share decision-making, and encourage.
- **Communication style**: "What do you think I should do? How can I help?"
- **Example**: Supporting a capable employee who's feeling overwhelmed or uncertain.

Delegating (Low Direction, Low Support)

- **When to use**: Person has high competence and high commitment.
- **Approach**: Turn over responsibility, monitor progress from a distance.
- **Communication style**: "You handle this and let me know how it goes."
- **Example**: Giving a proven performer autonomy on familiar tasks.

The GROW Coaching Model

When coaching is the appropriate approach, use the GROW model, which provides a structured framework for coaching conversations that develop thinking and ownership:

G - Goal: What do you want to achieve?

The first step in any coaching conversation is helping the person clarify what they're trying to accomplish. This isn't just about task completion; it's about understanding their underlying objectives and success criteria.

Effective goal-setting questions:

- "What would you like to achieve in this situation?"
- "What outcome would represent success for you?"
- "If you could wave a magic wand, what would happen?"
- "What's the ideal scenario from your perspective?"

R - Reality: What's the current situation?

Once the goal is clear, the next step is helping the person accurately assess the current situation. This involves exploring facts, circumstances, challenges, and resources available.

Effective reality-checking questions:

- "What's happening now?"
- "What have you tried so far?"
- "What obstacles are you facing?"
- "What resources do you have available?"
- "What's working well in this situation?"

O - Options: What are the possibilities?

This is often the most creative phase of the coaching conversation. Instead of jumping to solutions, you help the person generate multiple options and consider different approaches.

Effective option-generating questions:

- "What options do you see?"
- "What else could you try?"
- "What would you do if you had unlimited resources?"
- "What advice would you give someone else in this situation?"
- "What hasn't been tried yet?"

W - Way Forward: What will you do?

The final phase focuses on commitment and action planning. This is where coaching conversations translate into concrete next steps and accountability.

Effective commitment questions:

- "What's your next step?"
- "When will you do this?"

- "How will you measure progress?"
- "What support do you need?"
- "What might get in the way, and how will you handle it?"

When Coaching Doesn't Work

While coaching is a powerful development tool, it's not appropriate in every situation. I've identified several circumstances where management approaches are more effective than coaching:

Crisis Situations: When immediate action is required to prevent serious problems, there isn't time for coaching conversations.

Safety Issues: When safety is at stake, compliance with procedures is more important than creative problem-solving.

New Employee Onboarding: People who are new to roles or organizations usually need clear direction and structure before they're ready for coaching.

Performance Problems: When someone isn't meeting basic performance standards, management approaches focused on clarity and accountability are usually more appropriate.

Lack of Basic Skills: If someone lacks fundamental knowledge or skills required for a task, they need training or instruction rather than coaching.

Time Constraints: When deadlines are tight and results are critical, management approaches that focus on efficiency may be more appropriate.

Your Coaching Development Plan

Here's the approach I recommend for developing stronger coaching capabilities:

Week 1: Situational Assessment Evaluate your current approach with different team members. Identify where you're managing when you could be coaching, and where you're attempting to coach when management would be more appropriate.

Week 2: GROW Model Practice Use the GROW model in lower-stakes situations. Focus on asking questions rather than giving advice.

Week 3: Listening Skills Development Focus on improving your listening skills. Practice listening for content, emotion, assumptions, and gaps.

Week 4: Questioning Skills Practice Develop your ability to ask powerful, open-ended questions. Practice avoiding leading questions and advice-giving.

Week 5: Coaching Conversation Practice Schedule formal coaching conversations with team members who are ready for development. Use the full GROW model and track the results.

Week 6: Transition Skills Development Practice moving smoothly between managing and coaching approaches based on situational needs.

Week 7: Resistance Management Practice coaching with people who prefer direction. Learn to make coaching feel supportive rather than frustrating.

Week 8: Culture Building Begin promoting coaching approaches with your peers and throughout your organization.

Start practicing both approaches consciously and watch how it transforms both your effectiveness and your satisfaction as a leader.

CHAPTER 11

Difficult Conversations - A Framework for Hard Conversations

The Avoidance Epidemic

Over the years, I found that most leaders will do almost anything to avoid difficult conversations. They hope problems will resolve themselves. They work around challenging people instead of addressing behavior directly. They let performance issues linger for months rather than having direct discussions about expectations and accountability.

This avoidance creates enormous costs for organizations and individuals. Problems that could be resolved quickly with direct conversation escalate into major conflicts. High performers become frustrated when poor performance goes unaddressed. Team dynamics deteriorate as issues fester beneath the surface. Leaders lose credibility when they fail to address obvious problems that everyone can see.

I've speculated that the average leader has at least three difficult conversations they're currently avoiding. These might involve performance problems, behavior issues, interpersonal conflicts, strategic disagreements, or career discussions. The longer these conversations are delayed, the more difficult they become and the more damage they create.

The COURAGE Framework

When helping leaders handle difficult conversations more effectively, use the COURAGE framework as a systematic approach that makes these conversations more productive and less stressful:

C - Clarify Your Purpose

Before entering any difficult conversation, you must be crystal clear about what you're trying to accomplish. Vague purposes lead to rambling conversations that create confusion rather than resolution.

Effective purpose clarification involves:

- *Specific outcomes*: What exactly do you want to achieve?
- *Behavior changes*: What needs to start, stop, or continue happening?
- *Relationship goals*: How do you want the relationship to be affected?
- *Organizational benefits*: How will addressing this serve larger objectives?

Example purpose statements:

- "I want to address the pattern of missed deadlines and establish clear expectations going forward."
- "I need to resolve the conflict between Sarah and Mike so my team can work effectively."
- "I want to discuss the feedback from your presentation and help you improve for next time."

O - Organize Your Thoughts

Difficult conversations require more preparation than routine discussions. You need to organize your thoughts, gather relevant information, and plan your approach.

Effective preparation includes:

- *Fact gathering*: What specific examples and evidence do you have?
- *Perspective taking*: How might they see the situation differently?
- *Emotional preparation*: What emotions might arise, and how will you manage them?
- *Response planning*: How will you handle likely reactions or objections?

U - Understand Their Perspective

One of the biggest mistakes in difficult conversations is starting with your perspective rather than seeking to understand theirs. People are more open to hearing difficult feedback after they feel heard and understood.

Understanding their perspective involves:

- *Active listening*: Really hearing what they're saying, not just waiting for your turn to talk
- *Empathetic inquiry*: Asking questions to understand their viewpoint, feelings, and concerns
- *Assumption checking*: Verifying your interpretations rather than assuming you know what they mean
- *Emotional acknowledgment*: Recognizing and validating their emotional experience

R - Relate with Empathy

Difficult conversations are fundamentally about relationships. How you show up emotionally and interpersonally often matters more than the specific words you use.

Relating with empathy involves:

- *Genuine care*: Demonstrating that you care about them as a person, not just their performance

- *Respectful communication*: Treating them with dignity, even when addressing problems
- *Emotional attunement*: Being sensitive to their emotional state and adjusting accordingly
- *Human connection*: Remembering that you're talking to a fellow human being with feelings, fears, and aspirations

A - Address Issues Directly

After you've clarified your purpose, organized your thoughts, understood their perspective, and established an empathetic connection, you must address the issues directly. This is where many leaders falter, because they do everything except have the actual difficult conversation.

Direct addressing involves:

- *Clear communication*: Speaking plainly about the problem without dancing around it
- *Specific examples*: Using concrete instances rather than vague generalizations
- *Behavioral focus*: Concentrating on observable actions rather than character judgments
- *Impact description*: Explaining how the behavior affects others, the team, or the organization

G - Generate Solutions Together

The most effective difficult conversations don't just identify problems, but they also create collaborative solutions. This involves the person in solving the problem rather than just imposing solutions on them.

Collaborative solution generation includes:

- *Joint problem-solving*: Working together to identify root causes and potential solutions

- *Multiple options*: Generating several possible approaches rather than just one
- *Ownership building*: Helping them take ownership of the solution, not just compliance
- *Resource identification*: Determining what support, training, or resources might be needed

E - Establish Clear Agreements

Difficult conversations must end with clear agreements about what will happen next. Vague conclusions lead to continued problems and the need for repeated difficult conversations.

Clear agreements include:

- *Specific actions*: Exactly what will be done differently
- *Clear timelines*: When changes will be implemented and results expected
- *Success measures*: How progress will be evaluated and measured
- *Follow-up plans*: When and how you'll check in on progress
- *Consequences*: What will happen if agreements aren't kept

Common Difficult Conversation Scenarios

Based on my consulting experience, I've identified several common scenarios that leaders frequently face and developed specific approaches for each:

Performance Below Standards

Approach: Focus on specific behaviors and measurable results rather than general performance. Use the conversation to understand obstacles and create development plans.

Example opening: "I want to discuss the project deadlines that have been missed over the past month. Let me share what I've observed, and then I'd like to understand your perspective on what's been happening."

Behavioral Issues

Approach: Address the behavior's impact on others and the organization rather than making character judgments. Focus on change rather than blame.

Example opening: "I need to address some feedback I've received about interactions in team meetings. I'd like to share what I've heard and get your perspective."

Interpersonal Conflicts

Approach: Focus on helping people work together effectively rather than determining who's right or wrong. Establish ground rules for professional interaction.

Example opening: "I've noticed some tension between you and Sarah that's affecting team dynamics. I'd like to understand both perspectives and help you work together more effectively."

Missed Commitments

Approach: Understand what led to the missed commitment and establish clear agreements about reliability going forward.

Example opening: "I need to talk about the commitment you made last week that wasn't delivered. Help me understand what happened, and let's figure out how to prevent this in the future."

Career Disappointments

Approach: Acknowledge their disappointment while providing clear, specific feedback about what needs to change for future opportunities.

Example opening: "I know you're disappointed about not getting the promotion. I'd like to explain the decision and discuss what you can focus on for future opportunities."

Your Difficult Conversation Development Plan

Here's the approach I recommend for building your capability in this critical leadership skill:

Week 1: Avoidance Assessment Identify three difficult conversations you're currently avoiding. Analyze what's making you avoid them and what it's costing you, your team, and your organization.

Week 2: Framework Learning Study the COURAGE framework and practice using it in lower-stakes conversations. Focus on preparation and purpose clarification.

Week 3: Communication Skills Practice Work on the fundamental communication skills: non-violent communication, active listening, and assertive expression. Practice these in routine conversations.

Week 4: Emotional Management Development Practice, managing your emotions under pressure and helping others manage theirs. Use breathing techniques, perspective-taking, and empathetic responses.

Week 5: First Difficult Conversation Have your first difficult conversation using the COURAGE framework. Choose something important but not the most difficult conversation you're avoiding.

Week 6: Skill Refinement Based on your experience, refine your approach. Seek feedback and identify areas for improvement.

Week 7: Second Difficult Conversation Have another avoided conversation, applying what you learned from the first one. Gradually increase the difficulty level.

Week 8: System Integration Begin making difficult conversations a regular part of your leadership practice rather than something you avoid or delay.

Your leadership effectiveness and personal satisfaction depend on your willingness to have the conversations that matter, even when they're difficult.

CHAPTER 12

Motivation - Discover What Really Drives People

Solving The Motivation Crisis

Often, leaders have no idea what truly motivates the people they're trying to lead. They default to outdated assumptions about money, job security, and career advancement that may have worked in previous generations but fail miserably with today's workforce.

I regularly encounter managers who are frustrated because their "generous" compensation packages aren't producing the engagement they expected. I see leaders who offer promotions and get turned down by people they were sure would jump at the opportunity. I work with executives who can't understand why their teams seem disengaged despite having "great jobs" with excellent benefits.

A Gallup survey (2023) reveals that only 32% of employees are engaged at work, while 17% are actively disengaged. This means the vast majority of people are showing up physically but not emotionally or intellectually. They're doing the minimum required rather than contributing their best efforts.

What I've Learned About Real Motivation

Through my research and consulting experience, I've identified several fundamental truths about motivation that contradict conventional wisdom:

Truth 1: Money Motivates Until It Doesn't

Money is important for motivation, but not in the way most leaders think. Seminal research by Herzberg (1959) and confirmed by decades of subsequent studies shows that compensation is primarily a "hygiene factor" (tangible) that can demotivate people when it's inadequate but increasing it beyond adequacy doesn't significantly increase motivation.

The real-world application: Ensure your people feel fairly compensated, then focus your motivational efforts on non-financial factors. Don't assume that throwing more money at motivation problems will solve them.

Truth 2: Recognition Works When It's Personal and Specific

Generic recognition programs fail because they treat all people the same way. I've found that what constitutes meaningful recognition varies dramatically among individuals. Some people want public acknowledgment; others prefer private appreciation. Some value peer recognition; others care more about supervisor feedback.

The real-world application: Learn how each individual prefers to be recognized and tailor your approach accordingly. Keep detailed notes about what types of recognition energize each team member most. No matter what your budget is, praise and recognition are always free!

Truth 3: Autonomy Trumps Control Every Time

The most significant shift in workplace motivation over the past two decades has been the increasing importance of autonomy. Modern workers, especially knowledge workers, are motivated more by having control over their work than by being controlled in their work.

The real-world application: Define clear outcomes and success measures, then give people maximum freedom in how they achieve those outcomes. Focus on results, not methods. Don't be a micromanager!

Truth 4: Purpose Beats Perks

I've observed that people will choose meaningful work with modest compensation over meaningless work with excellent benefits. Purpose isn't just about saving the world; it's about understanding how your work contributes to something larger than yourself.

The real-world application: Help each person understand how their specific role contributes to team success, organizational mission, and customer value. Make the connection explicit and regular. Help followers understand how they fit in the greater organization.

Truth 5: Growth Opportunities Energize More Than Comfort

Contrary to popular belief, people aren't primarily motivated by comfort and security (Maslow). They're motivated by challenge, learning, and growth. Stagnation is demotivating even when it's comfortable or highly paid.

The real-world application: Continuously provide growth assignments, learning opportunities, and new challenges. Don't assume that making people's jobs easier will make them more motivated.

The Individual Motivation (Self-Determination) Matrix

One of my most important discoveries is that motivation is highly individual. What energizes one person may drain another. What challenges one person may overwhelm another. Effective leaders develop what I call "motivation literacy," which is the ability to understand and respond to each person's unique motivational drivers.

Dimension 1: Internal vs. External Motivation

Internally Motivated People:

- Driven by personal satisfaction and achievement
- Value autonomy and self-direction
- Motivated by mastery and competence
- Need clear goals but minimal supervision
- **Real-world application**: Give them challenging projects, clear success criteria, and freedom to figure out how to achieve results

Externally Motivated People:

- Driven by recognition, rewards, and social approval
- Value feedback and acknowledgment
- Motivated by competition and comparison
- Need regular check-ins and validation
- **Real-world application**: Provide frequent recognition, public acknowledgment, and competitive opportunities

The Motivation Diagnostic Process

Before you can motivate someone effectively, you must understand what drives them. Use this systematic process for diagnosing individual motivation that goes beyond assumptions and generalizations:

Step 1: The Motivation Interview

Schedule individual conversations with each team member, focused specifically on understanding their motivations.

Key questions to explore:

- "Tell me about a time when you felt most engaged and energized at work. What made that experience so positive?"
- "What aspects of your current role give you the most energy? What aspects drain you?"
- "When you think about your ideal work environment, what would it look like?"
- "How do you prefer to receive feedback and recognition?"
- "What would make your work feel more meaningful to you?"
- "What are you hoping to learn or develop in the next year?"

Step 2: The Energy Audit

Have each person track their energy levels throughout different types of work for a week. When do they feel most engaged? What activities energize them versus drain them?

Step 3: The Values Assessment

Understand what each person values most in their work experience. Values drive motivation more than skills or interests.

Step 4: The Motivational Profile Creation

Based on the interview, energy audit, and values assessment, create a motivational profile for each person that captures:

- Primary motivational drivers
- Preferred recognition style
- Optimal work environment characteristics
- Development interests and goals
- Potential demotivators to avoid

Real-World Motivation Strategies That Work

Strategy 1: The Customized Challenge Approach

Instead of giving everyone the same assignments, create customized challenges based on each person's motivational profile. That's the point of individual motivation!

Strategy 2: The Meaningful Connection Method

Help each person understand specifically how their work contributes to larger objectives that they care about. Help people "fit" into the organization.

Real-world application: Instead of just assigning tasks, spend time explaining the "why" behind each assignment in terms that connect to what motivates that specific person.

Strategy 3: The Growth-Focused Goal Setting

Replace simple task completion goals with development-focused objectives that help people grow while accomplishing work.

Traditional goal: "Complete the quarterly report by Friday."

Growth-focused goal: "Complete the quarterly report by Friday and use this as an opportunity to practice the data visualization skills you wanted to develop."

Your Motivation Leadership Development Plan

Here's a comprehensive approach to developing your ability to motivate others effectively:

Week 1: Motivation Assessment Complete motivational profiles for each of your team members using the Individual Motivation Matrix and diagnostic process I've outlined.

Week 2: Personal Motivation Analysis Analyze your own motivational drivers and biases. What motivates you may not motivate others, and your assumptions about motivation may limit your effectiveness.

Week 3: Customization Practice Begin customizing your approach to each team member based on their motivational profile. Practice different recognition styles, communication approaches, and assignment methods.

Week 4: Environment Evaluation Assess your team environment for factors that enhance or diminish motivation. Identify specific changes you can make to create more motivating conditions.

Week 5: Difficult Motivation Conversations Have direct conversations with team members who seem disengaged or demotivated. Use diagnostic questions to understand what's affecting their motivation.

Week 6: Systems and Process Review Examine organizational systems, processes, and policies that may be creating motivation barriers. Identify what you can change and what you need to work around.

Week 7: Recognition and Celebration Enhancement Implement more systematic and personalized approaches to recognition and celebration. Focus on progress as much as final results.

Week 8: Long-term Development Planning Create individual development plans that connect each person's growth interests with organizational needs. Make motivation part of your ongoing leadership practice.

Your success as a leader ultimately depends not on your own motivation but on your ability to create conditions where others can access and express their best motivation.

CHAPTER 13

Feedback That Works - An Approach to Growth Conversations

The Feedback Failure

In my decades of consulting, I've witnessed a massive failure in how leaders give feedback. Most feedback conversations are either so vague they provide no useful guidance, "Great job on that project," or so harsh they create defensiveness rather than improvement, "Your presentation was terrible". The result is organizations where people rarely receive the specific, actionable information they need to grow and improve.

I regularly encounter high-performing professionals who tell us they haven't received meaningful feedback from their supervisor in months or even years. I see talented people making the same mistakes repeatedly because no one has taken the time to give them specific guidance about what to change. I work with leaders who are frustrated by poor performance but have never had direct conversations about their expectations and observations.

The latest research by Zenger and Folkman (2022) reveals that 67% of employees say they want more feedback than they currently receive, yet 78% of managers say they regularly provide feedback to their teams. This gap suggests that what managers think is feedback isn't actually experienced as useful feedback by the people receiving it.

Feedback That Creates Change

When I talk about effective feedback, I am not referring to annual performance reviews, generic praise, or critical comments. I mean specific, actionable information delivered in ways that help people understand their impact and improve their effectiveness.

Feedback that creates change has several characteristics I've identified:

Specific and Observable: It describes particular behaviors and their effects rather than making general statements about personality or performance.

Timely and Relevant: It's delivered close to when the behavior occurred and connects to current priorities and challenges.

Balanced and Fair: It acknowledges what's working well while addressing what needs improvement.

Actionable and Clear: It provides specific suggestions for what to start, stop, or continue doing.

Growth-Oriented: It frames feedback in terms of development opportunities rather than personal failures.

Dialogue-Based: It creates conversation rather than one-way communication, seeking to understand before seeking to be understood.

The SBI-I Framework To Use for All Feedback Using Cognitive Evaluation Theory (CET)

After testing numerous feedback models, I've found that the SBI-I framework is the most effective for creating productive feedback conversations – always give the "why":

S - Situation: Describe when and where the behavior occurred.
B - Behavior: Explain the specific, observable behavior.
I - Impact: Describe the effect of the behavior.
I - Intent: Explore the intent behind the behavior and collaborate on improvement

Real-World Example of SBI-I in Action:

Situation: "In yesterday's client meeting with the Johnson account..."

Behavior: "I noticed that when Sarah raised concerns about the timeline, you interrupted her twice and said the timeline was non-negotiable without asking questions about her concerns."

Impact: "The impact was that Sarah stopped contributing to the discussion, and I could see the client looking uncomfortable. I may have missed important information about potential obstacles, and the client might have concerns about how I handle internal disagreements."

Intent: "I'm curious about what was going through your mind at that moment. What were you trying to accomplish? And how do you think I could handle similar situations in the future to get better outcomes?"

Notice how this framework provides specific information without attacking character, explores impact without assuming intent, and creates opportunity for learning rather than defensiveness.

The Five Types of Feedback Every Leader Must Master

Through my consulting experience, I've identified five distinct types of feedback that leaders need to give regularly. Each type requires different approaches and skills:

Type 1: Performance Feedback

This addresses gaps between expected and actual results, whether positive or negative.

When to use: After projects, during regular check-ins, when performance standards aren't being met

Example opening: "Let's review the results from the quarterly campaign. I had targeted a 15% engagement rate, and the actual results were 9%. I want to understand what contributed to the gap and how I can improve next quarter."

Type 2: Behavioral Feedback

This addresses how someone's actions affect others and the work environment.

When to use: When you observe behaviors that help or hinder team effectiveness

Example opening: "I want to discuss something I observed in team meetings. When others are presenting ideas, I've noticed you checking your phone and laptop. The impact is that people feel like their ideas aren't valued, and they are missing opportunities for good discussion."

Type 3: Development Feedback

This identifies growth opportunities and helps people build new capabilities.

When to use: During coaching conversations, career discussions, and after stretch assignments

Example opening: "I see real potential for you to take on more strategic responsibilities. To get there, I think developing your presentation skills would be valuable. I noticed in your last two presentations that the content was excellent, but the delivery could be more engaging."

Type 4: Recognition Feedback

This acknowledges excellent performance and reinforces positive behaviors.

When to use: Immediately after observing excellent performance, during team meetings, in formal reviews

Example opening: "I want to recognize how you handled the crisis with the Miller account. You stayed calm under pressure, kept the client informed every step of the way, and found a creative solution that strengthened the relationship. This is exactly the kind of client leadership I need."

Type 5: Corrective Feedback

This addresses serious performance or behavior problems that must change.

When to use: When behavior violates standards, policies, or values

Example opening: "I need to address the pattern of missed deadlines over the past month. This is affecting team morale and client relationships. I need to see immediate improvement in meeting commitments. Let's discuss what's contributing to this pattern and how I can fix it."

The Real-World Feedback Calendar

Most leaders give feedback randomly or only during formal review periods. I've found that systematic, regular feedback is much more effective than sporadic, intense feedback sessions.

Daily Feedback Opportunities:

- Brief recognition for specific contributions
- Quick course corrections on immediate issues
- Acknowledgment of effort and progress
- Simple appreciation for good work

Real-world application: End each day by giving at least one piece of specific positive feedback to someone on your team.

Weekly Feedback Rhythms:

- Individual check-ins with direct reports
- Project progress discussions
- Team dynamic observations
- Development conversations

Real-world application: Use your one-on-ones for systematic feedback, not just status updates.

Monthly Feedback Focus:

- Comprehensive performance discussions
- Career development conversations
- Skill development progress
- Goal achievement assessment

Real-world application: Schedule monthly development conversations that go deeper than weekly check-ins.

Quarterly Feedback Intensives:

- Formal performance reviews
- 360-degree feedback sessions
- Career planning discussions
- Annual goal setting and review

Real-world application: Make quarterly reviews genuine development conversations, not just documentation exercises.

The Difficult Feedback Situations

Scenario 1: The High Performer with Blind Spots

The challenge: Excellent results but problematic behaviors that affect others

Example conversation: "Your technical work is consistently excellent, and clients really value your expertise. I want to talk about something that could help you advance to senior roles. I've received feedback that in team meetings, you sometimes dismiss others' ideas quickly. For leadership positions, you'll need to be seen as someone who builds on others' ideas, not just evaluates them."

Scenario 2: The Defensive Receiver

The challenge: Someone who becomes argumentative or shuts down when receiving feedback

Example conversation: "I can see you're feeling frustrated about this feedback. Help me understand your perspective on the situation. What did you think happened during that meeting?"

Scenario 3: The Consistent Underperformer

The challenge: Someone whose performance is consistently below standards despite previous feedback

Example conversation: "I've talked about meeting deadlines three times in the past two months, and I'm still seeing the same pattern. This has to change immediately. Let's figure out if this is a capacity issue, a priority issue, or a commitment issue."

Your Feedback Mastery Development Plan

Helping leaders improve their feedback skills, here's a comprehensive development approach:

Week 1: Current State Assessment Evaluate your current feedback practices using the SBI-I framework. Record yourself giving feedback (with permission) and analyze your effectiveness.

Week 2: Framework Practice Practice the SBI-I framework in low-stakes situations. Focus on specific observations and impact descriptions rather than general evaluations.

Week 3: Delivery Skills Development Work on emotional regulation, language precision, and question-based dialogue. Practice with trusted colleagues before using it with team members.

Week 4: Difficult Situation Practice Identify one challenging feedback conversation you've been avoiding and plan your approach using the frameworks and skills you've developed.

Week 5: Recognition Enhancement Focus on improving your positive feedback skills. Practice giving specific, timely recognition that reinforces desired behaviors.

Week 6: Systematic Implementation Implement regular feedback rhythms with your team. Schedule weekly development conversations using structured approaches.

Week 7: Peer and Upward Feedback Practice giving feedback to colleagues and supervisors using appropriate approaches for each relationship.

Week 8: Culture Building Begin promoting a feedback culture within your sphere of influence. Train others, model excellent feedback, and create systems that support continuous feedback.

Your effectiveness as a leader will ultimately be measured not by your own performance, but by how much you help others improve their performance. Feedback is the primary tool for creating that improvement.

PART IV

TEAM LEADERSHIP — LEADING GROUPS

CHAPTER 14

Team Dynamics - What Is Observed in High-Performing Teams

Addressing The Team Dysfunction Crisis

Most groups of people working together do not function as teams. They're collections of individuals who happen to share the same manager, attend the same meetings, and work toward loosely related objectives. The result is mediocre performance, interpersonal friction, and enormous waste of human potential.

I regularly observe teams where members work in silos, competing rather than collaborating. I see groups where meetings are painful exercises in information sharing rather than dynamic problem-solving sessions. I encounter teams where one or two people do most of the work while others coast or actively undermine progress. Most tragically, I work with teams that have tremendous individual talent but produce collective results that are worse than the sum of their parts.

Research by Gallup (2023) shows that only 23% of teams are truly engaged and highly performing, while 18% are actively disengaged and creating negative value for their organizations. This means that the majority of teams are functioning somewhere between mediocre and dysfunctional, representing a massive opportunity cost for organizations and career limitations for individuals.

The Five Stages of Team Development

Based on my work with hundreds of teams, I've found that most teams progress through the predictable stages of development by Bruce Tuckman. Understanding these stages helps leaders provide appropriate support and accelerate team development.

Stage 1: Forming - "Getting Started"

Characteristics:

- High dependence on the leader for direction and decision-making
- Individual behavior is driven by the desire to be accepted by the group
- Processes and procedures are undefined or unclear
- Team members are testing boundaries and trying to understand expectations
- Limited trust and sharing among members

Leader behaviors that help:

- Provide clear structure, roles, and expectations
- Facilitate introductions and relationship building
- Establish a team charter with purpose, goals, and operating agreements
- Create psychological safety for sharing and participation
- Make decisions quickly to maintain momentum

Real-world application: Don't assume people understand their roles or how to work together. Invest significant time in clarification and structure during this stage.

Stage 2: Storming - "Working Through Differences"

Characteristics:

- Conflicts emerge about roles, responsibilities, and approaches
- Competition for position and influence within the team
- Questioning of the leader's authority and team objectives
- Formation of subgroups and coalitions
- Emotional reactions and interpersonal tensions

Leader behaviors that help:

- Address conflicts directly rather than hoping they'll resolve themselves
- Facilitate healthy debate about approaches and processes
- Clarify roles and decision-making authority
- Coach individuals through interpersonal challenges
- Maintain focus on shared objectives while allowing discussion of methods

Real-world application: Don't avoid or suppress conflict during this stage. Guide the team through disagreements to reach better solutions and stronger relationships.

Stage 3: Norming - "Finding My Rhythm"

Characteristics:

- Agreement on team processes and individual roles
- Development of trust and mutual respect among members
- Establishment of team identity and shared practices
- Increased collaboration and mutual support
- Focus on team objectives rather than individual agendas

Leader behaviors that help:

- Support emerging team norms that enhance performance

121

- Delegate more decision-making authority to the team
- Recognize and celebrate team achievements
- Provide resources and remove obstacles
- Coach the team on continuous improvement processes

Real-world application: Allow the team more autonomy while providing support and resources. Focus on strengthening positive patterns that are emerging.

Stage 4: Performing - "Achieving Excellence"

Characteristics:

- High levels of interdependence and collaboration
- Shared leadership with different members leading in different situations
- Focus on the achievement of shared objectives
- Continuous learning and adaptation
- High trust and psychological safety

Leader behaviors that help:

- Provide strategic direction while allowing tactical autonomy
- Focus on removing external obstacles rather than managing internal processes
- Challenge the team with stretch goals and new opportunities
- Facilitate knowledge sharing and capability development
- Recognize both team and individual contributions

Real-world application: Step back from day-to-day management and focus on strategic support. Trust the team to manage their own processes and relationships.

Stage 5: Transforming - "Evolving and Renewing"

Characteristics:

- Continuous adaptation to new challenges and opportunities
- Innovation in approaches and solutions
- Development of other teams and leaders
- Sustainable high performance over extended periods
- Legacy building and knowledge transfer

Leader behaviors that help:

- Focus on long-term development and capability building
- Create opportunities for the team to teach and mentor others
- Continuously raise standards and expectations
- Facilitate strategic thinking and planning
- Prepare for leadership transition and team evolution

Real-world application: Focus on sustainability and multiplication of team capabilities. Help the team become a model for other teams in the organization.

The Team Dynamics Assessment

Before you can improve team performance, you must accurately assess current team dynamics. Use this comprehensive assessment that examines eight critical dimensions of team effectiveness:

Dimension 1: Purpose and Direction Clarity

Assessment questions:

- Can every team member clearly articulate the team's purpose and objectives?
- Do individual goals align with team goals?
- Are priorities clear and consistent?
- Does the team have meaningful success measures?

Red flags: Different answers to "What's my main objective?" Confusion about priorities. Lack of clear success metrics.

Green flags: Consistent understanding of purpose. Clear connections between individual and team goals. Regular discussion of progress toward objectives.

Dimension 2: Role Definition and Accountability

Assessment questions:

- Does each person understand their specific role and responsibilities?
- Are there clear accountability mechanisms for individual and collective performance?
- Are there gaps or overlaps in responsibilities?
- Do people know who to go to for different types of decisions?

Red flags: Confusion about "who does what." Duplicated efforts. Important tasks falling through cracks.

Green flags: Clear role descriptions. Understood decision-making authority. Effective handoffs between team members.

Real-World Team Development Interventions

Based on my assessment results, I implement specific interventions designed to address the team's highest-priority development needs:

Intervention 1: Team Charter Development

When to use: New teams, teams with unclear purpose, teams experiencing direction confusion

Intervention 2: Communication Process Design

When to use: Teams with meeting problems, information sharing issues, or communication breakdowns

Intervention 3: Trust Building Activities

When to use: Teams with low trust, new team members, teams after conflicts or crises

Your Team Development Leadership Plan

Here's a comprehensive approach to developing your team leadership capabilities:

Week 1: Team Assessment Complete a comprehensive assessment of your team's current development stage and performance across the eight dimensions I outlined. Gather input from all team members.

Week 2: Development Priority Identification Based on assessment results, identify the top three development priorities that would most improve team performance. Focus on areas with the greatest impact potential.

Week 3: Individual Conversations Meet individually with each team member to understand their perspective on team dynamics, their individual goals, and their ideas for team improvement.

Week 4: Team Development Planning Facilitate team session to share assessment results, discuss development priorities, and create improvement plans that everyone commits to implementing.

Week 5: First Intervention Implementation. Begin implementing your highest-priority team development intervention. Monitor progress and gather feedback on effectiveness.

Week 6: Process and Norm Development Work with the team to establish or improve processes and norms that support better collaboration and performance.

Week 7: Conflict and Communication Enhancement Address any communication or conflict issues that are limiting team effectiveness. Provide skill-building and practice opportunities.

Week 8: Performance Optimization Implement systems for goal alignment, resource optimization, process improvement, and capability development that will sustain long-term team growth.

Your success as a leader increasingly depends not on your individual capabilities, but on your ability to build and lead teams that achieve results no individual could accomplish alone.

CHAPTER 15

Psychological Safety - How We Create Trust

The Safety Crisis Destroying Team Performance

I've discovered that most workplace environments are psychologically unsafe. People are afraid to speak up with ideas, concerns, or mistakes. They're hesitant to ask questions that might make them look incompetent. They avoid taking risks that could lead to innovation because they fear punishment if those risks don't pay off.

This psychological fear is destroying organizational performance in ways that most leaders don't recognize or understand. I regularly encounter teams where the best ideas never get shared because people don't feel safe expressing them. I see organizations where critical problems go unaddressed because employees are afraid to raise concerns. I work with companies that claim to value innovation but have created cultures where people are punished for the failures that inevitably accompany experimentation. Leaders must have the courage to encourage innovation and protect those with good intent who are unsuccessful. Make innovation an important part of your culture!

Google's Project Aristotle found that psychological safety was the number one factor distinguishing high-performing teams from average ones, as more important than individual talent, team composition, or even resources. Yet Gallup's research shows that only 3 in 10 employees strongly agree that their opinions count at work, and fewer than half feel comfortable expressing disagreement with their supervisors.

Psychological Safety

Psychological safety is not about being nice, avoiding conflict, or creating comfortable environments where people never feel challenged. It's about creating conditions where people feel safe to be vulnerable in the service of better performance and continuous learning.

Edmondson defines psychological safety as "a belief that one can speak up without risk of punishment or humiliation." The following is a more comprehensive understanding that includes several specific dimensions:

Intellectual Safety: The ability to ask questions, admit ignorance, and challenge ideas without being seen as incompetent or disruptive.

Emotional Safety: The freedom to express genuine emotions and reactions without being judged, dismissed, or punished for having human feelings.

Social Safety: The confidence that you belong and are valued as a team member, even when you make mistakes or disagree with others.

Creative Safety: The permission to experiment, take risks, and try new approaches without fear of punishment if they don't work perfectly.

Ethical Safety: The ability to raise moral concerns, report problems, and challenge questionable practices without retaliation or ostracism.

The Four Levels of Psychological Safety

Through my work with organizational teams, I've identified four progressive levels of psychological safety that teams can develop:

Level 1: Basic Safety - "I Won't Be Punished"

Characteristics:

- People feel safe from retaliation for normal workplace interactions
- Basic civility and respect are maintained
- Obvious mistakes don't result in severe punishment
- People can ask basic questions without being ridiculed

Leader behaviors that create this level:

- Respond to mistakes with curiosity rather than blame
- Treat all team members with consistent respect
- Address hostile or disrespectful behavior immediately
- Create clear expectations about acceptable workplace conduct

Real-world assessment: People will admit obvious mistakes and ask clarifying questions about their work without fear of punishment.

Level 2: Learning Safety - "I Can Learn and Grow"

Characteristics:

- People feel safe admitting ignorance and asking for help
- Mistakes are treated as learning opportunities
- Questions are welcomed and answered helpfully
- Development and growth are supported and encouraged

Leader behaviors that create this level:

- Admit your own learning needs and knowledge gaps
- Ask questions frequently to model curiosity
- Respond positively to requests for help and development
- Share your own mistakes and what you learned from them

Real-world assessment: People regularly ask for help, admit when they don't understand something, and discuss their development needs openly.

Level 3: Inclusion Safety - "I Belong and Am Valued"

Characteristics:

- People feel included in important discussions and decisions
- Diverse perspectives are actively sought and valued
- Team members support each other during challenges
- Everyone feels like their contributions matter

Leader behaviors that create this level:

- Actively seek input from all team members
- Value and build on different perspectives and approaches
- Create opportunities for people to contribute their unique strengths
- Address exclusion or favoritism immediately

Real-world assessment: All team members contribute actively to discussions, people build on each other's ideas, and diverse viewpoints are expressed and valued.

Level 4: Innovation Safety - "I Can Take Risks and Challenge Ideas"

Characteristics:

- People feel safe proposing new ideas and approaches
- Failure is viewed as part of learning and innovation

- Challenging existing practices and assumptions is encouraged
- Experimentation and calculated risk-taking are supported

Leader behaviors that create this level:

- Encourage experimentation and new approaches
- Celebrate intelligent failures and learning from them
- Challenge your own assumptions and invite others to do the same
- Provide resources and support for testing new ideas

Real-world assessment: People regularly propose new ideas, challenge existing approaches, and experiment with different methods without fear of punishment for failures.

Real-World Safety Building Strategies

Helping teams build psychological safety, I've identified specific strategies that consistently produce results:

Strategy 1: Leader Vulnerability Modeling

The fastest way to build psychological safety is for leaders to model the vulnerability they want to see from others.

Strategy 2: Question-Based Leadership

Replace statement-based leadership with question-based leadership to encourage thinking and contribution.

Real-world application: Instead of announcing decisions, start with questions that invite input and exploration. Instead of giving answers, ask questions that help people develop their own thinking.

Strategy 3: Failure Celebration Systems

Create systematic approaches to celebrating intelligent failures and learning from them.

Your Psychological Safety Development Plan

Building psychological safety requires systematic effort over months, not days. Here's my recommended approach:

Week 1: Safety Assessment Complete comprehensive assessment of current psychological safety levels using surveys, observations, and conversations. Identify specific areas needing improvement.

Week 2: Leader Behavior Analysis Assess your own behaviors that might be destroying or building psychological safety. Get feedback from trusted team members about your impact on team safety.

Week 3: Vulnerability Modeling Practice Begin systematically modeling the vulnerability you want to see from others. Share mistakes, admit uncertainties, and ask for help and feedback.

Week 4: Question-Based Leadership Implementation Replace statement-based leadership with question-based leadership. Practice asking questions that invite thinking and contribution rather than giving answers.

Week 5: Failure Normalization Begin normalizing intelligent failures and learning from them. Create opportunities to celebrate experiments that didn't work but generated valuable learning.

Week 6: Inclusive Process Design Implement decision-making and communication processes that actively include all team members and value diverse perspectives.

Week 7: Conflict Skill Building Help team members develop skills for productive disagreement and conflict resolution. Practice addressing conflicts as learning opportunities.

Week 8: Safety Reinforcement Systems Create ongoing systems and practices that reinforce psychological safety over time. Build safety maintenance into your regular leadership practices.

Your effectiveness as a leader increasingly depends on your ability to create environments where people can bring their full capabilities to work. Psychological safety is the foundation of those environments.

CHAPTER 16

Productive Conflict - Why We Embrace Disagreement

Solving The Conflict Avoidance Crisis

When discussing organizational conflict, I've witnessed a pervasive and damaging pattern that costs organizations millions of dollars and countless opportunities: most leaders and teams treat conflict as something to be avoided, minimized, or quickly resolved rather than as a valuable source of better decisions and stronger relationships. This conflict avoidance creates enormous hidden costs that most organizations don't recognize or measure, but that I see destroying performance every day.

I regularly encounter teams where important strategic discussions are derailed the moment someone disagrees with the proposed direction. These teams spend hours in meetings where everyone nods politely while harboring serious concerns that never get voiced. I see organizations where critical problems persist for months or even years because addressing them would require difficult conversations between departments that have learned to work around each other rather than work through their differences. I work with leaders who pride themselves on "keeping the peace" while their teams consistently make poor decisions because diverse perspectives were never heard, challenged, or considered.

The irony is profound and costly. Organizations hire smart, experienced people precisely because they bring different perspectives and expertise, then create cultures that discourage them from sharing those differences. They invest millions in diversity initiatives while simultaneously training people to avoid the productive disagreement that makes diversity valuable. They claim to want innovation while punishing the creative conflict that generates breakthrough ideas. Remember that "Out of conflict often comes creativity!"

The latest research by Lencioni and CPP Global reveals that teams and organizations that engage in productive conflict make better decisions, solve problems faster, and develop stronger relationships over time. Yet 85% of employees experience workplace conflict as destructive rather than productive, and 76% of leaders report that they avoid difficult conversations that could resolve conflicts constructively. This represents one of the largest untapped opportunities for organizational improvement that I encounter in my consulting work.

Productive Conflict

When I advocate for embracing conflict, I am not suggesting that teams should argue constantly or create unnecessary drama. I am not promoting the kind of destructive conflict that damages relationships and undermines performance. I am talking about productive conflict, which is disagreement that's focused on ideas, issues, and approaches rather than personalities, and that's conducted with the explicit goal of reaching better outcomes for everyone involved.

Productive conflict is fundamentally different from the destructive conflict that most people have experienced in their personal and professional lives. Destructive conflict is about winning and being right.

Productive conflict is about learning and being better. Destructive conflict attacks people and positions. Productive conflict explores ideas and possibilities. Destructive conflict creates winners and losers. Productive conflict creates better solutions for everyone.

I've learned that productive conflict has several essential characteristics that distinguish it from the destructive variety. It's issue-focused rather than person-focused, meaning the disagreement centers on problems, approaches, or decisions rather than personal characteristics or past grievances. It's solution-oriented rather than blame-oriented, with the goal being to find better answers rather than to prove others wrong or assign responsibility for past problems.

Productive conflict is respectful in the deepest sense. People can disagree strongly with ideas while maintaining genuine respect for the individuals who hold those ideas. It's time-bounded rather than ongoing, meaning conflicts are addressed directly and resolved efficiently rather than being allowed to fester indefinitely or resurface repeatedly. It's learning-based rather than position-based, with participants entering conflicts with genuine curiosity about other perspectives and willingness to change their minds based on new information or better reasoning.

Most importantly, productive conflict is relationship-strengthening rather than relationship-damaging. When handled skillfully, disagreement builds trust and understanding among team members because it demonstrates that people can work through differences together and that diverse perspectives are valued and considered seriously.

The Five Types of Workplace Conflict I Navigate Daily

I've identified five distinct types of conflict that occur regularly in workplace settings. Understanding these different types is crucial because each requires different approaches, skills, and leadership interventions. Many conflicts become destructive simply because people are trying to resolve one type of conflict using approaches that work for a different type.

Task Conflict involves disagreement about goals, objectives, or work assignments. This might include disputes about priorities, resource allocation, or strategic direction. Task conflict often emerges when teams are facing resource constraints, competing deadlines, or unclear organizational priorities. For example, a marketing team might disagree about whether to focus its limited budget on digital advertising or trade show participation, with compelling arguments on both sides.

Task conflict becomes productive when it leads to better resource allocation, clearer priorities, and more thoughtful decision-making. It becomes destructive when it creates paralysis, undermines the execution of agreed-upon decisions, or turns into personal attacks on those who proposed different approaches. The key to managing task conflict effectively is to facilitate data-based discussion, clarify decision-making authority, and establish clear timelines for resolution so that analysis doesn't become perpetual delay.

Process Conflict involves disagreement about methods, procedures, or approaches to accomplishing work. This type of conflict is increasingly common in organizations that are trying to become more agile, efficient, or innovative. Teams often have strong opinions about the best ways to accomplish objectives, and these disagreements can either lead to better processes or create endless debate that prevents any approach from being implemented effectively.

A common example is an engineering team debating whether to use agile or waterfall methodology for a new project, with experienced team members having strong preferences based on their past successes and failures with different approaches. Process conflict becomes productive when it leads to more efficient workflows, better coordination, and systematic improvement in how work gets done. It becomes destructive when it prevents any method from being implemented effectively or when it turns into arguments about whose approach is superior rather than which approach fits the current situation best.

Role Conflict involves disagreement about responsibilities, authority, or decision-making rights. This type of conflict is particularly common in matrix organizations, cross-functional teams, and rapidly growing companies where roles and responsibilities haven't been clearly defined or have evolved faster than formal job descriptions. Role conflict often masquerades as other types of conflict because people are reluctant to admit they're confused about who should do what.

A typical example involves sales and marketing teams disagreeing about who is responsible for lead qualification and follow-up, with each group believing the other should handle more of the process. Role conflict becomes productive when it leads to clearer role definitions, better coordination between functions, and more effective handoffs. It becomes destructive when it creates gaps in coverage, duplicated efforts, or ongoing turf battles that waste energy and create customer confusion.

Relationship Conflict involves personal tensions, communication problems, or interpersonal friction between team members. This is often the most difficult type of conflict to address because it involves emotions, personality differences, and sometimes long histories of misunderstanding or hurt feelings. Relationship conflict often develops gradually as small irritations accumulate over time, or it can emerge suddenly when people are under stress, and their normal diplomatic filters break down.

Relationship conflict might involve two team members who have developed mutual distrust based on different work styles, communication preferences, or past misunderstandings that were never addressed directly. This type of conflict becomes productive when it leads to better understanding, improved working relationships, and clearer agreements about how people will interact with each other. It becomes destructive when it creates lasting hostility, undermines team effectiveness, or spreads to involve other team members who feel forced to choose sides.

Values Conflict involves disagreement about priorities, principles, or organizational values. This is often the deepest and most challenging type of conflict because it touches on fundamental beliefs about what's important and how organizations should operate. Values conflicts often emerge when organizations are facing difficult trade-offs between competing goods, such as short-term profitability versus long-term sustainability, individual performance versus team collaboration, or innovation versus risk management.

A leadership team might experience values conflict when deciding whether to prioritize quarterly earnings expectations or invest in employee development programs that won't show returns for years. Values conflict becomes productive when it leads to clearer organizational principles, more aligned decision-making, and explicit discussions about trade-offs and priorities. It becomes destructive when it creates irreconcilable divisions, undermines organizational unity, or prevents necessary decisions from being made.

The RESOLVE Framework for Managing Conflict

When facilitating conflict resolution sessions across every type of organization and conflict situation, use the RESOLVE framework; systematic approach for turning destructive conflict into productive dialogue. This framework provides a step-by-step process that leaders can use to navigate conflicts skillfully, regardless of their complexity or emotional intensity.

R - Recognizing the Real Issues is the essential first step that many leaders skip in their eagerness to resolve conflicts quickly. Before attempting to resolve any conflict, you must accurately identify what the disagreement is really about. Surface-level arguments often mask deeper concerns or issues, and trying to solve the wrong problem inevitably leads to temporary fixes that don't address root causes.

This recognition phase involves asking probing questions to understand what's really driving the conflict. What specifically am I disagreeing about? What interests or concerns are driving each perspective? Am I arguing about the real issue or just a symptom of something deeper? What would need to be different for everyone to feel satisfied with the outcome? Often, what appears to be a task conflict about resource allocation is a role conflict about decision-making authority, or what seems like a process disagreement is really a values conflict about organizational priorities.

E - Establish Ground Rules for the conflict discussion is crucial because productive conflict requires agreed-upon boundaries and expectations for how the conversation will be conducted. Without clear ground rules, conflicts quickly deteriorate into blame sessions, personal attacks, or power struggles that make resolution impossible and damage relationships permanently.

Essential ground rules include focusing on issues and behaviors rather than personalities or character, seeking to understand before seeking to be understood, sharing all relevant information rather than withholding important facts, looking for solutions that work for everyone involved, and committing to support whatever solution is ultimately chosen. These ground rules should be discussed and agreed upon at the beginning of every conflict conversation, and participants should feel empowered to reference them if the discussion gets off track.

S - Share Perspectives Completely ensures that each party has the opportunity to share their viewpoint fully without interruption or immediate judgment. This sharing phase is critical because people can't move toward resolution until they feel heard and understood. Rushing to problem-solving before perspectives are fully shared inevitably leads to solutions that don't address everyone's core concerns.

The structured sharing process involves each person presenting their view of the situation without interruption, others listening for understanding rather than preparing rebuttals, asking clarifying questions to ensure accurate understanding, and acknowledging legitimate concerns and interests from all parties. This phase often takes longer than people expect but investing time in a complete understanding dramatically accelerates the solution development phase.

O - Options Generation focuses the group's energy on creating multiple possible solutions rather than arguing about preferred approaches. This phase separates creativity from evaluation, encouraging people to generate as many possibilities as they can before discussing the merits of any particular approach. The goal is to expand the solution space rather than immediately narrowing it.

Effective options generation involves brainstorming multiple possible solutions without immediate evaluation, building on each other's ideas rather than dismissing them, looking for creative approaches that address everyone's core concerns, and considering partial solutions and pilot approaches that allow for experimentation and learning. The key is to resist the temptation to evaluate ideas as they're proposed, which kills creativity and returns the group to argumentative mode.

L - Look for Common Ground by identifying areas of agreement and shared interests that can serve as the foundation for solution development. Even in the most heated conflicts, there are usually more areas of agreement than disagreement, but these commonalities often get lost in the focus on differences. Deliberately identifying shared ground creates a positive foundation for collaborative problem-solving.

Common ground discovery involves asking what outcomes everyone wants to achieve, what concerns are shared across different perspectives, what principles everyone can support, and where interests are aligned rather than opposed. Starting solution development with shared interests and working outward to areas of disagreement is much more effective than starting with the most contentious issues.

V - Viable Solutions Development creates specific, actionable approaches that address the core concerns of all parties involved. These solutions must be practical, given available resources and constraints, acceptable to all parties who must implement them, and specific enough to guide actual behavior and decision-making.

Solutions should address root causes rather than just symptoms, be workable given available resources and organizational constraints, be acceptable to all parties who must implement them, and include specific actions, timelines, and accountability measures. The best solutions often combine elements from different proposed approaches rather than simply choosing one person's preferred solution.

E - Agreements and Follow-Up concludes the conflict resolution process with clear commitments about what will happen next and how progress will be monitored. Conflicts often resurface not because the solutions were poor, but because the agreements were vague and follow-up was inadequate.

Essential agreements include specific actions each party will take, timelines for implementation and review, success measures and evaluation criteria, processes for addressing future disagreements, and follow-up schedules to monitor progress. These agreements should be documented and reviewed regularly to ensure that conflict resolution translates into sustained behavior change.

Your Productive Conflict Development Plan

Building your capability to lead productive conflict requires systematic practice over time. Here's my recommended eight-week development approach based on helping leaders improve their conflict management skills:

Week 1: Conflict Assessment and Pattern Recognition involves analyzing your current approach to conflict and identifying patterns in how you and your team handle disagreement. Complete a comprehensive assessment of how conflicts are currently managed in your area of responsibility, identify conflicts you're currently avoiding and the costs of that avoidance, analyze your personal conflict style and triggers that make conflict difficult for you, and gather feedback from team members about how conflicts are typically handled.

Week 2: Productive Conflict Skill Building focuses on developing the fundamental skills needed for healthy disagreement. Practice the RESOLVE framework in lower-stakes situations, work on emotional regulation and staying calm during disagreements, develop your ability to separate issues from personalities, and learn to ask questions that explore rather than attack different perspectives.

Week 3: Creating Conflict-Safe Environments involves establishing conditions that make productive conflict possible within your team. Establish ground rules for team discussions that encourage healthy disagreement, model productive conflict yourself by respectfully challenging ideas and inviting challenges to your own thinking, address any team dynamics that punish disagreement or reward false harmony, and begin making disagreement safe and expected rather than avoided.

Week 4: Facilitating Team Conflicts develops your ability to help others work through their disagreements productively. Practice facilitating conflicts between team members using structured processes, learn to remain neutral while helping others explore different perspectives, develop skills for keeping discussions focused on issues rather than personalities, and create opportunities for team members to practice productive conflict in safe settings.

Week 5: Leading Strategic Disagreements focuses on using conflict to improve decision-making and strategic thinking. Structure decision-making processes that deliberately surface different perspectives and potential concerns, assign team members to argue for different approaches regardless of their personal preferences, create "red team" exercises that challenge important proposals before they're finalized, and practice making disagreement a valued contribution rather than something people do reluctantly.

Week 6: Managing Difficult Conflict Situations prepares you for the most challenging conflict scenarios you're likely to encounter. Practice managing conflicts involving senior stakeholders or people with strong personalities, develop approaches for addressing conflicts that have been avoided for extended periods, learn to handle conflicts that involve multiple parties with different interests, and build skills for addressing relationship conflicts that are affecting team performance.

Week 7: Organizational Conflict Systems expands your focus beyond your immediate team to broader organizational dynamics. Identify and address systemic factors that create unnecessary conflict or prevent productive resolution, work with other leaders to create consistent approaches to conflict management across the organization, develop processes for escalating and resolving conflicts that cross departmental boundaries, and begin building organizational capability for productive conflict at scale.

Week 8: Conflict Leadership Integration makes productive conflict management a permanent part of your leadership practice rather than something you do occasionally. Integrate conflict management into your regular leadership routines and team processes, create ongoing systems for surfacing and addressing conflicts before they become destructive, develop your team's collective capability for managing disagreements independently, and establish metrics for tracking the health of conflict dynamics within your area of responsibility.

Remember that building comfort and skill with productive conflict takes time and practice. Start with lower-stakes situations and gradually work up to more challenging conflicts as your confidence and capability grow. The goal isn't to eliminate conflict from your workplace; it's to transform conflict from a destructive force into a powerful tool for better decisions, stronger relationships, and improved performance.

CHAPTER 17

Delegation Done Right - Your System for Empowerment

The Delegation Crisis Limiting Every Leader

Consulting with leaders at every organizational level, I've identified another leadership failure: the inability to delegate effectively. Most leaders I work with are drowning in tasks that others could and should be handling, while simultaneously complaining that their people aren't developing fast enough and aren't taking sufficient ownership of their work. This creates a vicious cycle where leaders become bottlenecks to organizational performance while inadvertently stunting the growth of the people they're supposed to be developing.

I regularly encounter senior executives who are working 60 to 70-hour workweeks on tasks that could be handled by people earning a fraction of their salary. I see managers who claim they want to develop their people but never give them opportunities to develop into new responsibilities. I work with leaders who are frustrated by their teams' lack of initiative while continuing to make all the decisions themselves. The irony is profound: leaders create the very problems they complain about through their inability to delegate effectively.

Research by Gallup and Harvard Business Review reveals that leaders who delegate effectively achieve 23% better results and report 24% lower stress levels than those who try to handle everything themselves. Yet studies consistently show that less than 30% of leaders believe they delegate well, and even fewer receive positive feedback from their teams about delegation practices. This represents one of the largest untapped opportunities for leadership improvement that I encounter in my consulting work.

The cost of poor delegation extends far beyond individual leader burnout. Organizations with leaders who can't delegate effectively experience slower decision-making, reduced innovation, higher turnover among high-potential employees, and systematic under-development of leadership capabilities throughout the organization. They become overly dependent on a few key individuals and struggle to scale their operations as they grow.

Delegation Done Right

When I talk about effective delegation, I am not referring to simply dumping tasks on other people or abdication of leadership responsibility. I am talking about a systematic approach to developing others' capabilities while achieving better results and freeing yourself to focus on your highest-value contributions. Real delegation is simultaneously a performance tool, a development strategy, and a leadership multiplication system.

Effective delegation has several essential characteristics that distinguish it from mere task assignment. It's development-focused rather than just task-focused, meaning the goal is building people's capabilities over time, not just getting immediate work completed. It's outcome-oriented rather than process-oriented, specifying what needs to be accomplished while giving people freedom to determine how to achieve those outcomes. It's supported rather than abandoned, providing resources, guidance, and feedback while avoiding micromanagement.

True delegation is relationship-building rather than relationship-avoiding, creating opportunities for coaching, mentoring, and collaborative problem-solving. It's strategic rather than random, aligning delegated responsibilities with both organizational needs and individual development goals. Most importantly, effective delegation is gradual and progressive, building people's capabilities systematically over time rather than overwhelming them with responsibilities they're not prepared to handle.

I've learned that delegation done right requires more initial investment of time and energy than doing tasks yourself, but it pays enormous dividends in increased capacity, improved results, and accelerated development of your people. Leaders who master delegation become force multipliers who achieve more through others than they ever could accomplish individually.

The Delegation Readiness Matrix

One of the biggest delegation mistakes I see is leaders treating all tasks and all people the same way. Effective delegation requires matching the right level of delegation to the specific task and the specific person's readiness for that responsibility. I've adopted and expanded Ken Blanchard's Situational Leadership II delegation readiness matrix to help leaders make these decisions systematically rather than randomly.

High Competence, High Commitment (Delegate Fully): When someone has both the skills to handle a responsibility and the motivation to do it well, you can delegate almost completely. These situations call for clear outcome expectations, adequate resources, and minimal supervision. Your role becomes strategic support rather than active management.

For example, if you have a senior team member who has successfully managed similar projects multiple times and is enthusiastic about taking on a new challenge, you can delegate the entire project with confidence. Provide clear success criteria, ensure they have the necessary resources, and schedule periodic check-ins to offer support rather than oversight. This level of delegation frees you to focus on higher-level responsibilities while giving the person valuable growth opportunities.

High Competence, Low Commitment (Delegate with Motivation Focus): When someone has the skills but lacks enthusiasm or commitment, delegation requires more attention to motivational factors. These situations often arise when people are burned out, feeling unappreciated, or unclear about how the work connects to their career goals.

Your approach should focus on understanding and addressing the commitment issues while leveraging their existing competence. This might involve connecting the work to their personal development goals, providing more recognition and feedback, or addressing obstacles that are undermining their motivation. The delegation can still be substantial but requires more relationship investment.

Low Competence, High Commitment (Delegate with Development Support): When someone is eager to take on new responsibilities but lacks the necessary skills or experience, delegation becomes a structured development opportunity. These situations require significant upfront investment in training, coaching, and support systems.

Your approach should include clear skill development plans, regular coaching sessions, graduated responsibility increases, and safety nets that prevent failures from becoming disasters. This type of delegation often takes longer initially but creates tremendous long-term value through capability building.

Low Competence, Low Commitment (Don't Delegate Yet): When someone lacks both the skills and the motivation for a responsibility, delegation is premature and likely to fail. These situations require addressing the fundamental competence and commitment issues before delegation becomes viable.

Your approach should focus on basic skill development, motivation building, and performance management. Rather than delegating significant responsibilities, focus on smaller tasks that can build both competence and confidence over time. This is often the most challenging delegation scenario and may require difficult decisions about whether the person is in the right role.

The EMPOWER Framework for Delegation

When helping leaders improve their delegation skills, use the EMPOWER framework; a systematic approach that ensures delegation serves both performance and development objectives while maintaining appropriate accountability and support.

E - Establish Clear Outcomes and Expectations is the foundation of all effective delegation. Vague expectations lead to frustration, disappointment, and failed delegation attempts that make leaders reluctant to delegate in the future. Clear outcomes include not just what needs to be accomplished, but success criteria, quality standards, deadlines, and resource constraints.

Effective outcome setting involves defining specific, measurable results rather than just activities or efforts. Instead of saying "work on the customer satisfaction initiative," specify "increase customer satisfaction scores from 7.2 to 8.0 within six months while maintaining current service costs." Include quality standards that define what excellent work looks like, timeline expectations that specify not just final deadlines but key milestones along the way, and resource parameters that clarify what budget, people, and tools are available.

You should also specify decision-making authority clearly, such as what decisions they can make independently, what decisions require consultation, and what decisions must be escalated. This prevents the common delegation failure where people either make decisions they shouldn't or fail to make decisions they should. Finally, establish communication expectations about how often you'll check in, what information you need, and how problems or questions should be handled.

M - Match Responsibility to Readiness ensures that delegation challenges people appropriately without setting them up for failure. This involves honestly assessing both the complexity of the task and the person's current capability level, then structuring the delegation accordingly.

For routine tasks with experienced people, delegation can be quite broad with minimal structure. For complex tasks or developing people, delegation requires more scaffolding, support, and gradual responsibility transfer. The goal is to stretch people just beyond their current comfort zone without overwhelming them.

Consider both technical readiness (do they have the skills and knowledge needed) and leadership readiness (can they influence others, make decisions, and manage projects). Sometimes people are technically capable but need development in project management, stakeholder communication, or team leadership skills.

P - Provide Authority and Resources means ensuring that people have what they need to be successful in their delegated responsibilities. Nothing undermines delegation faster than giving someone responsibility without corresponding authority or adequate resources to fulfill that responsibility.

Authority includes decision-making power appropriate to the level of delegation, access to information and systems needed to do the work, ability to represent you or the organization in relevant contexts, and influence over other people whose cooperation is needed. Resources include budget authority for necessary expenditures, access to tools, technology, and facilities required, time allocation that recognizes the work requires attention, and support staff or expertise when needed.

You should also provide access to your own networks and relationships when that would help them be successful. Sometimes the most valuable resource you can provide is an introduction to key stakeholders or an endorsement that opens doors they couldn't open independently.

O - Offer Support Without Micromanaging requires finding the delicate balance between providing adequate guidance and maintaining appropriate autonomy. The goal is to be available for consultation while avoiding the temptation to take back control when things don't go exactly as you would do them.

Effective support includes regular check-ins that focus on removing obstacles rather than monitoring every detail, coaching conversations that help people think through challenges rather than providing all the answers, resource provision when people encounter barriers beyond their control, and course correction when major adjustments are needed.

The key is to be responsive to requests for help while avoiding unsolicited intervention. Let people know that asking for help is expected and valued, not a sign of weakness or incompetence. At the same time, resist the urge to jump in and fix things when you can accomplish tasks faster yourself.

W - Work Through Mistakes and Learning recognizes that delegation inevitably involves some failures and mistakes, and these should be treated as learning opportunities rather than reasons to stop delegating. How you handle mistakes determines whether delegation builds capability and confidence or creates fear and dependence.

When mistakes happen, focus on understanding what went wrong and how to prevent similar problems in the future rather than assigning blame or taking back control. Use mistakes as coaching opportunities to develop better judgment, planning skills, or risk management capabilities. Help people distinguish between mistakes that indicate they weren't ready for the responsibility and mistakes that are normal parts of learning and development.

Sometimes mistakes reveal that your initial delegation was poorly structured due to unclear expectations, inadequate resources, or insufficient authority. Be willing to acknowledge your own contribution to delegation failures and adjust your approach accordingly.

E - Evaluate Results and Recognize Success ensures that delegation contributes to both immediate performance and long-term development. This involves measuring both the quality of outcomes achieved and the learning and growth that occurred through the delegation process.

Evaluation should focus on results achieved relative to expectations, quality of work relative to standards, timeliness and efficiency of execution, and development of new capabilities and confidence. Recognition should acknowledge both successful outcomes and effective learning from challenges or setbacks.

Use evaluation conversations to discuss what worked well, what could be improved, and what the person learned about themselves, their work, or the organization. This information helps you calibrate future delegation decisions and helps the person understand their own development progress.

R - Reward Growth and Expand Opportunities creates positive momentum for both continued development and future delegation. People who handle delegated responsibilities well should see expanded opportunities, increased autonomy, and recognition for their growth.

Rewards might include increased responsibility and authority, public recognition of achievements and growth, input into their own development planning, and opportunities to teach or mentor others. The goal is to create a positive cycle where successful delegation leads to more delegation, greater capability development, and increased contribution to organizational success.

Your Delegation Mastery Development Plan

Building effective delegation skills requires systematic practice and gradual capability building. Here's my recommended eight-week development approach based on helping leaders become more effective delegators:

Week 1: Delegation Assessment and Opportunity Identification involves analyzing your current delegation patterns and identifying opportunities for improvement. Complete a comprehensive inventory of tasks you're currently handling that could potentially be delegated, assess the readiness levels of your team members for different types of responsibilities, identify delegation failures from your past and analyze what went wrong, and calculate the time and energy costs of your current approach versus the benefits of more effective delegation.

Week 2: Delegation Readiness Analysis focuses on systematically evaluating delegation opportunities using the readiness matrix I've described. For each potential delegation opportunity, assess the person's competence and commitment levels, determine what type of support and structure would be needed, identify what development would be required before delegation becomes viable, and prioritize delegation opportunities based on both immediate benefits and long-term development value.

Week 3: First Delegation Implementation involves selecting your highest-priority delegation opportunity and implementing it using the EMPOWER framework. Choose a delegation opportunity that's important enough to matter but not so critical that failure would be catastrophic, practice using the framework systematically rather than relying on intuition, document your delegation conversation so you can reference agreements later, and establish clear check-in schedules and communication expectations.

Week 4: Support and Monitoring Systems develops your ability to provide appropriate support without micromanaging. Practice checking in on progress without taking back control, learn to coach through challenges rather than providing all the answers, work on providing resources and removing obstacles when needed, and resist the temptation to intervene when people approach tasks differently than you would.

Week 5: Advanced Delegation Scenarios prepares you for more complex delegation situations involving higher stakes, multiple people, or cross-functional coordination. Practice delegating projects that involve influencing others outside your direct authority, work on delegating responsibilities that require representing you or the organization, develop skills for delegating to remote or virtual team members, and learn to delegate strategic responsibilities rather than just operational tasks.

Week 6: Delegation Failure Recovery builds your capability to handle delegation mistakes and setbacks constructively. Practice responding to delegation failures with curiosity rather than blame, learn to distinguish between people problems and system problems when delegation doesn't work, develop skills for course-correcting delegation without completely taking back control, and work on using mistakes as development opportunities rather than reasons to stop delegating.

Week 7: Systematic Delegation Planning creates ongoing systems for identifying and implementing delegation opportunities rather than handling them randomly. Develop regular processes for assessing team members' readiness for expanded responsibilities, create development planning that includes systematic responsibility increases over time, establish organizational systems that support effective delegation across multiple levels, and work with other leaders to create consistent delegation practices and standards.

Week 8: Delegation Culture Building expands your focus from individual delegation skills to creating organizational cultures that support effective delegation at scale. Model effective delegation practices that others can observe and learn from, train other leaders in your organization on systematic delegation approaches, create recognition and reward systems that value development of others rather than just individual performance, and establish metrics for tracking delegation effectiveness and organizational capability development over time.

Remember that effective delegation is one of the highest-leverage leadership skills you can develop. Every person you successfully develop multiplies your impact and creates capabilities that continue producing value long after specific projects are completed. The initial investment in learning to delegate well pays dividends throughout your entire leadership career.

CHAPTER 18

Performance Culture - How We Build Excellence

Confronting The Performance Mediocrity Crisis

I've clearly identified another major culture problem: the widespread acceptance of mediocre performance as normal and acceptable. Most organizations have cultures that tolerate average work, avoid difficult performance conversations, and inadvertently reward compliance over excellence. The result is a vast wasteland of human potential where capable people produce ordinary results because extraordinary performance is neither expected, supported, nor consistently recognized.

I regularly encounter teams where high performers become frustrated and eventually leave because their excellence isn't valued or rewarded differently from average performance. I see organizations where people learn to do just enough to avoid negative consequences rather than striving for outstanding results. I work with leaders who claim they want high performance but have created systems, processes, and cultural norms that make excellence difficult and mediocrity comfortable.

This performance mediocrity isn't just about individual under-achievement, but it's about systematic organizational failure to create conditions where people can and will do their best work. It represents one of the largest opportunities for competitive advantage that most organizations completely ignore. While they invest millions in technology, marketing, and strategic planning, they fail to address the fundamental cultural factors that determine whether those investments will be executed with excellence or mediocrity.

The latest research by McKinsey and Gallup reveals that organizations with truly high-performance cultures achieve 2.5 times the revenue growth, 1.9 times the return to shareholders, and 40% lower turnover than organizations with average performance cultures. Yet studies consistently show that less than 15% of organizations believe they have strong performance cultures, and fewer have systematic approaches for building and maintaining them.

The cost of accepting mediocre performance extends far beyond missed financial results. Organizations with weak performance cultures experience slower innovation, reduced customer satisfaction, higher employee turnover, and systematic under-development of leadership capabilities. They become vulnerable to disruption by competitors who create cultures that unleash rather than constrain human potential.

High-Performance Culture

When I talk about building performance culture, I am not advocating for creating high-pressure, fear-based environments where people are constantly stressed about meeting unrealistic expectations. I am talking about systematic approaches to creating conditions where people consistently perform at or near their best capabilities because they're supported, challenged, recognized, and developed in ways that bring out their natural drive for excellence.

True performance culture has several essential characteristics that distinguish it from both toxic high-pressure environments and comfortable low-expectation cultures. It's standards-based rather than fear-based, meaning excellence is defined clearly and pursued systematically rather than demanded through threats or punishment. It's development-focused rather than evaluation-focused, treating performance gaps as development opportunities rather than personal failures.

High-performance culture is support-intensive rather than sink-or-swim, providing people with the resources, training, and coaching they need to meet high standards rather than simply expecting them to figure it out independently. It's recognition-rich rather than criticism-heavy, celebrating and reinforcing excellent performance while addressing substandard performance constructively. Most importantly, it's sustainable rather than sprint-based, creating conditions that enable consistently high performance over time rather than unsustainable bursts of activity.

I've learned that authentic high-performance cultures are simultaneously demanding and supportive, challenging and caring, results-oriented and people-focused. They don't sacrifice human dignity or work-life balance in pursuit of results; instead, they create conditions where people want to do excellent work because it's personally satisfying and organizationally valued.

The Performance Culture Foundation

Creating a genuine high-performance culture requires addressing four foundational elements that most organizations either ignore or handle superficially. These elements work together as an integrated system because weakness in any single area undermines the entire performance culture effort.

Foundation 1: Clarity of Expectations and Standards

High performance is impossible when people don't understand what excellence looks like in their specific roles and responsibilities. Most organizations have vague performance expectations that leave people guessing about what's really important and how their work will be evaluated. This ambiguity inevitably leads to mediocre performance because people default to minimum acceptable standards when maximum expectations aren't clear.

Creating clarity requires defining excellence behaviorally rather than conceptually, meaning people understand not just what results are expected but what actions and approaches lead to those results. It involves establishing specific success criteria for all important responsibilities, not just the ones that are easily measured. It means communicating expectations in ways that people can translate into daily decisions and actions rather than abstract concepts they have to interpret.

Clarity also requires consistency across different leaders, departments, and time periods so that people don't receive conflicting messages about what's really important. When expectations change frequently or vary dramatically between different parts of the organization, people learn to focus on political navigation rather than performance excellence.

I help organizations create clarity by developing performance standards collaboratively with the people who will be held accountable for meeting them. This ensures that standards are both challenging and achievable, and that people understand the reasoning behind expectations rather than simply being told what to do.

Foundation 2: Capability Development and Support

Expecting high performance without providing the capability development and support needed to achieve it is both unfair and ineffective. Most organizations set high standards but fail to invest adequately in developing people's ability to meet those standards. This creates frustration for both leaders and team members when good intentions don't translate into better results.

Effective capability development goes beyond traditional training programs to include systematic skill building, ongoing coaching and mentoring, stretch assignments that build new capabilities, and access to tools, resources, and information needed for excellence. It involves helping people understand not just what to do but how to think about their work more strategically and effectively.

Capability development must be personalized rather than generic, addressing each person's specific development needs and learning style. It should be continuous rather than event-based, providing ongoing growth opportunities rather than relying on periodic training sessions. Most importantly, it should be connected to real work rather than abstract learning, giving people opportunities to practice new skills in meaningful contexts.

Support also includes removing obstacles that prevent excellent performance, such as bureaucratic processes, resource constraints, or organizational silos that make coordination difficult. Leaders must be willing to address systemic barriers rather than simply telling people to work harder within dysfunctional systems.

Foundation 3: Recognition and Accountability Systems

High-performance cultures require systematic approaches to recognizing and reinforcing excellent performance while addressing substandard performance constructively. Most organizations are terrible at both recognition and accountability, either ignoring good performance or handling poor performance ineffectively.

Effective recognition systems celebrate both results achieved, and behaviors demonstrated, helping people understand what excellent performance looks like in practice. Recognition should be timely, specific, and meaningful to the individuals receiving it rather than generic and disconnected from what really motivates people. It should acknowledge progress and improvement as well as final results, encouraging people to continue developing rather than only celebrating those who are already high performers.

Accountability systems must address performance gaps quickly and constructively rather than allowing problems to persist or escalate.

This involves having direct conversations about expectations and performance, providing additional support and development when needed, and making difficult decisions about people who consistently fail to meet standards despite adequate support and opportunity.

The key is balancing recognition and accountability so that people feel supported in their efforts to improve while understanding that sustained poor performance is not acceptable. This balance creates psychological safety for development while maintaining clear expectations for results.

Foundation 4: Leadership Modeling and Reinforcement

Performance culture is ultimately created and sustained by leadership behavior at every level of the organization. People watch what leaders do more than they listen to what leaders say, and they adjust their own performance accordingly. Leaders who accept mediocre performance from themselves or others inevitably create cultures where mediocrity becomes the norm.

Leadership modeling involves demonstrating the behaviors, standards, and approaches that are expected from others to "walk the talk.". This includes how leaders prepare for meetings, respond to challenges, interact with customers and colleagues, and handle both successes and failures. It involves leaders being transparent about their own development needs and learning efforts rather than pretending they have nothing to improve.

Reinforcement involves leaders consistently supporting and defending high-performance standards even when it's difficult or uncomfortable. This means having difficult conversations when performance standards aren't met, celebrating excellence even when it requires acknowledging that others haven't performed as well, and making resource allocation decisions that prioritize performance over politics or convenience.

Leaders must also model work-life integration that demonstrates that high performance doesn't require sacrificing personal well-being or family relationships. Sustainable high performance requires leaders who take care of themselves and support others in doing the same.

The EXCEL Framework for Performance Culture

When helping organizations build authentic high-performance cultures, use the EXCEL framework; a systematic approach that addresses all the critical elements needed for sustainable performance excellence.

E - Expectations: Clear, Challenging, and Achievable Standards

The foundation of any performance culture is a crystal-clear understanding of what excellence looks like in every important area of responsibility. This involves much more than annual goal-setting or general job descriptions. It requires ongoing dialogue about standards, regular calibration of expectations, and systematic communication about what high performance means in practice.

Effective expectations are specific enough to guide daily decisions and actions, challenging enough to require people to stretch and grow, achievable enough that people believe they can succeed with appropriate effort and support, and measurable enough that progress can be tracked and celebrated. They should connect individual performance to team and organizational success so that people understand how their excellence contributes to larger objectives.

Setting expectations effectively requires involving people in defining what excellence looks like rather than simply imposing standards from above. When people participate in creating performance standards, they're more likely to understand, accept, and commit to meeting them. This collaborative approach also ensures that standards are realistic, given available resources and constraints.

Expectations must also be dynamic rather than static, evolving as circumstances change and as people develop greater capabilities. Regular review and adjustment of expectations ensures that they remain relevant and motivating rather than becoming outdated or discouraging.

X - Excellence: Models, Examples, and Exemplars

People need to see what excellence looks like in practice, not just hear about it in theory. This requires creating and sharing concrete examples of outstanding performance, both from within the organization and from external sources that can serve as inspiration and learning opportunities.

Excellence modeling involves identifying and studying peak performance examples, sharing stories of exceptional achievement and the approaches that made them possible, creating opportunities for people to observe high performers in action, and providing access to best practices and proven methodologies from both internal and external sources.

I help organizations create "excellence libraries" that document outstanding performance examples, including what was accomplished, how it was achieved, what obstacles were overcome, and what lessons can be applied to other situations. These libraries become valuable resources for development and inspiration.

Excellence modeling also involves leaders sharing their own performance journeys, including failures and learning experiences that contributed to their development. This helps people understand that excellence is developed over time through consistent effort and learning rather than being an innate characteristic that some people possess and others don't.

C - Capability: Development, Training, and Coaching

High performance requires high capability, which must be developed systematically rather than left to chance. This involves creating comprehensive approaches to skill building that address both technical competencies and leadership capabilities needed for excellence.

Effective capability development includes formal training programs that provide foundational knowledge and skills, ongoing coaching that helps people apply learning to real situations, mentoring relationships that provide guidance and support from experienced performers and stretch assignments that challenge people to develop new capabilities through meaningful work.

Capability development must be personalized based on individual learning styles, development needs, and career aspirations. It should be continuous rather than episodic, providing ongoing growth opportunities rather than relying on periodic training events. Most importantly, it should be connected to performance expectations so that people understand what capabilities they need to develop to meet higher standards.

I also focus on developing organizational capabilities that support individual excellence, such as systems, processes, and tools that make high performance easier and more likely. Sometimes the biggest barriers to excellence are organizational constraints rather than individual limitations.

E - Engagement: Purpose, Commitment, Ownership

Getting employees to be engaged is more than morality or feeling good in the workplace. It is a measurable leadership outcome rooted in meaning, trust, and psychological ownership of the work. Engagement reflects the degree to which individuals are emotionally and cognitively invested in their roles, their leaders, and the mission of the organization. When engagement is present, effort is no longer transactional. It becomes discretionary.

Engaged employees do not simply comply with expectations. They internalize them. This internalization occurs when individuals understand why their work matters, how it contributes to something larger than themselves, and where they fit within the organizational narrative. Leaders drive engagement by connecting daily tasks to purpose, consistently communicating vision, and demonstrating alignment between stated values and actual behavior. Engagement erodes quickly when leaders say one thing and reward another.

At its core, engagement is sustained through relationships. Trust in leadership, perceived fairness, and psychological safety all serve as prerequisites. When employees believe their voice matters, that their contributions are recognized, and that mistakes are treated as learning rather than liability, engagement deepens. Conversely, environments characterized by inconsistency, favoritism, or silence produce compliance at best and disengagement at worst.

High engagement produces outcomes that cannot be mandated. Creativity, adaptability, resilience, and organizational citizenship behaviors emerge naturally when individuals feel invested rather than managed. For leaders, engagement is not an abstract concept to be delegated to human resources. It is a daily leadership responsibility, reinforced through presence, credibility, and intentional action.

L - Learning: Continuous Improvement and Adaptation

High-performance cultures are characterized by relentless focus on learning and improvement at both individual and organizational levels. This involves creating systematic approaches to capturing lessons from both successes and failures, sharing learning across the organization, and applying insights to improve future performance.

Learning culture includes conducting thorough after-action reviews of important projects and initiatives, creating safe spaces for discussing mistakes and failures without blame or punishment, establishing communities of practice where people can share challenges and solutions, and implementing systematic approaches to process improvement and innovation.

I help organizations develop learning disciplines that make improvement automatic rather than accidental. This includes regular reflection practices, systematic feedback collection and analysis, experimentation and pilot programs for testing new approaches, and knowledge management systems that preserve and share organizational learning.

Learning culture also involves developing people's ability to seek feedback, reflect on their performance, and take ownership of their own development rather than waiting for others to provide direction or correction.

Your Performance Culture Development Plan

Building a high-performance culture requires sustained effort over months and years rather than quick fixes or short-term initiatives. Here's my recommended approach to helping organizations create lasting performance improvements:

Weeks 1-2: Culture Assessment and Gap Analysis involves systematically evaluating your current performance culture against the standards and characteristics I've described. Complete a comprehensive assessment of current performance standards, expectations, and communication, analyze recognition and accountability systems to identify gaps and inconsistencies, evaluate capability development programs and support systems, and gather feedback from team members about their experience of performance culture.

Weeks 3-4: Foundation Building focuses on establishing the basic elements needed for performance culture. Work with your team to clarify performance expectations and standards for all important responsibilities, identify and address immediate obstacles that prevent excellent performance, establish basic recognition and feedback systems that reinforce desired behaviors, and begin modeling the leadership behaviors that support high performance.

Weeks 5-6: Excellence Definition and Communication involves creating clear, specific examples of what high performance looks like in your context. Document examples of excellent performance from within your team or organization, create performance standards that people can understand and apply to their daily work, establish regular communication processes for discussing performance expectations and results, and begin systematic recognition of excellent performance when it occurs.

Weeks 7-8: Capability Development Planning creates systematic approaches to developing people's ability to meet high-performance standards. Assess individual development needs related to performance expectations, create personalized development plans that address both technical and leadership capabilities, establish coaching and mentoring relationships that support ongoing growth, and provide access to training, resources, and tools needed for excellence.

Weeks 9-10: Learning and Improvement Systems implements processes for continuous performance improvement at both individual and team levels. Establish regular reflection and feedback processes that help people learn from their experiences, create systematic approaches to sharing best practices and lessons learned, implement process improvement initiatives that address performance barriers, and develop measurement systems that track both results and progress.

Weeks 11-12: Cultural Reinforcement and Sustainability focuses on making performance culture permanent rather than temporary. Create organizational systems and processes that support performance culture over time, train other leaders on performance culture principles and practices, establish metrics and review processes that ensure performance culture is maintained and strengthened, and begin expanding performance culture approaches to other parts of the organization.

Remember that building authentic high-performance culture is one of the most challenging and rewarding leadership responsibilities you can undertake. It requires consistent effort, patience with setbacks, and unwavering commitment to both high standards and high support. The results, for both organizational performance and individual satisfaction, make the investment worthwhile for everyone involved.

PART V

ORGANIZATIONAL LEADERSHIP — LEADING SYSTEMS

CHAPTER 19

Vision and Strategy - Your Approach to Direction Setting

Solving The Strategic Confusion Crisis

Let's examine the widespread inability of leaders to create clear, compelling direction that guides decisions and actions throughout an organization. Most organizations have vision statements that sound impressive but provide no practical guidance, strategic plans that collect dust on shelves, and leadership teams that spend countless hours in planning sessions that produce documents rather than direction.

I regularly encounter organizations where different departments are pursuing conflicting priorities because there's no clear organizational direction. I see leadership teams that can't articulate their strategy in simple terms that frontline employees can understand and apply. I work with executives who change strategic directions frequently based on conferences they attend or articles they read, creating confusion and cynicism throughout their organizations.

This strategic confusion isn't just about poor planning; it's about fundamental failure to understand the difference between strategic thinking and strategic planning, between vision as inspiration and vision as practical guidance, between strategy as document and strategy as decision-making framework. The result is organizations that waste enormous energy on initiatives that don't support clear objectives and miss opportunities because people don't understand how to prioritize their efforts.

The latest research by Harvard Business School and McKinsey reveals that organizations with clear, well-communicated strategies achieve 67% better financial performance than those with unclear or frequently changing strategic direction. Yet studies consistently show that less than 23% of employees can clearly articulate their organization's strategy, and fewer than 14% believe their organization's strategic plans guide daily decision-making.

The cost of strategic confusion extends far beyond missed financial targets. Organizations without clear direction experience reduced employee engagement, slower decision-making, increased internal conflict, and systematic misallocation of resources. They become reactive rather than proactive, responding to immediate pressures rather than pursuing long-term objectives that create sustainable competitive advantage.

Vision and Strategy That Works

When I talk about effective vision and strategy, I am not referring to elaborate planning documents, inspirational poster campaigns, or complex strategic frameworks that require MBA training to understand. I am talking about clear, practical direction that helps people throughout the organization make better decisions every day and understand how their work contributes to meaningful objectives.

Effective vision and strategy have several essential characteristics that distinguish them from the ineffective approaches I see in most organizations. They're simple enough to remember and communicate rather than so complex that people need reference materials to understand them. They're specific enough to guide decisions rather than so vague that they can justify any course of action. They're stable enough to provide consistent direction rather than changing so frequently that people stop paying attention.

True organizational direction is compelling rather than merely logical, connecting with people's deeper motivations and aspirations rather than just their professional obligations. It's practical rather than purely aspirational, providing concrete guidance for resource allocation, priority setting, and opportunity evaluation. Most importantly, it's living rather than being static, evolving thoughtfully as circumstances change rather than being ignored or abandoned when implementation becomes challenging.

I've learned that vision and strategy work best when they're developed collaboratively rather than imposed from above, communicated through stories and examples rather than bullet points and slides, and reinforced through decisions and actions rather than just words and documents. The most effective organizational direction feels both aspirational and achievable, challenging people to stretch while providing confidence that success is possible with appropriate effort and focus.

The Vision-Strategy Integration

One of the biggest problems I encounter in organizational direction-setting is the artificial separation between vision and strategy, with vision treated as inspiring but impractical dreaming and strategy treated as analytical but uninspiring planning. This separation creates organizations where people are either motivated but directionless or focused but uninspired.

Effective organizational direction integrates vision and strategy into coherent frameworks that provide both emotional engagement and practical guidance. Vision without strategy becomes wishful thinking that doesn't influence daily decisions. Strategy without vision becomes mechanical planning that doesn't engage people's best efforts and creativity.

Vision as Future Reality Description involves creating vivid, specific pictures of what the organization will look like when it's successful rather than abstract aspirational statements about values or intentions. Effective vision describes what customers will experience, what employees will accomplish, what problems will be solved, and what value will be created in concrete terms that people can visualize and understand.

This approach to vision creates emotional connection because people can imagine themselves as part of the future reality being described. It provides practical guidance because people can evaluate current decisions and actions against the future they're trying to create. It enables measurement because progress toward the vision can be tracked through observable changes in customer experience, employee capability, and organizational performance.

Strategy as Path Definition complements vision by describing how the organization will move from its current reality to its desired future. Strategy answers the practical questions that vision raises: What capabilities must I develop? What markets should I prioritize? What resources will I need? What obstacles must I overcome? How will I differentiate ourselves from competitors?

Effective strategy provides a logical sequence of steps that connects current reality to future vision, with specific milestones and decision points along the way. It identifies the critical few priorities that must be executed excellently rather than trying to do everything at once. It acknowledges resource constraints and trade-offs while maintaining focus on the most important opportunities.

Strategy also provides frameworks for making decisions when new opportunities or challenges arise. Rather than requiring constant leadership input, good strategy enables people throughout the organization to evaluate options against strategic criteria and make choices that advance the organization toward its vision.

Integration Through Story and Example brings vision and strategy together through narratives that help people understand both where the organization is going and how it will get there. These stories make abstract concepts concrete and help people see how their individual contributions fit into the larger organizational journey.

I help organizations create "strategy stories" that describe the customer problems they're solving, the unique approaches they're taking, the capabilities they're building, and the results they're achieving. These stories evolve over time as the organization learns and adapts, but they maintain consistency in core direction and values.

The COMPASS Framework for Direction Setting

When helping organizations create clear, effective direction, use the COMPASS framework as a systematic approach that ensures organizational direction provides both inspiration and practical guidance for decision-making and action.

C - Context Analysis and Environmental Scanning

Effective direction-setting begins with thorough understanding of the environment in which the organization operates. This involves analyzing not just current conditions but emerging trends, potential disruptions, and evolving stakeholder expectations that will shape future success requirements.

Context analysis includes systematic examination of customer needs and expectations, competitive dynamics and positioning opportunities, technological trends that could affect the organization, regulatory and social changes that might create constraints or opportunities, and internal capabilities and constraints that affect strategic options.

The goal isn't to predict the future with certainty, but to understand the range of possibilities and identify the factors most likely to influence organizational success. This analysis provides the foundation for direction-setting decisions and helps ensure that vision and strategy are grounded in reality rather than wishful thinking.

I help organizations create "environmental monitoring systems" that track key indicators and emerging trends on an ongoing basis rather than conducting analysis only during formal planning cycles. This enables more dynamic and responsive direction-setting that adapts to changing conditions while maintaining strategic consistency.

O - Opportunity Identification and Evaluation

Once the environmental context is understood, the next step involves identifying and evaluating specific opportunities that align with organizational capabilities and aspirations. This requires disciplined analysis that considers both the attractiveness of opportunities and the organization's ability to pursue them successfully.

Opportunity evaluation includes assessing market size and growth potential, competitive intensity and differentiation possibilities, required capabilities and resources versus current organizational strengths, potential returns and risks associated with pursuing different options, and alignment with organizational values and long-term aspirations.

The key is identifying the few critical opportunities that represent the best combination of attractiveness and organizational fit rather than trying to pursue every possibility. This requires making difficult choices about what not to do as much as deciding what to pursue actively.

I help organizations develop "opportunity portfolios" that balance different types of opportunities; some that build on existing strengths, some that develop new capabilities, some that offer short-term returns, and some that position the organization for long-term success.

M - Mission and Purpose Clarification

Before setting specific strategic directions, organizations must be clear about their fundamental purpose and mission. This involves answering basic questions about why the organization exists, what value it creates, and what problems it solves for which stakeholders.

Mission clarification goes beyond writing mission statements to understanding the core purpose that should guide all strategic decisions. This includes identifying the fundamental needs the organization meets, the unique value proposition that differentiates it from alternatives, the stakeholders who benefit from its success, and the principles that should guide its operations and decisions.

Clear mission provides the foundation for evaluating strategic options and ensuring that organizational direction remains consistent with fundamental purpose. It also provides a source of meaning and motivation for people throughout the organization who want to understand how their work contributes to something larger than immediate tasks.

I help organizations test their mission clarity by examining whether it provides useful guidance for difficult decisions, whether it resonates with key stakeholders, and whether it differentiates the organization from others in meaningful ways.

P - Priorities and Focus Areas Determination

With clear understanding of context, opportunities, and mission, organizations can identify the critical few priorities that will receive primary attention and resources. This involves making difficult trade-off decisions about what will be emphasized versus what will be maintained or eliminated.

Priority setting requires acknowledging that organizational attention and resources are limited, so choices must be made about where to focus efforts for maximum impact. Effective priorities are specific enough to guide resource allocation decisions, challenging enough to require organizational stretching and development, and few enough that people can remember and focus on them consistently.

Priorities should connect directly to the vision of future success while being achievable given current organizational capabilities and available resources. They should also be sequenced logically so that early successes build capabilities needed for later achievements.

I help organizations limit their strategic priorities to no more than three to five major focus areas, with clear success measures and resource commitments for each priority. This prevents the "strategic priority inflation" that occurs when everything becomes a priority and therefore nothing receives adequate attention.

A - Actions and Initiatives Planning

Strategic priorities must be translated into specific actions and initiatives that move the organization toward its vision. This involves creating detailed implementation plans that specify what will be done, by whom, when, and with what resources.

Action planning includes identifying specific projects and initiatives that support strategic priorities, assigning clear accountability for results and timelines, allocating necessary resources including budget, people, and systems, and establishing monitoring and review processes to track progress and make adjustments.

The goal is ensuring that strategy influences daily work rather than remaining at the conceptual level. This requires connecting strategic initiatives to operational plans, individual goals, and performance management systems throughout the organization.

I help organizations create "strategy implementation dashboards" that track progress on key initiatives and provide early warning signals when adjustments are needed. These dashboards focus on leading indicators of success rather than just lagging results.

S - Success Measures and Milestones Definition

Finally, effective direction-setting requires a clear definition of how success will be measured and what milestones will indicate progress toward the vision. This involves establishing both quantitative metrics and qualitative indicators that provide a comprehensive assessment of organizational advancement.

Success measures should include financial results that demonstrate organizational sustainability and growth, customer outcomes that indicate value creation and satisfaction, employee indicators that show engagement and capability development, and operational metrics that track efficiency and quality improvement.

Milestones provide intermediate targets that maintain motivation and enable course correction before major problems develop. They should be specific enough to be measurable, frequent enough to provide regular feedback, and meaningful enough that achieving them represents genuine progress toward larger objectives.

I help organizations develop "balanced scorecards" that track multiple dimensions of success and ensure that short-term performance doesn't undermine long-term strategic objectives. These scorecards are used for both organizational performance management and strategic review processes.

S - Stakeholder Alignment and Communication

The second "S" in my framework recognizes that even the best direction-setting work is worthless unless key stakeholders understand, support, and act in the strategic direction. This requires systematic communication and alignment efforts that go far beyond formal presentations or document distribution.

Stakeholder alignment involves identifying all groups whose support or cooperation is needed for strategic success, understanding their interests and concerns related to the strategic direction, developing tailored communication approaches that address their specific needs and perspectives, and creating mechanisms for ongoing feedback and dialogue about strategic implementation.

Communication should use multiple channels and formats to ensure that complex strategic concepts are understood by people with different learning styles and information preferences. This includes storytelling that makes strategy memorable, examples that make strategy concrete, and interactive discussions that allow for questions and clarification.

I help organizations create "communication cascades" that ensure strategic direction is communicated consistently throughout the organization, with each level of leadership taking responsibility for translating strategy into terms that are relevant for their specific audiences.

Your Vision and Strategy Development Plan

Creating effective organizational direction requires systematic work over several months rather than intensive planning retreats or quick strategy sessions. Here's my recommended approach to helping organizations develop clear, compelling direction:

Weeks 1-2: Current State Assessment and Stakeholder Input involves systematically evaluating your organization's current strategic position and gathering input from key stakeholders about opportunities and challenges. Complete a comprehensive analysis of organizational strengths, weaknesses, opportunities, and threats, conduct stakeholder interviews to understand different perspectives on organizational direction, review current vision and strategy documents to identify gaps and inconsistencies, and assess the effectiveness of current direction-setting and communication processes.

Weeks 3-4: Environmental Analysis and Trend Assessment focuses on understanding the external factors that will influence your organization's future success. Analyze market trends and competitive dynamics that affect your industry, identify technological and social changes that could create opportunities or threats, examine regulatory and economic factors that might influence strategic options, and assess customer needs and expectations that should guide strategic decisions.

Weeks 5-6: Mission and Purpose Clarification ensures that strategic direction is grounded in a clear understanding of organizational purpose and values. Facilitate discussions about fundamental organizational purpose and value creation, clarify the unique value proposition that differentiates your organization, identify core values and principles that should guide strategic decisions, and test mission clarity through stakeholder feedback and decision-making scenarios.

Weeks 7-8: Vision Development and Communication creates compelling pictures of future success that inspire and guide organizational action. Develop specific, vivid descriptions of what success will look like for customers, employees, and other stakeholders, create vision statements that are memorable and actionable rather than generic and abstract, test vision concepts with key stakeholders to ensure resonance and understanding, and begin initial communication of vision concepts to build excitement and commitment.

Weeks 9-10: Strategy Formulation and Priority Setting translates vision into specific strategic choices and priorities that guide resource allocation and decision-making. Identify strategic options and evaluate them against mission, vision, and organizational capabilities, select the critical few priorities that will receive primary attention and resources, develop strategic logic that connects current reality to future vision through specific actions and capabilities, and create decision-making frameworks that enable consistent strategic choices throughout the organization.

Weeks 11-12: Implementation Planning and Success Measures ensures that strategic direction translates into concrete actions and measurable results. Develop specific implementation plans for strategic priorities, including timelines, resource requirements, and accountability assignments; establish success measures and milestones that track progress toward strategic objectives, create communication and review processes that maintain strategic focus over time, and begin systematic implementation of strategic initiatives with regular monitoring and adjustment.

Remember that creating effective organizational direction is one of the most important and challenging responsibilities of senior leadership. It requires balancing analysis with intuition, involving others while maintaining decision-making efficiency, and providing stability while enabling adaptation to changing circumstances. The investment in getting direction right pays dividends in every aspect of organizational performance and provides the foundation for all other leadership activities.

CHAPTER 20

Culture Change - How We Transform Organizations

Addressing The Culture Change Failure

Culture and changing culture are often a large leadership challenge: the widespread failure of culture change initiatives. Despite spending billions of dollars annually on culture transformation programs, most organizations see little lasting change in how people behave, make decisions, or interact with each other. The result is cynicism about change efforts, wasted resources, and continued organizational dysfunction that limits performance and satisfaction.

I regularly encounter organizations that have launched multiple culture change initiatives over the years, each with different themes, approaches, and consultants, but with remarkably similar results, such as initial enthusiasm followed by gradual reversion to previous patterns. I see leaders who can articulate sophisticated theories about culture change but struggle to influence the actual behaviors and decisions that determine organizational effectiveness. I work with companies that have beautiful culture statements prominently displayed, while their actual cultures reward behaviors that directly contradict those stated values.

This widespread failure isn't due to a lack of good intentions or insufficient investment. Most culture change efforts fail because they're based on fundamental misunderstandings about what culture is, how it changes, and what leaders must do to influence it effectively. They treat culture as something that can be changed through communication campaigns, training programs, or policy modifications rather than understanding it as the complex system of beliefs, behaviors, and consequences that emerges from daily organizational practices.

The latest research by McKinsey, Deloitte, and Harvard Business Review reveals that organizations with strong, aligned cultures achieve 60% better financial performance than those with weak or misaligned cultures. Yet studies consistently show that 70% of culture change initiatives fail to achieve their intended results, and fewer than 25% of organizations believe they have successfully transformed their cultures when needed.

I've found that the most successful culture transformations follow a systematic approach based on John Kotter's research on leading change but adapted specifically for cultural transformation rather than general organizational change. Culture change requires addressing both the emotional and practical aspects of how people work together, and Kotter's framework provides a roadmap for navigating both dimensions effectively.

Culture and How It Actually Changes

When I talk about organizational culture, I am not referring to surface-level artifacts like office design, company swag, or social events. I am talking about the deep patterns of beliefs, behaviors, and consequences that determine how work gets done when no one is watching. Culture is the invisible force that influences every decision, interaction, and priority throughout the organization.

True organizational culture has several essential characteristics that distinguish it from superficial cultural programs. It's behavioral rather than aspirational, meaning it's defined by what people do rather than what they say they value. It's systematic rather than random, with consistent patterns that reinforce certain approaches and discourage others. It's consequential rather than neutral, directly affecting organizational performance, employee satisfaction, and competitive advantage.

Culture is also largely unconscious rather than deliberate, operating through assumptions and habits that people rarely examine or question. It's socially reinforced rather than individually controlled, maintained through peer pressure, leadership modeling, and organizational systems that reward certain behaviors while punishing others. Most importantly, culture is emergent rather than designed, arising from the complex interactions between people, processes, and environmental pressures over time.

Understanding how culture changes requires recognizing that it's not something leaders can mandate or program. Culture changes through systematic modification of the experiences that shape people's beliefs about how they should behave to be successful in the organization. This includes what gets measured and rewarded, what gets punished or ignored, what leaders pay attention to and model, and what systems and processes make it easy or difficult.

Kotter's 8 Steps Applied to Culture Change

I've adapted Kotter's seminal research on leading change specifically for cultural transformation. Each step requires particular attention to the unique challenges of changing deeply embedded behavioral patterns and belief systems.

Step 1: Create a Sense of Urgency Around Culture

Culture change will not succeed unless people throughout the organization understand that cultural transformation is essential for survival and success, not just a nice-to-have improvement. Creating urgency requires demonstrating the real costs of the current culture and the risks of not changing.

Building Cultural Urgency Through Data and Stories

Effective urgency creation involves gathering and sharing concrete evidence of how the current culture is limiting organizational performance. This includes customer feedback that reveals how internal dysfunction affects external relationships, competitive analysis that shows how other organizations are outperforming you due to cultural advantages, employee engagement data that demonstrates the costs of cultural problems, and financial analysis that quantifies the business impact of cultural issues.

Sharing External Perspectives and Benchmarks

Sometimes internal people become blind to cultural problems that are obvious to outsiders. Bringing in external perspectives through customer interviews, industry benchmarking, or third-party assessments can help people see their culture more objectively.

Implementation approach: Conduct systematic customer interviews focused specifically on their experience of your organizational culture. Ask questions like "How would you describe working with my organization?" and "What frustrates you most about how I operate?" Share these insights broadly throughout the organization, including specific quotes and examples that illustrate cultural issues.

Connecting Culture to Strategic Threats and Opportunities

People need to understand that culture change isn't just about making work more pleasant, but it's about organizational survival and competitive advantage. This requires connecting cultural patterns to strategic challenges the organization is facing.

Step 2: Form a Powerful Coalition for Culture Change

Culture change cannot be led effectively by a single person or a small group. It requires a coalition of influential people throughout the organization who are committed to modeling and reinforcing new cultural patterns. This coalition must include both formal leaders and informal influencers who can affect behavior change across different levels and functions.

Identifying and Recruiting Culture Champions

Effective coalitions include people with formal authority who can change systems and processes, informal influencers who are respected by their peers and can model new behaviors, diverse representation from different levels, functions, and demographics, and early adopters who are excited about culture change and willing to experiment with new approaches.

Implementation strategy: Map the informal influence networks in your organization to identify people whom others look to for cues about acceptable behavior. These informal leaders are often more important for culture change than formal managers. Recruit them through one-on-one conversations where you listen to their concerns and ideas rather than just trying to convince them to support your agenda.

Developing Coalition Capability and Commitment

Simply recruiting people to a culture change coalition isn't enough, because they need to understand their role and have the skills needed to lead change effectively. This involves education about culture change principles and processes, skill development in change leadership and difficult conversations, alignment around vision and strategy for culture change, and regular communication and coordination among coalition members.

Maintaining Coalition Energy and Focus

Culture change takes years, not months, so coalition energy and commitment must be sustained over time. This requires regular meetings to share progress and address challenges, ongoing development and support for coalition members, celebration of successes and learning from setbacks, and periodic refreshing of coalition membership as people's roles and circumstances change.

Step 3: Create a Vision for Culture Change

Culture change requires a clear, compelling picture of what the organization will look like when the transformation is successful. This vision must be specific enough to guide behavior change while being inspiring enough to motivate people through the inevitable challenges of change.

Developing Behavioral Vision Statements

Effective culture vision goes beyond abstract values to describe specific behaviors and practices that will characterize the new culture. This includes how decisions will be made differently, how people will interact with customers and each other, how conflicts will be handled, how innovation and risk-taking will be supported, and how success will be measured and celebrated.

Implementation approach: Use "future day in the life" exercises where people imagine and describe what typical workdays will look like when the culture change is successful. Have different groups create these scenarios for different roles and functions, then identify common themes that become part of the cultural vision.

Connecting Culture Vision to Business Strategy

Culture vision must connect clearly to organizational strategy and business objectives so that people understand how cultural transformation supports larger organizational success. This involves demonstrating how desired culture changes will improve customer satisfaction, operational efficiency, innovation capability, and financial performance.

Making Vision Memorable and Actionable

Culture vision must be communicated in ways that people can remember and apply to daily decisions. This often involves creating stories, metaphors, or simple frameworks that capture the essence of desired culture change.

Implementation strategy: Develop a simple framework or set of principles that capture your culture vision. For example, one organization used "Own It, Share It, Improve It" as their framework: Own It (take responsibility), Share It (collaborate openly), Improve It (continuously learn and adapt). This gave people a practical tool for making culture-aligned decisions.

Step 4: Communicate the Culture Change Vision

Even the best culture vision is worthless unless people throughout the organization understand it, believe in it, and know how to apply it to their daily work. Communication must be frequent, consistent, and multi-channel to overcome the natural resistance to change and competing priorities for people's attention.

Using Multiple Communication Channels and Formats

Different people receive and process information differently, so cultural vision communication must use various approaches to reach everyone effectively. This includes formal presentations and documents, informal conversations and storytelling, visual displays and symbols, interactive workshops and discussions, and experiential learning through pilot programs and practice sessions.

Leaders Modeling Vision Through Actions

People pay more attention to what leaders do than what they say, so culture vision communication must include consistent leadership modeling of desired behaviors. Leaders must demonstrate the culture they want to create rather than just talking about it.

Implementation approach: Create specific behavioral commitments for leaders that demonstrate cultural vision in practice. For example, if collaboration is part of your culture vision, leaders might commit to including diverse perspectives in important decisions and sharing credit publicly when teams achieve results.

Addressing Concerns and Resistance Openly

Culture change inevitably creates anxiety and resistance, which must be addressed directly rather than ignored or dismissed. This involves acknowledging that change is difficult and may create short-term challenges, listening to concerns and adapting approaches based on valid feedback, addressing misconceptions and fears that undermine support for change, and providing support and resources to help people navigate transition successfully.

Step 5: Empower Broad-Based Action

Culture change requires action from people throughout the organization, not just from leaders or designated change agents. This means removing obstacles that prevent people from acting on cultural vision and creating opportunities for people to practice new behaviors safely.

Removing System and Process Barriers

Many cultural problems are maintained by organizational systems and processes that reward old behaviors while making new behaviors difficult or risky. Empowering action requires identifying and modifying these systemic barriers.

Providing Skills and Resources for Change

People need more than permission to act differently because they need the skills and resources required to be successful with new behaviors. This includes training in new approaches and competencies, coaching and mentoring support during transition, tools and resources that make new behaviors easier, and psychological safety to experiment and learn from mistakes.

Implementation strategy: Identify the specific skills people need to demonstrate desired culture behaviors and create systematic development opportunities. For example, if your culture vision includes better conflict resolution, provide training and practice opportunities in constructive disagreement and problem-solving.

Creating Safe-to-Fail Experiments

Culture change involves risk because people must try new behaviors before they're confident they'll be successful. Creating safe-to-fail experiments allows people to practice culture change in low-risk environments where mistakes become learning opportunities rather than career disasters.

Step 6: Generate Short-Term Wins

Culture change takes years to complete, so people need evidence of progress along the way to maintain motivation and commitment. Short-term wins provide proof that culture change is working and build momentum for continued transformation.

Identifying and Celebrating Behavioral Changes

Effective short-term wins focus on observable changes in behavior rather than just good intentions or participation in culture change activities. This includes examples of people demonstrating new cultural behaviors, improvements in team collaboration and communication, better conflict resolution and problem-solving, and positive customer or stakeholder feedback about cultural changes.

Implementation approach: Create systematic ways to identify and document culture change examples throughout the organization. This might include regular reporting from department managers about culture change examples they've observed, employee nomination systems for culture change recognition, customer feedback collection focused on cultural improvements, and measurement of specific behavioral indicators.

Communicating Progress and Impact

Short-term wins must be communicated effectively throughout the organization to build confidence and momentum for continued change. This involves sharing specific stories and examples of culture change success, connecting behavioral changes to business results when possible, recognizing people who have contributed to culture change progress, and using wins to address skepticism and resistance.

Building on Success to Accelerate Change

Short-term wins should be used strategically to accelerate culture change rather than just celebrated and forgotten. This involves analyzing what made wins possible and scaling successful approaches, using success examples to encourage similar behavior in other areas, building confidence and capability among change leaders, and maintaining momentum during inevitable setbacks and challenges.

Step 7: Sustain Acceleration

The biggest risk in culture change comes after initial successes when people may assume the transformation is complete and attention shifts to other priorities. Sustaining acceleration requires maintaining focus on culture change while continuously expanding and deepening transformation efforts.

Avoiding Premature Victory Declarations

Leaders must resist the temptation to declare culture change successful after early wins. True culture change requires years of sustained effort and continuous reinforcement of new behavioral patterns.

Implementation strategy: Establish long-term milestones for culture change that extend 3-5 years beyond initial wins. Regularly communicate that culture change is a journey rather than a destination and that continued effort is needed to make changes permanent.

Continuously Expanding Change Efforts

As culture change gains momentum in some areas, it must be expanded systematically to other parts of the organization. This involves bringing additional departments and functions into culture change efforts, developing new change leaders throughout the organization, addressing more complex and challenging cultural issues, and deepening changes in areas where initial progress has been made.

Learning and Adapting Based on Experience

Culture change is complex and unpredictable, so approaches must be refined continuously based on experience and results. This involves regular assessment of what's working and what isn't, adaptation of strategies and tactics based on feedback and results, learning from both successes and failures, and incorporation of new insights and best practices from external sources.

Step 8: Anchor New Approaches in Culture

The final step involves making culture changes permanent by embedding them in organizational systems, processes, and practices that will persist regardless of leadership changes or competing priorities.

Modifying Organizational Systems and Processes

True culture change requires systematic modification of organizational infrastructure to support and reinforce new behavioral patterns. This includes performance management systems that measure and reward cultural behaviors, hiring and promotion processes that select for cultural fit, training and development programs that build cultural competencies, and communication and decision-making processes that reflect cultural values.

Developing Cultural Competence in Leaders

Organizational culture is everything! Leaders at all levels must understand their role in maintaining and developing organizational culture. This involves training current leaders on cultural leadership principles and practices, selecting and developing future leaders who demonstrate cultural competence, creating accountability for leaders to model and reinforce cultural behaviors, and establishing cultural leadership as a core leadership competency throughout the organization.

Creating Culture Maintenance Systems

Even a successful culture change will deteriorate over time without systematic maintenance and reinforcement. This involves regular culture assessment and monitoring processes, ongoing culture development and learning opportunities, new employee orientation programs that transmit cultural knowledge, and governance processes that maintain focus on culture during busy operational periods.

Implementation strategy: Establish annual "culture health checks" that assess the strength of cultural patterns and identify areas needing attention. Create culture development goals for all leaders and include culture metrics in regular business reviews.

Your Culture Change Development Plan

Leading culture change is a complex and challenging responsibility in organizational leadership. Here's my recommended approach based on Kotter's eight steps and my experience with successful culture transformations:

Months 1-2: Urgency Creation and Data Gathering involves building the case for culture change through systematic assessment of current cultural patterns and their business impact. Conduct a comprehensive culture assessment using surveys, interviews, and behavioral observation, gather customer and stakeholder feedback about their experience of your organizational culture, analyze business metrics that are affected by cultural issues, and create compelling documentation of the costs and risks of not changing culture.

Months 3-4: Coalition Building and Vision Development focuses on recruiting change leaders and creating a clear direction for culture transformation. Identify and recruit formal and informal leaders who can champion culture change, provide coalition training on culture change principles and leadership skills, develop a clear, behavioral vision for the desired culture that connects to business strategy, and begin communicating the culture change vision throughout the organization.

Months 5-8: System Changes and Early Implementation involves removing barriers to culture change and beginning systematic transformation efforts. Modify organizational systems and processes that conflict with desired culture, provide skills training and development opportunities that support new behavioral expectations, launch pilot programs and safe-to-fail experiments that allow practice of new cultural behaviors, and implement measurement systems that track cultural progress and behavioral changes.

Months 9-18: Scaling and Acceleration expands culture change efforts throughout the organization while maintaining momentum from early successes. Generate and communicate short-term wins that demonstrate culture change progress, expand culture change efforts to additional departments and functions, continuously adapt approaches based on learning and feedback, and develop additional change leaders throughout the organization.

Months 19-36: Anchoring and Institutionalization makes culture changes permanent through systematic embedding in organizational infrastructure. Modify all major organizational systems to align with and reinforce desired culture, develop cultural competence in leaders at all levels, create ongoing culture maintenance and development systems, and establish governance processes that sustain focus on culture over time.

Remember that culture change is one of the most challenging and important leadership responsibilities you can undertake. It requires patience, persistence, and unwavering commitment to both the vision and the process. The organizations that successfully transform their cultures create sustainable competitive advantages that persist for decades, while those that fail miss opportunities to unleash the full potential of their people and capabilities.

CHAPTER 21

Systems Thinking - The Lens We Use for Complex Problems

Linear Thinking Can Destroy Organizations

I found that leaders who primarily use linear thinking continue to hurt their organizations: the widespread tendency to approach complex organizational problems with linear, cause-and-effect thinking that ignores the interconnected nature of organizational systems and culture. Most leaders are trained to break problems down into components, find root causes, and implement solutions, which is an approach that works well for simple problems but fails catastrophically when applied to complex organizational challenges.

I regularly encounter executives who implement solutions that solve immediate problems while creating larger, more complex issues elsewhere in the organization. I see leaders who are frustrated when their carefully planned initiatives produce unexpected results or unintended consequences that seem to come from nowhere. I work with organizations that jump from crisis to crisis, addressing symptoms rather than understanding the underlying system dynamics that create those symptoms repeatedly.

This linear thinking crisis manifests in countless ways throughout modern organizations. Sales teams implement aggressive tactics that boost short-term revenue while damaging long-term customer relationships. Operations departments optimize efficiency in ways that reduce quality and employee satisfaction. HR departments create policies that solve specific problems while undermining the cultural flexibility needed for innovation and adaptation.

Research by MIT, Harvard Business School, and leading consulting firms reveals that organizations led by systems thinkers achieve 45% better long-term performance and show significantly greater resilience during disruptions and crises. Yet studies consistently show that fewer than 15% of senior executives demonstrate strong systems thinking capabilities, and most organizational decision-making processes are designed around linear rather than systemic analysis.

The cost of linear thinking in complex environments is enormous and often invisible until it's too late. Organizations become vulnerable to disruption because they optimize individual components rather than overall system performance. They create cultural dysfunction by implementing well-intentioned policies that conflict with human motivation and organizational dynamics. They miss strategic opportunities because they can't see the interconnections that create leverage points for transformation.

Systems Thinking

When I talk about systems thinking, I am not referring to abstract academic theories or complex analytical frameworks that require advanced degrees to understand. I am talking about practical approaches to understanding how different parts of organizations interact with each other and how those interactions create the patterns of performance, behavior, and results that leaders spend their time trying to influence.

Systems thinking is fundamentally about seeing connections rather than just components, understanding patterns rather than just events, and recognizing that the structure of relationships often determines outcomes more than the intentions or efforts of individual people. It's about developing the ability to see the forest and the trees, understanding how individual actions ripple through organizational networks in ways that either reinforce desired patterns or undermine them.

Effective systems thinking has several essential characteristics that distinguish it from traditional analytical approaches. It's holistic rather than reductionist, seeking to understand wholes rather than just analyzing parts. It's dynamic rather than static, recognizing that organizational systems are constantly changing and evolving rather than fixed entities that can be understood through snapshots.

Systems thinking is also circular rather than linear, understanding that causes and effects often loop back on each other in ways that create reinforcing cycles or balancing feedback loops. It's contextual rather than universal, recognizing that the same action can produce different results in different system contexts. Most importantly, it's leverage-focused rather than effort-focused, seeking high-impact intervention points rather than just working harder on obvious problems.

I've learned that systems thinking is both a mindset and a set of practical tools for understanding and influencing complex organizational dynamics. It requires developing comfort with ambiguity and interconnection while maintaining focus on actionable insights that can guide better decisions and interventions.

The Five Core Systems Thinking Principles You Apply

Through my work helping organizations solve complex challenges, I've identified five fundamental principles that guide effective systems thinking in organizational contexts. These principles work together to create a comprehensive approach to understanding and influencing complex organizational dynamics.

Principle 1: Structure Drives Behavior

One of the most important insights from systems thinking is that people's behavior is largely shaped by the systems and structures within which they operate rather than just their individual personalities, motivations, or intentions. When you see persistent behavioral patterns in organizations, whether positive or negative, you should look first at the systems that are creating and reinforcing those patterns rather than focusing solely on changing individuals.

This principle helps explain why well-intentioned people often produce results they don't want and why behavior change initiatives that focus only on individuals typically fail to create lasting change. If you want to change behavior patterns sustainably, you must change the underlying structures that influence those behaviors.

Application approach: When you encounter persistent behavioral patterns, ask yourself: "What systems or structures might be creating these behaviors?" Look at reward systems, performance measures, organizational processes, decision-making structures, and resource allocation patterns that might be influencing behavior in ways that conflict with stated intentions.

Principle 2: Policy Resistance Creates Unintended Consequences

When systems resist change efforts, it's often because the interventions conflict with underlying system dynamics that push back against the desired changes. This policy resistance explains why many organizational improvement efforts not only fail to achieve their intended results but often make situations worse through unintended consequences.

Understanding policy resistance helps leaders anticipate and address the systemic forces that will oppose change efforts rather than being surprised when initiatives don't work as planned. It also helps them design interventions that work with system dynamics rather than against them.

Application approach: Before implementing solutions, identify the stakeholders who might be negatively affected by your proposed changes and consider how they might respond in ways that undermine your objectives. Design interventions that address these potential resistance points rather than ignoring them.

Principle 3: Leverage Points Amplify Impact

Systems thinking seeks to identify the places within complex systems where small changes can produce significant improvements. This is what systems theorist Donella Meadows called "leverage points." These are often counterintuitive locations where minimal effort can create maximum impact because they address fundamental drivers of system behavior rather than just symptoms.

Understanding leverage points helps leaders focus their limited time and resources on interventions that will produce the greatest return on investment rather than working harder on approaches that address symptoms rather than causes.

Application approach: Look for problems or opportunities that affect multiple parts of your organization. These intersections often represent leverage points where focused intervention can create a broad impact. Also, look for upstream factors that influence many downstream outcomes.

Principle 4: Delays Between Actions and Results Create Learning Difficulties

In complex systems, there are often significant delays between when actions are taken and when results become apparent. These delays make it difficult to learn from experience because people can't easily connect their actions to outcomes, leading to poor decision-making and ineffective problem-solving.

Understanding system delays helps leaders maintain focus on long-term interventions even when short-term results aren't immediately visible. It also helps them avoid overreacting to short-term fluctuations that may not represent meaningful trends.

Application approach: When implementing systemic changes, establish both leading indicators (early signs that interventions are working) and lagging indicators (ultimate outcome measures). This helps you track progress during delay periods and maintain confidence in approaches that may take time to show results.

Principle 5: Mental Models Shape What We See and Do

The mental models that people use to understand situations largely determine what they pay attention to, how they interpret events, and what solutions they consider. These mental models often operate unconsciously but have an enormous influence on decision-making and problem-solving effectiveness.

Systems thinking involves surfacing and examining mental models to understand how they might be limiting effectiveness or creating blind spots. It also involves developing new mental models that provide better frameworks for understanding and influencing complex situations.

Application approach: Regularly examine the assumptions and beliefs that guide your decision-making. Ask questions like "What am I assuming about this situation?" and "What other ways could I interpret these events?" Seek diverse perspectives that might reveal blind spots in your own mental models.

The SYSTEMS Framework for Complex Problem-Solving

The SYSTEMS framework as a practical approach that helps leaders navigate complex problems systematically while avoiding the pitfalls of linear thinking.

S - Situation Mapping and Stakeholder Analysis

Effective systems thinking begins with a comprehensive understanding of the situation, including all the stakeholders who are affected by or can influence the issues you're trying to address. This involves mapping the current situation from multiple perspectives rather than just analyzing it from your own viewpoint.

Situation mapping includes identifying all stakeholders who are affected by or can influence the situation, understanding each stakeholder's interests, concerns, and constraints, mapping the relationships and interactions between different stakeholders, and analyzing the power dynamics and influence patterns that affect decision-making and implementation.

Implementation approach: Create visual maps that show stakeholder relationships and interactions. Use tools like stakeholder analysis matrices, influence network diagrams, and process flow charts to understand the complexity of relationships within your system.

Y - Yesterday's Solutions Analysis

Before developing new approaches, it's crucial to understand why previous attempts to address similar issues have failed or created unintended consequences. This historical analysis often reveals system dynamics that will affect current intervention attempts.

Yesterday's solutions analysis includes reviewing previous attempts to address similar issues and their results, identifying unintended consequences or system resistance that undermined past efforts, understanding what aspects of previous solutions worked well and why, and recognizing recurring patterns that suggest underlying system dynamics.

Implementation approach: Conduct systematic post-mortems of previous change efforts to understand what worked, what didn't, and

202

why. Look for patterns across different initiatives that might reveal systemic barriers to change.

S - Structure and Process Examination

The formal and informal structures and processes within organizations often create the constraints and incentives that drive behavioral patterns. Understanding these structural elements is essential for designing effective interventions.

Structure examination includes analyzing formal organizational structures like reporting relationships and decision-making processes, examining informal networks and communication patterns that influence how work gets done, identifying system constraints and bottlenecks that limit performance, and understanding resource allocation and incentive systems that shape behavior.

Implementation approach: Map both formal and informal organizational structures. Look for disconnects between how work is supposed to flow and how it flows. Pay particular attention to handoffs between departments or functions where problems often occur.

T - Thinking Patterns and Mental Models Exploration

The mental models and thinking patterns that people use to understand situations largely determine what solutions they consider and how they interpret results. Systems interventions often require changing these underlying thought patterns.

Mental model exploration includes surfacing the assumptions and beliefs that guide current decision-making, identifying cognitive biases or thinking patterns that might be limiting effectiveness, understanding how different groups or departments think about the same issues, and exploring alternative frameworks that might provide better guidance for action.

Implementation approach: Facilitate sessions where people share their assumptions about causes and solutions for complex problems. Look for areas where different groups have conflicting mental models that might explain coordination difficulties.

E - Energy and Motivation Assessment

Complex problems often persist because the people who could solve them lack the energy, motivation, or capability to do so effectively. Understanding these human factors is essential for designing interventions that will be implemented successfully.

Energy assessment includes understanding what motivates or demotivates key stakeholders around the issues you're addressing, identifying capacity constraints that might limit people's ability to implement solutions, analyzing competing priorities that might divert attention from your initiatives, and recognizing emotional or political factors that affect willingness to change.

Implementation approach: Conduct confidential interviews with key stakeholders to understand their perspective on the problems and their energy for addressing them. Look for intervention points that align with rather than conflict with stakeholder motivations.

M - Measurement and Feedback Systems Analysis

Organizations get the behaviors they measure and reward, so understanding current measurement and feedback systems is crucial for predicting how interventions will affect behavior and performance.

Measurement analysis includes examining what metrics are currently tracked and how they influence behavior, identifying gaps between what's measured and what's important for overall system performance, understanding how feedback loops either reinforce desired patterns or create unintended consequences, and analyzing how different parts of the organization receive information about their performance and impact.

Implementation approach: Map the key performance indicators used throughout your organization and analyze how they might be creating unintended consequences or conflicts between different functions.

S - Solutions Design and Implementation Planning

Finally, systems thinking approaches solution design by focusing on interventions that address multiple leverage points simultaneously rather than just tackling individual problems in isolation.

Systems solutions design includes identifying multiple intervention points that can work together synergistically, designing approaches that address both symptoms and underlying causes, planning for potential system resistance and unintended consequences, and creating monitoring systems that track both intended results and unexpected effects.

Implementation approach: Design intervention portfolios that address multiple aspects of complex problems simultaneously. Plan for how different parts of your solution will interact with each other and with existing system dynamics.

Your Systems Thinking Development Plan

Developing systems thinking capability requires consistent practice over time rather than just intellectual understanding of concepts. Here's my recommended approach based on helping leaders develop systems thinking skills:

Weeks 1-2: Mental Model Awareness Development focuses on recognizing how your current thinking patterns might be limiting your effectiveness with complex problems. Practice identifying your assumptions about causes and effects, notice when you're thinking linearly about complex situations, seek feedback from others about blind spots in your perspective, and begin experimenting with alternative ways of interpreting organizational challenges.

Weeks 3-4: Relationship and Connection Mapping develops your ability to see how different parts of your organization interact with each other. Practice creating visual maps of stakeholder relationships and interactions, identify formal and informal communication and influence patterns, look for unexpected connections between seemingly separate issues, and begin recognizing how changes in one area might affect other areas.

Weeks 5-6: Pattern Recognition and Leverage Point Identification builds your capability to see recurring patterns and identify high-impact intervention points. Look for problems that affect multiple parts of your organization, identify upstream factors that influence many downstream outcomes, practice asking "why" multiple times to understand deeper causes, and begin recognizing where small changes might create large improvements.

Weeks 7-8: Systems Intervention Design develops your ability to create solutions that work with rather than against system dynamics. Practice designing interventions that address multiple aspects of complex problems simultaneously, anticipate potential system resistance and unintended consequences, create feedback loops that provide information about intervention effectiveness, and develop monitoring approaches that track both intended and unexpected results.

Weeks 9-12: Advanced Systems Leadership Practice integrates systems thinking into your regular leadership practice and decision-making processes. Apply systems thinking frameworks to current organizational challenges, facilitate systems thinking conversations with your team and colleagues, implement systems-based solutions and track their effectiveness over time, and develop your organization's collective capability for systems thinking and complex problem-solving.

Remember that systems thinking is both a mindset and a practical capability that improves with practice. The most effective systems thinkers I work with combine intellectual understanding with practical application, using systems principles to guide their daily decision-making and problem-solving rather than just applying them to major organizational initiatives.

CHAPTER 22

Change Management - A Methodology That Actually Works

Solving The Change Management Failure Epidemic

I've identified another persistent problem in modern organizations: the spectacular failure rate of organizational change initiatives. Despite investing billions of dollars annually in change management consulting, training, and technology, most organizations see their transformation efforts fail to achieve intended results or sustain lasting improvement. The statistics are sobering and consistent across industries, as 70% of change initiatives fail to meet their objectives, and fewer than 30% of organizations report successful change implementation.

I regularly encounter executives who have launched multiple change initiatives over the years, each promising to transform organizational performance, only to see them fade into memory without creating lasting impact. I see employees who have become cynical about change because they've experienced numerous "transformation" efforts that disrupted their work without delivering promised benefits. I work with organizations that have changed initiative fatigue, where people automatically resist new improvement efforts because they've learned that most changes don't stick.

This widespread failure isn't due to lack of good intentions, sophisticated planning, or adequate resources. Most change efforts fail because they're based on fundamental misunderstandings about how organizations change and what leaders must do to navigate the complex human and technical challenges that transformation requires. They treat change as a project management challenge rather than understanding it as a complex adaptive process that requires different skills and approaches.

The latest research by McKinsey, Prosci, and leading business schools reveals that organizations with mature change management capabilities achieve 67% better financial results from change initiatives and report 143% better adoption rates for new processes and technologies. Yet studies consistently show that fewer than 25% of organizations have systematic change management capabilities, and most change efforts rely on intuition and good intentions rather than proven methodologies.

The cost of change failure extends far beyond wasted consulting fees and lost time. Organizations that repeatedly fail at change become less competitive, less adaptable, and less able to respond to market disruptions. They develop cultures of cynicism where people resist improvement efforts and become resigned to mediocre performance. They miss strategic opportunities because they can't execute the transformations needed to capitalize on changing market conditions.

Change Management That Actually Works

When I talk about effective change management, I am not referring to communication campaigns, training programs, or project management approaches that treat change as a series of tasks to be completed. I am talking about systematic approaches to helping organizations and individuals navigate the complex psychological, cultural, and technical challenges that accompany any significant transformation effort.

Effective change management recognizes that change is fundamentally about people, how they think, feel, and behave, rather than just processes, systems, or structures. While technical aspects of change are important, the human side of change determines whether transformation efforts succeed or fail. This requires understanding how people experience change emotionally, what motivates them to adopt new approaches, and what barriers prevent them from letting go of familiar ways of working.

True change management has several essential characteristics that distinguish it from ineffective approaches. It's human-centered rather than just process-focused, recognizing that people's emotions, concerns, and motivations determine adoption success. It's systematic rather than random, following proven methodologies that address predictable challenges rather than relying on intuition or trial-and-error approaches.

Effective change management is also proactive rather than reactive, anticipating and addressing resistance before it undermines change efforts rather than just responding to problems after they emerge. It's sustained rather than episodic, providing ongoing support throughout the change journey, rather than just during initial implementation. Most importantly, it's adaptive rather than rigid, adjusting approaches based on feedback and changing circumstances rather than following predetermined plans regardless of emerging realities.

I've learned that change management is simultaneously an art and a science as it requires understanding proven principles and methodologies while adapting them skillfully to unique organizational contexts, challenges, and cultures. The most effective change leaders combine analytical rigor with emotional intelligence, systematic planning with flexible adaptation, and technical competence with human sensitivity.

The Change Journey Framework

Leading successful organizational transformations, I've identified a predictable journey that both organizations and individuals go through during significant change efforts. Understanding this journey helps leaders provide appropriate support and intervention at each stage rather than treating change as a uniform process.

Stage 1: Status Quo Comfort

Before change begins, people and organizations operate in patterns that feel familiar, predictable, and safe, even when those patterns aren't producing optimal results. This status quo comfort provides psychological security and operational efficiency because people know what to expect and how to navigate existing systems and relationships.

During this stage, people often resist acknowledging problems or opportunities that might require change because admitting the need for change threatens their sense of competence and security. Organizations may continue using outdated approaches simply because they're familiar rather than because they're effective.

Change leadership focus: Help people recognize the costs and risks of maintaining the status quo while building awareness of opportunities that change could create. Create urgency without creating panic or defensiveness.

Stage 2: Disruption and Resistance

When change is introduced, it inevitably disrupts familiar patterns and creates anxiety, confusion, and resistance. People experience loss of competence as they struggle with new approaches, loss of relationships as organizational structures change, and loss of identity as their roles and responsibilities evolve.

This disruption stage is often the most challenging phase of change because emotions run high and performance often decreases temporarily as people learn new ways of working. Many change efforts fail during this stage because leaders underestimate the intensity of emotional reactions or try to minimize them rather than addressing them directly.

Change leadership focus: Acknowledge the emotional impact of change and provide support for people's concerns and fears. Communicate frequently about progress and provide resources to help people develop new competencies. Address resistance constructively rather than dismissively.

Stage 3: Exploration and Learning

As people begin developing competence with new approaches, they enter an exploration phase where they experiment with different ways of implementing changes and start seeing some positive results. This phase is characterized by increasing confidence and gradual performance improvement, though results are still inconsistent.

During exploration, people begin to see possibilities that weren't apparent during the disruption phase, but they may also experience setbacks that create temporary discouragement. Support and encouragement are crucial during this stage to maintain momentum and prevent reversion to old patterns.

Change leadership focus: Celebrate early successes and learning progress while providing continued support for challenges and setbacks. Help people see their growing competence and confidence with new approaches.

Stage 4: Commitment and Integration

As people develop mastery with new approaches and begin seeing consistent positive results, they move into the commitment phase, where they embrace changes as improvements rather than just requirements.

During this stage, new approaches become natural and preferred rather than forced.

Integration involves embedding new patterns into personal and organizational habits so that they persist without constant attention and reinforcement. This is when change becomes sustainable and begins generating the intended benefits consistently.

Change leadership focus: Reinforce new patterns through recognition, measurement, and system integration. Help people become advocates for changes they've successfully adopted. Begin planning for spreading successful changes to other parts of the organization.

The BRIDGE Framework for Change Implementation

When leading successful change initiatives, use the BRIDGE framework. This is a systematic methodology that addresses both the technical and human aspects of organizational transformation while providing practical steps for navigating complex change challenges.

B - Build Awareness and Understanding

Successful change begins with helping people understand what's changing, why it's necessary, and how it will affect them personally. This awareness building must address both rational and emotional aspects of change, providing logical reasons while acknowledging emotional concerns.

Building awareness includes communicating the business case for change in terms that people can understand and relate to, explaining specifically what will be different and what will remain the same, addressing concerns and questions honestly rather than dismissively, and helping people understand their role in the change process.

Implementation approach: Use multiple communication channels and formats to reach different learning styles and preferences. Include face-to-face discussions that allow for questions and dialogue rather than just one-way presentations. Share information gradually rather than overwhelming people with complex details all at once.

R - Remove Barriers and Obstacles

Change efforts often fail because people encounter obstacles that prevent them from adopting new approaches successfully. These barriers might be technical, procedural, cultural, or skill related. Systematic barrier removal is essential for enabling successful change adoption.

Barrier removal includes identifying technical obstacles like inadequate systems or tools, addressing skill gaps through training and development opportunities, modifying organizational policies and procedures that conflict with new approaches, and changing cultural factors that discourage new behaviors.

Implementation approach: Conduct systematic analysis of potential barriers before implementing changes rather than waiting for people to encounter them. Create rapid response systems for addressing unexpected obstacles as they emerge. Involve front-line people in identifying barriers they're likely to encounter.

I - Involve People in the Change Process

I believe that people are less adverse to change than they are to a perceived loss of status. Meaning, "How will this change [negatively] affect me?" Remember, people are more likely to support changes they help create rather than changes imposed on them. Involvement creates ownership, improves solution quality, and reduces resistance by making people partners in change rather than passive recipients.

Involvement strategies include including key stakeholders in change planning and design decisions, creating opportunities for people to contribute ideas and feedback throughout implementation, establishing change champion networks that provide peer support and advocacy, and using pilot programs that allow experimentation and learning before full-scale implementation.

Implementation approach: Identify formal and informal leaders throughout the organization who can influence adoption success. Involve them in meaningful ways that use their expertise and insights rather than just seeking their endorsement. Create feedback loops that allow you to adjust approaches based on their experience and recommendations.

D - Develop Skills and Capabilities

Change often requires people to develop new competencies, and skill development must be systematic rather than accidental. This includes both technical skills needed to operate new systems or processes and adaptive skills needed to navigate ongoing change and uncertainty.

Skill development includes providing formal training that addresses specific competency gaps, creating coaching and mentoring relationships that support on-the-job learning, establishing communities of practice where people can share experiences and solutions, and offering stretch assignments that allow people to practice new skills in supportive environments.

Implementation approach: Assess current capabilities against future requirements to identify specific development needs. Provide multiple learning opportunities that accommodate different learning styles and schedules. Focus on building capability for continued learning rather than just addressing immediate skill gaps.

G - Generate Quick Wins and Momentum

Change is easier when people see evidence that new approaches are working and producing benefits. Quick wins provide proof that change efforts are worthwhile and build confidence for tackling more challenging aspects of transformation.

Generating wins includes identifying opportunities for early success that demonstrate change benefits, celebrating progress and achievements to maintain motivation and momentum, using success stories to encourage adoption in other areas, and building on initial successes to tackle more complex change challenges.

Implementation approach: Look for change opportunities that are likely to succeed and provide visible benefits relatively quickly. Communicate successes broadly throughout the organization. Use wins to address skepticism and resistance from people who are hesitant about change.

E - Embed Changes in Systems and Culture

Sustainable change requires embedding new approaches in organizational systems, processes, and culture so they persist without constant attention and reinforcement. This institutionalization phase is often overlooked but is essential for preventing reversion to old patterns.

Embedding changes includes modifying performance management systems to measure and reward new behaviors, updating policies and procedures to reflect new approaches, integrating new methods into training and development programs, and creating organizational structures that support rather than undermine change objectives.

Implementation approach: Identify all organizational systems that influence the behaviors you're trying to change and modify them systematically. Create governance processes that maintain focus on new approaches even during busy operational periods. Develop internal change capability so that the organization can continue adapting without external support.

Addressing the Human Side of Change

While technical aspects of change are important, the human side typically determines success or failure. People experience change emotionally as well as logically, and effective change management must address both dimensions systematically.

Understanding Change Psychology

Change threatens people's sense of competence, relationships, and identity, creating predictable emotional reactions that must be acknowledged and addressed rather than ignored or minimized. These reactions include anxiety about their ability to succeed with new approaches, grief about losing familiar ways of working, anger about having change imposed on them, and excitement about opportunities that change might create.

Change leadership approach: Normalize emotional reactions to change rather than treating them as problems to be solved. Provide emotional support and reassurance while maintaining focus on change objectives. Help people see change as a growth opportunity rather than just disruption or loss.

Building Change Resilience

Some people adapt to change more easily than others, but change resilience can be developed through appropriate support and skill building. Resilience factors include optimism about the future and confidence in the ability to adapt, social support from colleagues and supervisors, a clear understanding of the change rationale and personal benefits, and previous positive experiences with change and learning.

Development strategies: Provide skills training that builds confidence with new approaches. Create support networks and mentoring relationships that help people navigate change challenges. Communicate frequently about progress and success stories that demonstrate change benefits.

Creating Psychological Safety for Change

People need to feel safe to experiment, make mistakes, and ask questions during change processes. Without psychological safety, people either resist change or comply superficially without truly adopting new approaches.

Safety creation approaches: Encourage questions and concerns rather than expecting immediate enthusiasm. Treat mistakes during change implementation as learning opportunities rather than performance failures. Model vulnerability by sharing your own change challenges and learning experiences.

Your Change Management Development Plan

Developing change management capability requires systematic practice with real organizational challenges rather than just theoretical understanding. Here's my recommended approach to helping leaders become more effective change agents:

Months 1-2: Change Assessment and Opportunity Identification involves evaluating your organization's current change management maturity and identifying opportunities for improvement. Assess previous change efforts to understand what worked well and what could be improved, evaluate current change management processes and capabilities, identify upcoming changes that could serve as development opportunities, and begin building your personal change management toolkit.

Months 3-4: Human-Centered Change Skills Development focuses on building your capability to understand and address the human aspects of change. Learn to recognize and respond appropriately to emotional reactions to change, develop skills in change communication that address both rational and emotional concerns, practice involving people in change processes in meaningful ways, and build capability for creating psychological safety during change efforts.

Months 5-6: Change Planning and Design Practice develops your ability to create systematic approaches to complex change challenges. Practice using the BRIDGE framework to plan change implementation strategies, learn to anticipate and address potential barriers and resistance points, develop skills in creating quick wins and building momentum for change, and practice adapting change approaches based on feedback and changing circumstances.

Months 7-8: Change Implementation and Facilitation builds your capability to lead change efforts effectively in real-world situations. Practice facilitating change planning sessions with diverse stakeholder groups, develop skills in managing resistance and conflict during change efforts, learn to monitor change progress and make necessary adjustments, and build capability for sustaining change momentum over extended time periods.

Months 9-12: Organizational Change Capability Building expands your focus from individual change projects to building systematic change management capability throughout your organization. Develop change management processes and tools that can be used consistently across different initiatives, train other leaders in change management principles and practices, create organizational learning systems that capture and share change management insights, and establish change management governance that maintains focus on change success factors.

Remember that change management is one of the most valuable and transferable leadership skills you can develop. In today's rapidly evolving business environment, the ability to lead successful change efforts is essential for organizational survival and competitive advantage. Organizations that develop strong change management capabilities can adapt quickly to market changes, implement strategic improvements effectively, and maintain high performance during periods of uncertainty and transformation.

CHAPTER 23

Ethical Leadership - The Standards You Won't Compromise

The Ethical Crisis Destroying Trust in Leadership

I've witnessed a troubling erosion of ethical standards that is destroying trust in leadership and undermining organizational effectiveness. This isn't just about high-profile scandals that make headlines, but it's about the daily compromises, corner-cutting, and ethical blind spots that have become normalized in too many organizations. The result is widespread cynicism about leadership integrity, reduced employee engagement, and organizational cultures where people feel they must choose between doing what's right and doing what's rewarded.

I regularly encounter leaders who consider themselves ethical while operating in organizations where questionable practices are routine. I see executives who make decisions based primarily on short-term financial pressure without considering broader stakeholder impact. I work with companies that have elaborate compliance programs while ignoring the cultural factors that drive ethical behavior throughout the organization.

This ethical crisis manifests in countless ways that most leaders don't recognize or acknowledge. Organizations promise customers value they can't deliver while meeting technical compliance requirements. Managers manipulate performance data to look better while staying within the bounds of formal policies. Leaders make commitments to employees they know they can't keep while justifying their actions as necessary for business success.

The latest research by Ethics and Compliance Initiative, Harvard Business School, and leading consulting firms reveals that organizations with strong ethical cultures achieve 85% better stock performance, 40% lower employee turnover, and significantly better customer loyalty than those with weak ethical climates. Yet studies consistently show that only 34% of employees believe their senior leaders demonstrate ethical behavior, and fewer than 42% would report ethical violations they observe.

The cost of ethical erosion extends far beyond legal risks and regulatory penalties. Organizations with weak ethical cultures experience reduced innovation because people are afraid to challenge questionable practices. They struggle to attract and retain top talent because ethical people don't want to work in environments that compromise their values. They face increased operational costs because ethical shortcuts often create larger problems that require expensive solutions later.

Ethical Leadership That Creates Trust

When I talk about ethical leadership, I am not referring to compliance with minimum legal standards or adherence to abstract ethical theories that have little practical application. I am talking about consistent demonstration of principled decision-making that considers the welfare of all stakeholders and builds trust through transparent, fair, and honest behavior in all circumstances, especially when it's difficult or costly to do so.

Ethical leadership is fundamentally about integrity, such as the alignment between values, words, and actions that creates consistency and predictability in how leaders operate. It's about making decisions based on principles rather than just immediate pressures, considering long-term consequences rather than just short-term benefits, and accepting responsibility for the broader impact of leadership choices rather than just focusing on narrow organizational interests.

True ethical leadership has several essential characteristics that distinguish it from mere compliance or situational ethics. It's principle-based rather than rule-based, meaning decisions are guided by core values and moral reasoning rather than just following policies and procedures. It's stakeholder-oriented rather than shareholder-focused, considering the impact of decisions on employees, customers, communities, and society as well as owners and investors.

Ethical leadership is also transparent rather than secretive, with decision-making processes that can be examined and explained rather than hidden from scrutiny. It's accountable rather than defensive, accepting responsibility for mistakes and working to make things right rather than shifting blame or minimizing problems. Most importantly, ethical leadership is courageous rather than convenient, willing to do what's right even when it's difficult, unpopular, or costly.

I've learned that ethical leadership isn't just about avoiding wrongdoing, but it's about actively creating conditions where ethical behavior is expected, supported, and rewarded throughout the organization. It requires building cultures where people feel safe to raise ethical concerns, where ethical dilemmas are discussed openly rather than ignored, and where ethical behavior is recognized as essential for long-term organizational success rather than just a constraint on business activity.

The Four Dimensions of Ethical Leadership

I've identified four interconnected dimensions of ethical leadership that must be developed systematically rather than left to chance or good intentions.

Dimension 1: Moral Awareness and Sensitivity

Ethical leadership begins with the ability to recognize ethical dimensions of decisions and situations that might appear to be purely business or technical issues. Many ethical failures occur not because people intend to do wrong, but because they fail to recognize the ethical implications of their choices until after problems have emerged.

Moral awareness includes recognizing when decisions affect stakeholder welfare in ways that might not be immediately obvious, understanding how business pressures and organizational dynamics can create ethical blind spots, identifying potential conflicts of interest or competing loyalties that might compromise judgment, and sensing when situations feel wrong even if they appear technically acceptable.

Development approach: Practice asking "Who else might be affected by this decision?" and "What are the potential unintended consequences?" before making important choices. Seek diverse perspectives on decisions to identify ethical dimensions you might miss. Pay attention to gut feelings that something doesn't feel right, even when logical analysis suggests it's acceptable.

Dimension 2: Moral Reasoning and Decision-Making

Once ethical dimensions are recognized, leaders must have frameworks for working through complex moral reasoning that considers multiple perspectives and potential consequences. This involves more than just following rules or policies; therefore, it requires principled thinking about competing values and stakeholder interests.

Moral reasoning includes understanding different ethical frameworks like rights-based, duty-based, and consequences-based approaches to

223

decision-making, developing the ability to weigh competing stake-holder interests and values when they conflict, creating systematic approaches to gathering information and perspectives needed for ethical decision-making, and building skill in communicating ethical reasoning to others who might disagree.

Development approach: Study different ethical frameworks and practice applying them to business decisions. Seek training in ethical decision-making processes that provide structure for working through complex moral dilemmas. Practice explaining your ethical reasoning to others and listening to alternative perspectives.

Dimension 3: Moral Courage and Action

Perhaps the most challenging aspect of ethical leadership is having the courage to act on ethical convictions when doing so involves personal or organizational risk. Many people recognize ethical issues and understand what should be done, but fail to follow through when action requires courage.

Moral courage includes the willingness to speak up about ethical concerns even when it's uncomfortable or risky, taking action to address ethical problems rather than hoping someone else will handle them, accepting personal costs when necessary to maintain ethical standards, and persisting in ethical action even when others pressure you to compromise.

Development approach: Start by taking action on smaller ethical issues to build confidence and skill for larger challenges. Build support networks of people who share your values and can provide encouragement when courage is needed. Practice speaking up about ethical concerns in low-risk situations to develop skills for higher-stakes moments.

Dimension 4: Ethical Culture Building

Individual ethical behavior is important but insufficient for organizational effectiveness. Ethical leaders must also create cultures where ethical behavior is expected, supported, and consistently reinforced throughout the organization rather than just demonstrated by individual leaders.

Culture building includes establishing clear ethical expectations and values that guide organizational decision-making, creating systems and processes that support ethical behavior and make unethical behavior difficult, modeling ethical leadership behavior that others can observe and emulate, and addressing ethical violations quickly and consistently when they occur.

Development approach: Examine organizational systems to identify factors that might encourage or discourage ethical behavior. Look for opportunities to recognize and reward ethical decision-making. Create forums for discussing ethical dilemmas and challenges openly rather than avoiding them.

The ETHICS Framework for Ethical Decision-Making

When helping leaders navigate complex ethical challenges, use the ETHICS framework. This is a systematic approach to ethical decision-making that provides practical guidance for situations where the right course of action isn't immediately obvious.

E - Evaluate the Situation and Stakeholders

Effective ethical decision-making begins with a comprehensive understanding of the situation and all parties who might be affected by your choices. This involves looking beyond immediate stakeholders to consider broader impacts that might not be immediately apparent.

Situation evaluation includes identifying all stakeholders who might be directly or indirectly affected by the decision, understanding what each stakeholder values most and how they might be impacted, recognizing the ethical dimensions and moral tensions within the situation, and clarifying what specific outcomes you're trying to achieve while maintaining ethical standards.

Implementation approach: Create comprehensive stakeholder maps that show everyone who might be affected by your decision, including second and third-order effects. Interview key stakeholders to understand their perspectives and concerns. Look for ethical principles that might be in tension with each other.

T - Think Through Principles and Values

Once you understand the situation comprehensively, the next step involves examining what fundamental principles and values should guide your decision-making. This requires moving beyond just considering practical consequences to examine deeper questions about right and wrong.

Principles consideration includes reviewing your personal and organizational core values and how they apply to this situation, examining universal ethical principles like honesty, fairness, respect for persons, and responsibility, identifying which values or principles might be in conflict and need to be prioritized, and considering what kind of precedent your decision might set for future similar situations.

Implementation approach: Write down your organization's stated values and honestly assess how different options align with those principles. Consider whether you would want your decision to become a universal rule that others follow in similar situations. Ask what decision would reflect the character and integrity you want to demonstrate.

H - Honor Different Perspectives

Ethical decision-making benefits significantly from diverse viewpoints because individual perspectives often have blind spots or biases that affect moral reasoning. Seeking and genuinely considering different perspectives helps identify considerations you might miss and tests your reasoning against alternative values and experiences.

Perspective honoring includes actively seeking input from people who represent different stakeholder interests and cultural backgrounds, consulting with individuals who have demonstrated wisdom in ethical reasoning, looking for perspectives from people who might disagree with your initial inclination, and considering how your decision might look from the viewpoint of different ethical traditions or value systems.

Implementation approach: Identify people whose judgment you respect and who bring different perspectives to the situation. Ask them not just what they would do, but what ethical considerations they think are most important. Create diverse advisory groups when facing complex ethical decisions.

I - Identify Options and Alternatives

Many ethical dilemmas appear to have only limited options, often involving painful trade-offs between competing values or stakeholder interests. Effective ethical decision-making involves creative problem-solving that might identify alternatives addressing multiple concerns simultaneously rather than just choosing between obvious options.

Options identification includes brainstorming multiple approaches beyond the most obvious alternatives, looking for innovative solutions that might address multiple stakeholder concerns, considering whether timing, sequencing, or partnerships might create additional options, and exploring whether additional resources or creative approaches might enable better outcomes for everyone involved.

Implementation approach: Resist the urge to choose quickly between obvious options. Invest time in creative problem-solving sessions that explore unconventional alternatives. Ask "What would need to be true for this to work for everyone?" and work backward from ideal outcomes.

C - Consider Consequences and Impacts

Ethical decision-making requires a thorough analysis of both immediate and long-term consequences that might result from different choices. This includes not just intended outcomes but also potential unintended effects that might emerge over time across different stakeholder groups.

Consequence consideration includes analyzing short-term and long-term effects of different options on all identified stakeholders, considering unintended consequences that might result from your choices, evaluating precedent effects and how your decision might influence future situations, and assessing whether potential benefits justify potential risks and costs to different parties.

Implementation approach: For each option, create scenarios showing how different stakeholders might be affected over various time horizons. Consider worst-case scenarios and how you would handle them. Think about ripple effects that might extend beyond immediate impacts.

S - Select and Implement with Integrity

Finally, ethical decision-making requires choosing a course of action and implementing it with transparency, accountability, and commitment to monitoring outcomes. This involves making difficult choices while remaining open to adjustment if circumstances change or unintended consequences emerge.

Implementation with integrity includes selecting the option that best balances ethical principles with practical realities, communicating your decision and reasoning transparently to affected stakeholders, taking full responsibility for outcomes rather than shifting blame if problems emerge, and establishing monitoring systems to ensure your decision achieves intended ethical outcomes.

Implementation approach: Choose the option that you can implement with complete integrity and explain convincingly to all stakeholders.

Communicate your decision openly, including the ethical reasoning that guided your choice. Create mechanisms for tracking whether your decision produces intended results, and be prepared to make adjustments.

Building Ethical Organizational Culture

Individual ethical behavior is important but insufficient for organizational effectiveness. Ethical leaders must create cultures where ethical behavior is expected, supported, and consistently reinforced throughout the organization.

Creating Ethical Infrastructure

Ethical culture requires systematic approaches to supporting ethical behavior rather than just hoping people will do the right thing naturally. This includes establishing clear codes of conduct that provide practical guidance for common ethical dilemmas, implementing ethics training programs that build moral reasoning skills rather than just compliance knowledge, creating reporting mechanisms that allow people to raise ethical concerns safely, and establishing investigation and resolution processes that address ethical violations fairly and consistently.

Implementation approach: Audit your current ethical infrastructure to identify gaps and improvement opportunities. Focus on creating systems that support ethical decision-making rather than just punish ethical violations. Make ethical resources easily accessible and well-known throughout the organization.

Recognizing and Reinforcing Ethical Behavior

What gets measured and rewarded gets repeated, so ethical culture requires systematic recognition of ethical behavior rather than just addressing ethical failures. This includes incorporating ethical behavior assessments into performance management systems, recognizing employees who demonstrate ethical courage in challenging situations, celebrating examples of ethical decision-making that serve as models for others, and ensuring that ethical behavior is considered in promotion and advancement decisions.

Implementation approach: Look for opportunities to recognize and celebrate ethical behavior publicly. Share stories of ethical decision-making that demonstrate organizational values in action. Make ethical leadership a visible requirement for advancement to leadership positions.

Addressing Ethical Violations Consistently

How organizations respond to ethical violations sends powerful messages about what behavior is actually tolerated versus what is merely stated as policy. Ethical culture requires consistent, fair, and timely responses to ethical problems rather than selective enforcement or cover-up attempts.

Implementation approach: Develop clear processes for investigating and responding to ethical violations that are applied consistently regardless of the position or performance of people involved. Focus on learning and improvement rather than just punishment when addressing ethical problems.

Your Ethical Leadership Development Plan

Developing ethical leadership capability requires intentional practice and systematic development over time. Here's my recommended approach to helping leaders strengthen their ethical leadership:

Weeks 1-2: Ethical Self-Assessment and Values Clarification involves examining your current ethical leadership patterns and clarifying the values that should guide your decision-making. Complete a comprehensive assessment of your ethical decision-making patterns and blind spots, clarify your core values and how they should influence your leadership choices, identify situations where you've compromised ethical standards and analyze what led to those compromises, and establish personal ethical standards that will guide your future decision-making.

Weeks 3-4: Ethical Awareness and Sensitivity Development focuses on improving your ability to recognize ethical dimensions of decisions and situations. Practice identifying ethical implications of business decisions before they become problems, seek diverse perspectives on decisions to identify ethical considerations you might miss, study examples of ethical failures to understand how good people make poor ethical choices, and develop sensitivity to situations that create ethical risks or temptations.

Weeks 5-6: Ethical Decision-Making Framework Practice builds your capability to work through complex ethical dilemmas systematically using proven frameworks. Practice using the COMPASS framework on current ethical challenges you're facing, learn about different ethical philosophies and how they apply to business situations, develop skills in stakeholder analysis and consequence assessment for ethical decisions, and practice communicating ethical reasoning clearly to others who might disagree.

Weeks 7-8: Moral Courage and Action Development strengthens your ability to act on ethical convictions even when it's difficult or risky. Identify situations where you should speak up about ethical concerns but haven't done so, practice raising ethical concerns in low-risk situations to build skills and confidence, build support networks of people who share your values and can provide encouragement, and take action on at least one ethical issue that you've been avoiding.

Weeks 9-12: Ethical Culture Building Practice expands your focus from individual ethical behavior to creating organizational cultures that support ethical leadership. Assess your organization's ethical culture and identify improvement opportunities, implement systems or processes that better support ethical decision-making, model ethical leadership behavior consistently in your daily interactions, and address at least one organizational practice that undermines ethical behavior.

Remember that ethical leadership is both a personal responsibility and an organizational necessity. In today's environment of increased transparency and stakeholder activism, ethical failures can destroy careers and organizations quickly, while ethical leadership creates sustainable competitive advantages through trust, loyalty, and reputation. The investment in developing strong ethical leadership capabilities pays dividends throughout your career and contributes to building organizations that serve all stakeholders effectively.

PART VI

EXTERNAL LEADERSHIP — LEADING STAKEHOLDERS

CHAPTER 24

Customer Leadership - How We Create Value

Addressing The Customer Disconnect Crisis

I've also witnessed an issue with creating value: the widespread disconnect between what organizations think they're providing customers with and what customers experience and value. Most leaders operate with outdated assumptions about customer needs, preferences, and decision-making processes that lead to strategies, products, and services that miss the mark despite good intentions and significant investment.

I regularly encounter executives who can recite detailed market research and customer segmentation data but struggle to explain why their customer satisfaction scores are declining or why they're losing market share to competitors. I see organizations that have invested millions in customer experience initiatives while maintaining internal processes, policies, and cultures that systematically frustrate the customers they claim to serve. I work with companies that pride themselves on customer focus while making decisions based primarily on internal convenience rather than customer impact.

This customer disconnect isn't just about poor service or inadequate products, but it's about fundamental failure to understand that customer leadership requires different skills, mindsets, and approaches than internal leadership. Leading customers means influencing people who have choices, who can leave without notice, and who owe you nothing beyond what you earn through value creation. It requires building trust, loyalty, and advocacy through consistent demonstration of customer-centered decision-making rather than through authority, position, or organizational hierarchy.

The latest research by Harvard Business School, McKinsey, and leading customer experience firms reveals that organizations with true customer leadership capabilities achieve 60% higher customer lifetime value, 50% better customer retention rates, and 40% faster revenue growth than those with traditional inside-out approaches to customer relationships. Yet studies consistently show that fewer than 23% of organizations consistently make decisions from the customer's perspective, and even fewer have systematic approaches to developing customer leadership capabilities throughout their organizations.

The cost of customer disconnect extends far beyond lost sales and reduced satisfaction scores. Organizations that fail at customer leadership miss strategic opportunities because they don't understand emerging customer needs. They waste resources on features, services, and initiatives that customers don't value while under-investing in areas that would create genuine differentiation. They become vulnerable to disruption by competitors who understand customer needs better and create more compelling value propositions.

Customer Leadership That Creates Value

When I talk about customer leadership, I am not referring to traditional customer service approaches, satisfaction survey programs, or marketing campaigns designed to persuade customers to want what you're already providing. I am talking about the ability to understand customers so deeply that you can anticipate their needs, influence their thinking about problems and solutions, and create value propositions that make you indispensable to their success.

Customer leadership is fundamentally about earning the right to influence customer decisions through demonstrated understanding of their challenges, goals, and success criteria. It's about becoming a trusted advisor who helps customers think through complex decisions rather than just a vendor who provides products or services. It's about creating customer advocacy and loyalty that persists even when competitors offer lower prices or seemingly better features.

True customer leadership has several essential characteristics that distinguish it from traditional sales and marketing approaches. It's insight-based rather than feature-based, focusing on helping customers understand their situations better rather than just promoting your capabilities. It's value-focused rather than price-focused, competing on the total value you create rather than just the immediate cost of your offerings.

Customer leadership is also proactive rather than reactive, anticipating customer needs and challenges before they become critical rather than just responding to expressed requirements. It's relationship-oriented rather than transaction-oriented, building long-term partnerships that create mutual value rather than just completing individual sales. Most importantly, customer leadership is authentic rather than manipulative, genuinely serving customer interests rather than just using customer language to advance your own agenda.

I've learned that customer leadership requires fundamentally different capabilities than internal leadership. While internal leadership often involves directing people who must follow your guidance, customer leadership requires influencing people who choose to follow your recommendations. This requires deeper understanding, greater credibility, and more compelling value creation than most organizations provide.

The Customer Value Creation Framework

I've identified five interconnected levels of customer value creation that determine your ability to influence customer decisions and build lasting relationships.

Level 1: Product and Service Excellence

The foundation of customer leadership is providing excellent products and services that reliably meet or exceed customer expectations. Without this basic level of competence, attempts at higher-level customer leadership will fail because customers won't trust your ability to deliver on promises or recommendations.

Product excellence includes delivering consistent quality that meets customer specifications and requirements, providing reliable performance that customers can depend on for their operations, offering features and capabilities that genuinely address customer needs, and maintaining competitive pricing that provides fair value for the quality delivered.

Service excellence involves responsive communication that keeps customers informed about relevant developments, proactive support that prevents problems rather than just fixing them after they occur, knowledgeable assistance that helps customers use your products and services effectively, and professional interactions that reflect respect for customer time and priorities.

Level 2: Customer Problem Solving

Beyond basic product and service delivery, customer leadership requires helping customers solve problems that extend beyond your immediate offerings. This involves understanding customer challenges comprehensively and contributing to solutions even when they don't directly benefit your organization.

Problem-solving leadership includes diagnosing customer challenges accurately rather than just promoting your existing solutions, developing a comprehensive understanding of customer operations and success factors, contributing insights and expertise that help customers think through complex decisions, and connecting customers with resources and solutions beyond your own offerings when appropriate.

This level requires investing time and effort in customer success without immediate return, which builds trust and positions you as a genuine partner rather than just a vendor pursuing your own interests.

Level 3: Customer Innovation and Growth

The next level of customer leadership involves helping customers identify and pursue growth opportunities they might not recognize independently. This requires understanding customer markets, strategies, and capabilities well enough to contribute to their strategic thinking.

Innovation leadership includes identifying opportunities for customers to improve their competitive position or operational effectiveness, sharing market insights and trends that affect customer success, introducing customers to new approaches, technologies, or strategies that could create value, and collaborating on innovation projects that benefit both organizations.

This level requires significant investment in understanding customer industries and markets, not just their immediate needs for your products or services.

Level 4: Customer Market Leadership

Advanced customer leadership involves helping customers become leaders in their own markets by sharing insights, capabilities, and strategies that improve their competitive position. This requires understanding customer competitive environments and contributing to their market success.

Market leadership support includes providing market intelligence and competitive insights that inform customer strategy, sharing best practices and capabilities that improve customer performance, introducing customers to potential partners or opportunities that advance their objectives, and advocating for customer interests in industry forums and discussions.

This level requires broad industry knowledge and network connections that provide value beyond your specific products or services.

Level 5: Customer Legacy and Transformation

The highest level of customer leadership involves helping customers achieve transformational change that creates lasting competitive advantage and market leadership. This requires deep partnership relationships and significant investment in customer success over extended time periods.

Transformational leadership includes helping customers envision and achieve breakthrough improvements in their operations or market position, providing access to cutting-edge capabilities, technologies, and strategies, supporting customers through major organizational changes and market transitions, and building capabilities that enable customer independence and continued success.

This level represents true partnership where customer success becomes as important as your own organizational success.

The SERVE Framework for Customer Leadership

Use the SERVE framework as a systematic approach to building customer relationships that create mutual value and lasting competitive advantage.

S - Study Customer Reality Deeply

Effective customer leadership begins with a comprehensive understanding of customer situations, challenges, goals, and success criteria. This requires going far beyond a surface-level needs assessment to understand the complex context within which customers operate.

Deep customer study includes understanding customer business models and how they create value for their own customers, analyzing customer competitive environments and market pressures, identifying customer strategic priorities and success metrics, and recognizing customer organizational dynamics and decision-making processes.

Implementation approach: Invest significant time learning about customer industries, markets, and challenges rather than just focusing on immediate sales opportunities. Conduct regular strategic conversations with customer leaders about their long-term objectives and concerns.

E - Empathize with Customer Pressures

Customer leadership requires a genuine understanding of and empathy for the pressures, constraints, and challenges that customers face daily. This emotional understanding enables you to provide support and solutions that address not just logical needs but also emotional concerns.

Customer empathy includes recognizing the personal and professional pressures facing customer decision-makers, understanding the consequences customers face if their decisions don't work out well, appreciating the competing priorities and resource constraints that affect customer choices, and acknowledging the risks and uncertainties that make customer decisions difficult.

Implementation approach: Spend time understanding the individual perspectives and concerns of customer decision-makers. Ask about their biggest challenges and fears, not just their requirements and preferences.

R - Recommend Solutions That Create Value

Based on deep customer understanding and genuine empathy, customer leadership involves recommending solutions that create real value for customers rather than just promoting your existing products and services. This requires an objective assessment of what customers need versus what you can provide.

Value-based recommendations include suggesting solutions that address customer priorities even if they don't maximize your immediate revenue, being honest about limitations of your offerings and recommending alternatives when appropriate, focusing on customer return on investment rather than just your product features, and developing custom approaches when standard offerings don't meet customer needs effectively.

Implementation approach: Train your customer-facing people to think like customer consultants rather than just sales representatives. Reward them for customer success outcomes rather than just sales

V - Validate Customer Success Continuously

Customer leadership requires ongoing attention to whether your customers are achieving the results they expect from your relationship. This involves systematic monitoring of customer outcomes rather than just satisfaction with your products or services.

Success validation includes tracking customer achievement of their stated objectives through your relationship, monitoring customer satisfaction with business outcomes rather than just product performance, identifying and addressing any gaps between customer expectations and actual results, and adjusting your approach when customer needs or circumstances change.

Implementation approach: Establish regular business reviews focused on customer outcomes and success metrics rather than just operational performance. Create early warning systems that identify when customer relationships need attention.

E - Evolve Relationships Through Value Creation

Finally, customer leadership involves continuously expanding the value you create for customers and deepening relationships through demonstrated contribution to their success. This requires ongoing innovation in how you serve customer needs and contribute to their objectives.

Relationship evolution includes identifying new ways to contribute to customer success as their needs and circumstances change, developing additional capabilities that increase your value to customers, connecting customers with opportunities and resources that advance their objectives, and building long-term partnerships that create value for both organizations.

Implementation approach: Regularly assess how your relationship with each major customer could create more value for them. Look for opportunities to contribute to customer success beyond your traditional product or service boundaries.

Your Customer Leadership Development Plan

Building customer leadership capability requires systematic development of both understanding and skills over extended time periods. Here's my recommended approach to helping organizations become more customer-centered:

Months 1-2: Customer Reality Assessment and Understanding Development involves systematically improving your understanding of current customer situations, challenges, and opportunities. Complete a comprehensive analysis of your most important customer relationships and their effectiveness, study customer industries, markets, and competitive environments to understand context beyond immediate needs, conduct strategic conversations with key customers about their long-term objectives and challenges, and assess gaps between customer expectations and your current value delivery.

Months 3-4: Customer Empathy and Insight Building focuses on developing a deeper emotional understanding of customer pressures and decision-making challenges. Practice seeing situations from customer perspectives rather than just your organizational viewpoint, identify personal and professional pressures facing customer decision-makers, understand customer success criteria and how they measure value from relationships, and develop skills in consultative conversation that uncover deeper customer needs and concerns.

Months 5-6: Value Creation and Solution Development builds your capability to create genuine value for customers beyond your traditional product or service offerings. Identify opportunities to contribute to customer success that extend beyond immediate sales, develop consulting and advisory capabilities that help customers think through complex challenges, create custom solutions and approaches that address unique customer situations, and establish outcome-based success measures that align your interests with customer results.

Months 7-8: Customer Success and Relationship Evolution develops systematic approaches to ensuring customer success and continuously expanding value creation. Implement regular business reviews focused on customer outcomes rather than just operational performance, create early warning systems that identify when customer relationships need attention or adjustment, develop new capabilities and services that increase your value to existing customers, and establish long-term partnership approaches that create mutual success and dependence.

Months 9-12: Customer Leadership Culture and Capability Building expands customer leadership from individual relationships to organizational capability and culture. Train customer-facing teams on consultative relationship management and value creation approaches, modify organizational systems and incentives to reward customer success rather than just sales volume, create industry expertise and thought leadership that positions your organization as a customer advisor, and establish customer leadership as a core organizational competency and competitive advantage.

Remember that customer leadership is increasingly essential for competitive advantage in markets where products and services are becoming commoditized. Organizations that master customer leadership create relationships that persist through competitive pressure, economic uncertainty, and market changes. The investment in developing these capabilities pays dividends throughout economic cycles and provides sustainable differentiation that competitors find difficult to replicate.

CHAPTER 25

Stakeholder Management - A Relationship Strategy

Navigating The Stakeholder Complexity Crisis

Working with leaders identified developing customer relationships as a challenging issue: the exponential increase in stakeholder complexity that leaders must navigate to achieve organizational success. Today's leaders must influence and coordinate with an unprecedented number of internal and external stakeholders who have different interests, priorities, decision-making processes, and success criteria. The result is organizational paralysis, strategic confusion, and leadership effectiveness that diminishes as stakeholder complexity increases.

I regularly encounter executives who can successfully lead their direct teams but struggle when they must influence people outside their immediate authority. I see leaders who excel at customer relationships but fail to build effective partnerships with suppliers, regulators, community groups, or other external stakeholders. I work with organizations that have clear internal alignment but consistently fail to achieve objectives because they can't coordinate effectively with the complex ecosystem of relationships required for success.

This stakeholder complexity isn't just about having more relationships to manage, but it's about the fundamental shift from hierarchical leadership within organizations to network leadership across organizational boundaries. Today's most important initiatives require coordination among stakeholders who don't report to you, who have different cultures and priorities, and who often have competing interests that must be balanced rather than simply directed.

The latest research by Harvard Business School, McKinsey, and leading management consulting firms reveals that organizational success increasingly depends on leaders' ability to build and maintain effective stakeholder networks. Projects with strong stakeholder management are 75% more likely to succeed than those without, yet studies consistently show that fewer than 30% of leaders have systematic approaches to stakeholder relationship management, and most organizations provide little training or support for the complex relationship skills required for stakeholder leadership.

The cost of poor stakeholder management extends far beyond project delays and increased costs. Organizations that fail at stakeholder leadership miss strategic opportunities because they can't coordinate complex partnerships. They face increased regulatory scrutiny because they don't build proactive relationships with government officials. They experience community opposition that could have been prevented through early engagement and relationship building. They lose competitive advantages because they can't create the ecosystem partnerships needed for innovation and market development.

Stakeholder Management That Creates Success

When I talk about effective stakeholder management, I am not referring to superficial relationship maintenance, networking events, or communication campaigns designed to manage stakeholder perceptions. I am talking about systematic approaches to building authentic relationships with all parties whose cooperation, support, or approval is needed for organizational success. This requires understanding each

247

stakeholder's interests, constraints, and decision-making processes well enough to create mutually beneficial outcomes.

Stakeholder management is fundamentally about creating alignment among diverse parties who have different priorities, different success criteria, and often competing interests. It's about building trust and credibility across cultural, organizational, and industry boundaries. It's about coordinating complex initiatives that require sustained cooperation from people who have many other priorities competing for their attention and resources.

True stakeholder management has several essential characteristics that distinguish it from traditional relationship management approaches. It's strategic rather than opportunistic, focusing on relationships that are essential for organizational success rather than just maintaining general goodwill. It's proactive rather than reactive, building relationships before you need them rather than scrambling to create influence when crises emerge.

Stakeholder management is also reciprocal rather than extractive, creating value for stakeholders rather than just trying to get them to support your agenda. It's systematic rather than random, following consistent approaches and maintaining organized information about stakeholder relationships. Most importantly, stakeholder management is authentic rather than manipulative, building genuine trust through honest communication and reliable follow-through rather than using relationship tactics to advance hidden agendas.

I've learned that stakeholder management is both an art and a science, because it requires analytical thinking to understand complex relationship dynamics while also requiring interpersonal skills to build trust and influence across diverse personalities and cultures. The most effective stakeholder leaders combine systematic planning with authentic relationship building, strategic thinking with emotional intelligence, and organizational awareness with personal credibility.

The Stakeholder Ecosystem Mapping

Before you can manage stakeholder relationships effectively, you must understand the complete ecosystem of relationships that affect your organization's success. This requires mapping not just obvious stakeholders but also indirect influencers, coalition partners, and potential opponents who might affect your ability to achieve objectives.

Primary Stakeholders: Direct Impact and Authority

Primary stakeholders are individuals and organizations that have direct authority over decisions affecting your success or direct impact from your organization's actions. These relationships typically require the most attention and investment because they can directly enable or prevent your success.

Primary stakeholders include customers who purchase your products or services and provide revenue for organizational operations, employees who execute organizational strategy and create value for customers, investors and board members who provide capital and governance oversight, regulators who establish rules and compliance requirements that affect operations, and direct suppliers and partners who provide essential capabilities or resources.

Management approach: Invest heavily in understanding primary stakeholder priorities and decision-making processes. Create systematic communication and engagement processes that maintain strong relationships. Develop contingency plans for managing conflicts or changes in primary stakeholder relationships.

Secondary Stakeholders: Indirect Influence and Impact

Secondary stakeholders don't have direct authority over your success, but can influence primary stakeholders or create conditions that affect your ability to operate effectively. These relationships often receive less attention but can become critically important during crises or major initiatives.

Secondary stakeholders include industry associations and trade groups that influence regulatory and market conditions, media organizations that shape public perception and stakeholder opinions, community groups that can support or oppose your operations, professional associations that influence employee loyalty and recruitment, and academic institutions that conduct research or provide talent pipeline.

Management approach: Monitor secondary stakeholder activities and opinions to identify potential issues before they become critical. Build relationship foundations that can be activated when needed. Look for opportunities to provide value to secondary stakeholders even when immediate benefits aren't apparent.

Influencer Networks: Hidden Power and Coalition Building

Many stakeholder relationships operate through informal networks of influence that aren't apparent from organizational charts or formal structures. Understanding and engaging these influencer networks can dramatically increase your stakeholder management effectiveness.

Influencer networks include informal thought leaders who shape opinion within stakeholder communities, coalition builders who can organize support or opposition across multiple stakeholder groups, issue advocates who focus on specific topics that affect your organization, and bridge connectors who have relationships across different stakeholder communities.

Management approach: Map informal influence networks within important stakeholder communities. Build relationships with key influencers who can amplify your messages or provide credible third-party validation. Look for opportunities to support influencer priorities that align with your organizational interests.

Opposition and Competitive Stakeholders: Managing Adversarial Relationships

Not all stakeholder relationships will be positive or collaborative. Some stakeholders may have interests that directly conflict with yours, requiring different management approaches that focus on limiting damage rather than building a partnership.

Opposition stakeholders include direct competitors who compete for the same customers and resources, activist groups that oppose your industry or specific practices, union organizations that may have conflicting interests with management priorities, and regulatory officials who view your organization skeptically based on past experience or industry reputation.

Management approach: Understand opposition stakeholder motivations and strategies so you can anticipate and prepare for their actions. Look for areas of potential common ground even with adversarial stakeholders. Build coalitions with friendly stakeholders who can provide balance against opposition voices.

The ALIGN Framework for Stakeholder Management

Use the ALIGN framework as a systematic approach to stakeholder management that creates sustainable influence and cooperation across complex relationship networks.

A - Analyze Stakeholder Interests and Influence

Effective stakeholder management begins with a comprehensive analysis of who your stakeholders are, what they care about, how much influence they have, and how your organization's success affects their interests. This analysis must go beyond surface-level identification to understand deeper motivations and constraints.

Stakeholder analysis includes identifying all parties who can affect or are affected by your organization's success, understanding each stakeholder's primary interests, goals, and success criteria, assessing each stakeholder's level of influence and decision-making authority, and recognizing potential conflicts or synergies between different stakeholder interests.

Implementation approach: Create comprehensive stakeholder maps that show relationships, influence patterns, and interest overlaps. Conduct regular interviews with key stakeholders to understand their evolving priorities and concerns. Use stakeholder analysis to identify coalition opportunities and potential conflict points.

L - Listen to Stakeholder Perspectives and Concerns

Stakeholder management requires genuine listening to understand stakeholder viewpoints rather than just communicating your own agenda. This involves creating multiple channels for stakeholder input and demonstrating that you value their perspectives through responsive action.

Active stakeholder listening includes conducting regular stakeholder interviews and surveys to understand evolving concerns and priorities, creating forums for stakeholder input on decisions that affect them, monitoring stakeholder communications and public statements for insights about their positions, and using advisory groups or committees that provide ongoing stakeholder counsel.

Implementation approach: Establish systematic processes for gathering stakeholder input rather than just communicating with them. Create safe spaces where stakeholders can share honest feedback without fear of retaliation. Show that you value stakeholder input by incorporating their perspectives into your decision-making.

I - Identify Mutual Value and Shared Interests

Sustainable stakeholder relationships are built on mutual benefit rather than one-sided extraction. This requires identifying ways that your organization's success can also advance stakeholder interests and priorities.

Mutual value identification includes looking for ways that your organizational objectives can also serve stakeholder goals, identifying resources or capabilities you can share that benefit stakeholders, finding opportunities to support stakeholder priorities that don't conflict with your interests, and creating joint initiatives that advance both your objectives and stakeholder goals.

Implementation approach: For each key stakeholder relationship, create explicit value propositions that show how your success benefits them. Look for opportunities to provide support or resources that strengthen stakeholders without significant cost to your organization. Develop joint initiatives that create shared wins.

G - Generate Trust Through Transparency and Reliability

Trust is the foundation of all effective stakeholder relationships, and it must be earned through consistent demonstration of honesty, competence, and reliability over time. This requires transparency about your intentions and constraints as well as reliable follow-through on commitments.

Trust building includes communicating honestly about your organization's capabilities, constraints, and intentions, following through consistently on commitments and promises made to stakeholders, sharing information proactively rather than waiting for stakeholders to request it, and admitting mistakes openly while working to correct them quickly.

Implementation approach: Establish communication standards that prioritize honesty over optimism in stakeholder interactions. Create systems for tracking and following up on commitments made to stakeholders. Be transparent about challenges and constraints rather than over-promising capabilities.

N - Navigate Conflicts and Build Coalitions

Stakeholder relationships inevitably involve conflicts and competing interests that must be managed skillfully rather than avoided. This requires diplomatic skills for managing disagreements while building coalitions that can advance shared objectives.

Conflict navigation includes addressing stakeholder conflicts directly rather than hoping they will resolve themselves, facilitating discussions between stakeholders who have competing interests, looking for creative solutions that address multiple stakeholder concerns simultaneously, and building coalitions of stakeholders who share common interests or objectives.

Implementation approach: Develop skills in facilitation and mediation for managing stakeholder conflicts. Look for opportunities to bring stakeholders together around shared interests rather than just managing them separately. Create formal and informal coalition-building processes.

Advanced Stakeholder Management Strategies

Strategy 1: Stakeholder Lifecycle Management

Different stakeholders become more or less important at different stages of organizational development or the project lifecycle. Effective stakeholder management requires understanding these patterns and adjusting relationship investment accordingly.

Lifecycle management includes identifying which stakeholders are most critical during different phases of projects or organizational development, building relationships before you need stakeholder support rather than waiting until crises emerge, maintaining dormant relationships that might become important in the future, and transitioning stakeholder relationship management as circumstances change.

Implementation approach: Map stakeholder importance across different scenarios and time periods. Invest in relationship building before stakeholder support becomes critical. Create systems for maintaining contact with dormant stakeholders who might become important.

Strategy 2: Cross-Cultural Stakeholder Engagement

As organizations become more global and diverse, stakeholder management increasingly requires skills for building relationships across cultural, linguistic, and value system differences.

Cross-cultural engagement includes understanding cultural differences in communication styles, decision-making processes, and relationship expectations, adapting your engagement approach to match stakeholder cultural preferences, building cultural competence within your stakeholder management team, and creating inclusive processes that work across different cultural backgrounds.

Implementation approach: Invest in cultural competence training for team members who manage key stakeholder relationships. Research cultural preferences and expectations for important stakeholder groups. Create engagement processes that accommodate different cultural styles.

Strategy 3: Digital Stakeholder Relationship Management

Modern stakeholder management increasingly requires sophisticated digital tools and platforms for managing complex relationship information and communications.

Digital relationship management includes using customer relationship management systems adapted for stakeholder management, monitoring social media and digital communications for stakeholder sentiment and issues, creating digital platforms for stakeholder engagement and collaboration, and analyzing stakeholder data to identify relationship patterns and opportunities.

Implementation approach: Implement systematic tools for tracking stakeholder interactions, preferences, and relationship history. Create digital engagement platforms that make it easy for stakeholders to provide input and stay informed. Use data analysis to improve stakeholder relationship effectiveness.

Your Stakeholder Management Development Plan

Building stakeholder management capability requires systematic development of both analytical and relationship skills over extended time periods. Here's my recommended approach to helping leaders become more effective at stakeholder relationship management:

Months 1-2: Stakeholder Analysis and Mapping involves systematically identifying and analyzing all stakeholders who affect or are affected by your organization's success. Complete comprehensive stakeholder mapping, including primary, secondary, and influencer networks, analyze each stakeholder's interests, influence, and potential impact on your success, identify current relationship strengths and gaps that need attention, and prioritize stakeholder relationships based on importance and relationship quality.

Months 3-4: Stakeholder Listening and Understanding Development focuses on building your capability to understand stakeholder perspectives and concerns accurately. Establish systematic processes for gathering stakeholder input and feedback, conduct strategic conversations with key stakeholders about their priorities and concerns, develop skills in cross-cultural communication and relationship building, and create stakeholder feedback systems that provide ongoing insight into relationship health.

Months 5-6: Mutual Value Creation and Trust Building develops your ability to create genuine value for stakeholders while advancing your organizational objectives. Identify specific ways your success can benefit each key stakeholder group, implement transparency and communication practices that build stakeholder trust, develop partnership initiatives that create shared value and stronger relationships, and establish reliability in stakeholder commitments and follow-through.

Months 7-8: Conflict Management and Coalition Building builds your capability to navigate stakeholder conflicts and build supportive coalitions. Develop skills in facilitating discussions between stakeholders with competing interests, practice building coalitions around shared objectives and mutual benefits, learn to manage opposition and adversarial stakeholder relationships effectively, and create processes for ongoing stakeholder relationship maintenance and development.

Months 9-12: Stakeholder Management Systems and Culture expands stakeholder relationship management from individual capability to organizational competency. Implement systems and tools that support systematic stakeholder relationship management, train other team members on stakeholder management principles and practices, create organizational processes that integrate stakeholder considerations into decision-making, and establish stakeholder relationship management as a core organizational capability and competitive advantage.

Remember that stakeholder management is increasingly essential for leadership success in my interconnected and complex business environment. Leaders who master stakeholder relationship management can achieve objectives that would be impossible through hierarchical authority alone. Organizations that build strong stakeholder management capabilities create networks of support and collaboration that provide sustainable competitive advantages and resilience during challenging periods.

CHAPTER 26

Crisis Leadership - What We Do When Everything Falls Apart

Closing The Crisis Leadership Preparation Gap

In my work with leaders, I've witnessed underdeveloped crisis leadership capabilities: the ability to lead effectively during crises when normal operations are disrupted, stakeholder confidence is shaken, and decisions must be made quickly with incomplete information. Most leaders excel during stable periods but struggle when facing the unique challenges that crises create, such as intense pressure, public scrutiny, resource constraints, and the need to maintain stakeholder confidence while navigating unprecedented situations.

I regularly encounter executives who have never experienced a true organizational crisis and therefore have no tested frameworks for crisis decision-making or stakeholder communication. I see leaders who become paralyzed during crises because they're used to deliberate analysis and consensus-building processes that don't work when time is critical, and information is limited. I work with organizations that have detailed crisis management plans that were never tested under realistic conditions and therefore fail when actual crises emerge.

This crisis leadership preparation gap isn't just about emergency response procedures or communication protocols. It's about the fundamental leadership capabilities needed to maintain organizational effectiveness and stakeholder confidence when everything familiar becomes uncertain. Crisis leadership requires different decision-making processes, communication approaches, and stakeholder management strategies than normal operations. It requires personal resilience and emotional regulation under extreme pressure while also providing stability and confidence for others who are looking for direction.

The latest research by Harvard Business School, Wharton, and leading crisis management consultancies reveals that organizations with leaders who have strong crisis leadership capabilities recover 60% faster from disruptions and emerge stronger from crisis experiences than those with unprepared leadership. Yet studies consistently show that fewer than 25% of senior leaders have experienced significant crisis leadership situations, and most organizations provide little training or preparation for crisis leadership challenges.

The cost of poor crisis leadership extends far beyond immediate crisis impacts. Organizations that handle crises poorly experience long-term reputation damage that affects customer relationships, employee retention, and stakeholder confidence. They miss opportunities to build competitive advantages during periods when strong leadership can differentiate them from less prepared competitors. They develop cultures of crisis avoidance rather than crisis resilience, making them more vulnerable to future disruptions.

Crisis Leadership That Builds Resilience

When I talk about effective crisis leadership, I am not referring to crisis management procedures, emergency response protocols, or communication campaigns designed to minimize damage during difficult periods. I am talking about leadership capabilities that enable organizations to navigate crises successfully while emerging stronger and more resilient than before the crisis occurred. This requires maintaining operational effectiveness while also building stakeholder confidence and creating learning opportunities that improve future crisis preparedness.

Crisis leadership is fundamentally about providing stability, direction, and confidence when normal organizational systems and processes are disrupted. It's about making effective decisions with incomplete information under time pressure while maintaining trust and credibility with stakeholders who are watching closely. It's about coordinating complex response efforts across multiple functions and stakeholders while adapting to rapidly changing circumstances.

True crisis leadership has several essential characteristics that distinguish it from normal operational leadership. It's decisive rather than deliberate, making necessary decisions quickly based on available information rather than waiting for perfect clarity. It's transparent rather than secretive, communicating honestly about crisis realities while maintaining stakeholder confidence through demonstrated competence and commitment.

Crisis leadership is also adaptive rather than rigid, adjusting strategies and tactics based on emerging information and changing circumstances rather than following predetermined plans regardless of their effectiveness. It's resilience-focused rather than damage-focused, looking for opportunities to build organizational strength during crisis periods rather than just minimizing harm. Most importantly, crisis leadership is learning-oriented rather than blame-oriented, treating crises as development opportunities that improve organizational capabilities rather than just problems to survive.

I've learned that crisis leadership requires both operational excellence and emotional intelligence; therefore, leaders must maintain organizational effectiveness while also managing the psychological and relationship challenges that crises create. The most effective crisis leaders combine analytical thinking with emotional resilience, decisive action with stakeholder sensitivity, and short-term responsiveness with long-term strategic thinking.

The Four Phases of Crisis Leadership

I've identified four distinct phases of crisis leadership that require different capabilities, approaches, and priorities. Understanding these phases helps leaders provide appropriate leadership at each stage rather than using the same approaches throughout crisis periods.

Phase 1: Crisis Recognition and Response Activation

The first phase of crisis leadership involves recognizing that a crisis situation exists and activating appropriate response mechanisms quickly and effectively. Many potential crises become actual disasters because leaders fail to recognize crisis signals early or delay activation of response systems while hoping situations will resolve themselves.

Crisis recognition includes monitoring leading indicators and early warning signals that suggest potential crisis development, distinguishing between routine problems and situations that could escalate into organizational crises, overcoming psychological tendencies to minimize or deny crisis indicators, and activating crisis response systems quickly once crisis conditions are confirmed.

Leadership focus: Develop sensitivity to crisis warning signals and create decision frameworks for crisis activation. Build an organizational culture that encourages rapid escalation of potential crisis indicators rather than local problem-solving attempts that delay appropriate response.

Phase 2: Crisis Stabilization and Immediate Response

Once crisis conditions are confirmed, the next phase involves stabilizing the situation, protecting critical stakeholders, and implementing immediate response measures that prevent crisis escalation while preserving organizational capability for sustained response efforts.

Crisis stabilization includes ensuring the safety and security of people who might be affected by the crisis, protecting critical organizational assets and capabilities that are essential for response and recovery, implementing emergency response procedures that address immediate crisis impacts, and establishing crisis command structures that enable coordinated decision-making and action.

Leadership focus: Provide clear direction and coordination for immediate response efforts while maintaining situational awareness and stakeholder communication. Balance speed of response with quality of decision-making to avoid creating additional problems through hasty actions.

Phase 3: Crisis Management and Sustained Response

The third phase involves managing ongoing crisis response efforts while maintaining organizational operations and stakeholder relationships throughout extended crisis periods. This phase often lasts much longer than initial stabilization and requires sustained leadership attention and resource allocation.

Sustained crisis management includes coordinating complex response efforts across multiple functions and external partners, maintaining organizational operations in areas not directly affected by the crisis, managing stakeholder communications and relationships throughout the crisis period, and adapting response strategies based on evolving circumstances and new information.

Leadership focus: Maintain organizational resilience and stakeholder confidence through sustained crisis response efforts. Balance crisis response activities with ongoing operational needs to ensure organizational survival and continued stakeholder service.

Phase 4: Crisis Recovery and Learning Integration

The final phase involves transitioning from crisis response to normal operations while capturing learning opportunities that improve future crisis preparedness and organizational resilience. This phase is often neglected but is essential for building organizational strength from crisis experiences.

Crisis recovery includes restoring normal operations while incorporating lessons learned from crisis response, conducting comprehensive crisis analysis to identify improvement opportunities, implementing organizational changes that increase crisis resilience and preparedness, and communicating crisis outcomes and learning to stakeholders who supported response efforts.

Leadership focus: Lead organizational learning and improvement efforts that build crisis resilience. Use crisis experiences to strengthen organizational capabilities and stakeholder relationships rather than just returning to previous conditions.

The STEADY Framework for Crisis Leadership

Use the STEADY framework as a systematic approach to crisis leadership that maintains organizational effectiveness while building stakeholder confidence and learning opportunities during crisis periods.

S - Situational Awareness and Intelligence Gathering

Effective crisis leadership begins with a comprehensive understanding of crisis conditions, stakeholder impacts, and available response options. This requires systematic information gathering and analysis that informs decision-making throughout crisis response efforts.

Situational awareness includes gathering accurate information about crisis scope, severity, and potential impacts, monitoring stakeholder reactions and concerns that affect response strategy, assessing available resources and capabilities for crisis response, and tracking external factors that might influence crisis development or resolution.

Implementation approach: Establish systematic information gathering processes that provide regular updates on crisis conditions and stakeholder impacts. Create decision support systems that organize crisis information for leadership decision-making. Assign specific people to monitor different aspects of crisis development.

T - Transparent Communication and Stakeholder Engagement

Crisis leadership requires honest, frequent communication with all stakeholders who are affected by or can influence crisis outcomes. This communication must balance transparency about crisis realities with confidence in organizational response capabilities.

Transparent communication includes providing accurate, timely information about crisis conditions and response efforts, acknowledging uncertainty and limitations in your understanding while maintaining confidence in response capabilities, addressing stakeholder concerns and questions directly rather than deflecting or avoiding difficult topics, and using multiple communication channels to reach different stakeholder groups effectively.

Implementation approach: Develop crisis communication protocols that prioritize transparency and frequency over perfection and completeness. Create stakeholder-specific communication strategies that address different group concerns and information needs. Establish regular communication schedules that provide predictable information updates.

E - Empathetic Leadership and Emotional Support

Crises create emotional stress and uncertainty for employees, customers, and other stakeholders who look to leaders for emotional stability and support. Crisis leadership must address both operational challenges and the emotional needs of people affected by crisis conditions.

Empathetic leadership includes acknowledging the emotional impact of crisis conditions on employees and other stakeholders, providing emotional support and resources that help people cope with crisis stress, maintaining personal emotional stability that provides confidence and reassurance for others, and demonstrating genuine care for stakeholder welfare rather than just organizational concerns.

Implementation approach: Include emotional support and stress management in crisis response planning. Train crisis leaders on recognizing and responding to emotional stress in themselves and others. Create employee assistance and stakeholder support resources that address crisis-related emotional needs.

A - Adaptive Decision-Making and Strategy Adjustment

Crisis conditions change rapidly and unpredictably, requiring decision-making approaches that can adapt to new information and changing circumstances rather than following predetermined plans regardless of their continued effectiveness.

Adaptive decision-making includes making decisions quickly based on available information rather than waiting for perfect clarity, monitoring decision outcomes and adjusting strategies based on results and new information, maintaining flexibility in response approaches rather than rigid adherence to crisis plans, and learning from decisions that don't work out as expected rather than repeating failed approaches.

Implementation approach: Create decision-making frameworks that balance speed with quality while enabling rapid strategy adjustment. Establish review cycles that assess response effectiveness and enable course corrections. Build organizational capability for rapid decision implementation and modification.

D - Decisive Action and Resource Mobilization

Crisis response requires mobilizing organizational resources quickly and decisively to address crisis challenges while maintaining essential operations. This often requires making resource allocation decisions that wouldn't be necessary during normal operations.

Decisive action includes allocating resources rapidly to address crisis priorities while maintaining essential organizational functions, making personnel and organizational structure adjustments that improve crisis response effectiveness, implementing emergency procedures that enable faster decision-making and action, and coordinating with external partners and resources that can augment organizational crisis response capabilities.

Implementation approach: Pre-plan resource mobilization processes that can be activated quickly during crisis conditions. Create emergency authority structures that enable rapid decision-making without normal approval processes. Establish partnerships and agreements that provide access to external resources during crisis periods.

Y - Yield Learning and Build Resilience

The final element of crisis leadership involves capturing learning opportunities that improve future crisis preparedness and build organizational resilience. This requires treating crises as development opportunities rather than just problems to be survived.

Learning and resilience building includes conducting systematic analysis of crisis response effectiveness and improvement opportunities, implementing organizational changes that increase crisis preparedness and resilience, sharing crisis learning with industry partners and stakeholder communities, and building crisis response capabilities that provide competitive advantages during future disruptions.

Implementation approach: Establish post-crisis analysis processes that identify what worked well and what could be improved. Create organizational learning systems that integrate crisis insights into standard operating procedures. Build crisis response capabilities that exceed minimum requirements and provide competitive advantages.

Building Crisis Leadership Capability

Crisis leadership capability must be developed before crises occur because there's no time for leadership development during actual crisis situations. This requires systematic preparation that includes both individual leader development and organizational crisis response capability building.

Personal Crisis Leadership Development

Individual crisis leadership capability includes emotional resilience that enables effective performance under extreme pressure, decision-making skills that work with incomplete information and time constraints, communication abilities that maintain stakeholder confidence during uncertain periods, and a learning orientation that treats crises as development opportunities rather than just problems to survive.

Development approach: Seek progressively challenging leadership experiences that build comfort with pressure and uncertainty. Practice decision-making with incomplete information in lower-stakes situations. Develop stress management and emotional regulation capabilities through mindfulness, exercise, and other resilience practices.

Organizational Crisis Preparedness

Organizational crisis capability includes crisis detection systems that provide early warning of potential crisis conditions, response procedures that enable rapid mobilization of resources and coordination of efforts, communication systems that maintain stakeholder relationships during crisis periods, and learning processes that improve crisis response capability over time.

Development approach: Conduct regular crisis simulations that test response procedures and develop leadership capabilities. Create cross-functional crisis response teams that can coordinate complex response efforts. Establish partnerships and resource agreements that augment organizational crisis response capabilities.

Stakeholder Crisis Relationship Management

Crisis leadership requires maintaining stakeholder relationships during periods of high stress and uncertainty when normal relationship patterns are disrupted. This requires understanding how different stakeholders react to crisis conditions and adapting relationship management approaches accordingly.

Development approach: Map stakeholder crisis concerns and communication preferences before crisis conditions emerge. Create stakeholder-specific crisis communication strategies that address different group needs and expectations. Build stakeholder relationship strength during normal periods that provides resilience during crisis situations.

Your Crisis Leadership Development Plan

Building crisis leadership capability requires systematic preparation and practice over extended time periods. Here's my recommended approach to helping leaders develop crisis leadership capabilities:

Months 1-2: Crisis Leadership Assessment and Preparation Planning involves evaluating your current crisis leadership capabilities and developing systematic preparation approaches. Assess your personal crisis leadership experience and capability gaps, evaluate your organization's crisis preparedness and response capabilities, identify potential crisis scenarios that could affect your organization, and create development plans that build both personal and organizational crisis leadership capabilities.

Months 3-4: Decision-Making and Communication Skills Development focuses on building the core capabilities needed for effective crisis leadership. Practice decision-making with incomplete information and time pressure through simulations and exercises, develop communication skills for maintaining stakeholder confidence during uncertain periods, build emotional resilience and stress management capabilities that enable effective performance under pressure, and create personal crisis leadership frameworks that guide decision-making during actual crisis situations.

Months 5-6: Crisis Response Planning and Team Development builds organizational capabilities for coordinated crisis response. Develop comprehensive crisis response plans that address likely crisis scenarios, create cross-functional crisis response teams with clear roles and responsibilities, establish communication systems and protocols that maintain stakeholder relationships during crisis periods, and conduct crisis simulations that test response procedures and develop team capabilities.

Months 7-8: Stakeholder Crisis Management and External Relationships develops capabilities for maintaining stakeholder relationships during crisis periods. Map stakeholder crisis concerns and communication preferences for different crisis scenarios, create stakeholder-specific crisis communication strategies and protocols, build partnerships and resource agreements that augment crisis response capabilities, and establish relationships with external crisis management resources and expertise.

Months 9-12: Crisis Leadership Integration and Continuous Improvement makes crisis leadership preparation a permanent organizational capability rather than a one-time planning exercise. Integrate crisis leadership development into regular leadership training and development programs, establish ongoing crisis preparedness monitoring and improvement processes, create organizational learning systems that capture crisis response insights and improvements, and build crisis leadership capabilities that provide competitive advantages and stakeholder confidence during uncertain periods.

Remember that crisis leadership is one of the most valuable and differentiating capabilities leaders can develop. Organizations that handle crises well build stakeholder confidence and competitive advantages that persist long after crisis conditions resolve. Leaders who develop strong crisis leadership capabilities are valuable assets to any organization and often emerge from crisis experiences with enhanced credibility and leadership effectiveness.

PART VII

LEGACY LEADERSHIP — WHAT YOU LEAVE BEHIND

CHAPTER 27

Developing Others - How To Multiply Your Impact

Solving The Development Neglect Crisis

I've identified leadership succession planning issues in organizations: the widespread neglect of developing others as a core leadership responsibility. Most leaders are so focused on achieving immediate results and managing current challenges that they consistently under-invest in developing the people who could multiply their impact and create sustainable organizational capability. The result is organizations full of underdeveloped talent, leadership pipelines that are inadequate for future needs, and leaders who become bottlenecks rather than multipliers of organizational effectiveness.

I regularly encounter senior executives who are excellent individual performers but have never developed anyone else to their level of capability. I see managers who complain about their people's lack of initiative while never providing the development experiences that would build initiative and ownership. I work with organizations that claim people are their most important asset while investing minimal time, attention, or resources in systematic people development.

This development neglect isn't just about inadequate training programs or performance management processes. It's about a fundamental misunderstanding of leadership's primary purpose: creating more leaders rather than just followers, building organizational capability rather than just completing tasks, and multiplying impact through others rather than just maximizing individual productivity. True leadership development is about creating leaders who can create other leaders, establishing cycles of capability building that continue long after individual leaders move on to other roles.

The latest research by Harvard Business School, McKinsey, and leading consulting firms reveals that organizations with leaders who prioritize development achieve 37% better long-term performance, have 40% higher employee engagement, and develop 60% more internal leadership capability than those with leaders who focus primarily on immediate results. Yet studies consistently show that fewer than 30% of leaders spend significant time developing others, and most development efforts focus on skills training rather than comprehensive leadership capability building.

The cost of development neglect extends far beyond current team performance. Organizations that don't develop people systematically become dependent on external hiring for leadership positions, missing opportunities to promote from within and retain institutional knowledge. They experience higher turnover because people leave to find development opportunities elsewhere. They become vulnerable to disruption because they lack the internal capability needed to adapt to changing market conditions or competitive challenges.

Development That Multiplies Impact

When I talk about developing others, I am not referring to traditional training programs, performance improvement plans, or mentoring relationships that focus primarily on fixing weaknesses or maintaining current performance levels. I am talking about systematic approaches to building other people's leadership capabilities, expanding their thinking and problem-solving abilities, and creating leaders who can achieve more than they previously thought possible while developing others in turn.

Effective development is fundamentally about multiplication rather than addition. The goal is to create people who can accomplish more, lead others more effectively, and contribute to organizational success at higher levels than before. It's about building capability that persists and grows over time rather than just addressing immediate skill gaps or performance issues. It's about creating leaders who become developers themselves, establishing sustainable cycles of capability building throughout the organization.

True development has several essential characteristics that distinguish it from traditional training or coaching approaches. It's growth-oriented rather than deficit-focused, building on people's strengths and potential rather than just addressing weaknesses or gaps. It's challenging rather than comfortable, providing stretch opportunities that require people to develop new capabilities rather than just applying existing skills.

Development is also personalized rather than generic, adapting to individual learning styles, career aspirations, and development needs rather than using one-size-fits-all approaches. It's relationship-based rather than program-based, creating ongoing developmental relationships that provide sustained support and challenge rather than just periodic training events. Most importantly, development is multiplicative rather than linear, creating people who can develop others rather than just improving their own performance.

I've learned that effective development requires both systematic approaches and genuine care for people's growth and success. The most effective developers combine structured development planning with authentic investment in people's long-term success, challenging assignments with supportive coaching, and high expectations with patient guidance through the inevitable setbacks that accompany significant growth.

The Development Multiplier Effect

The true power of developing others lies not in the immediate improvement of individual performance but in the multiplier effect that occurs when developed people become developers themselves. This creates exponential rather than linear growth in organizational capability and impact.

Level 1: Individual Performance Enhancement

The first level of development involves helping individuals improve their current performance and expand their capabilities within their existing roles. This includes building technical skills and knowledge needed for excellence in current responsibilities, developing problem-solving and decision-making capabilities that improve work quality, enhancing communication and relationship skills that increase interpersonal effectiveness, and building confidence and ownership that leads to greater initiative and accountability.

While this level of development is important, it represents the smallest multiplier effect because it improves only one person's performance without necessarily creating broader organizational impact.

Level 2: Team and Function Leadership Development

The second level involves developing people's ability to lead others and coordinate team efforts effectively. This creates multiplication because one person's enhanced leadership capability improves the performance of everyone they influence.

Team leadership development includes building skills in delegation, coaching, and performance management that improve team effectiveness, developing abilities to facilitate collaboration and coordinate complex group efforts, enhancing strategic thinking capabilities that enable better team direction and priority setting, and building change leadership skills that help teams adapt to new challenges and opportunities.

This level creates significant multiplication because leadership improvements affect everyone the person leads, potentially improving the performance of entire teams or functions.

Level 3: Organizational System and Culture Development

The third level involves developing people who can influence and improve organizational systems, processes, and culture. This creates even greater multiplication because systemic improvements affect everyone in the organization, regardless of reporting relationships.

System leadership development includes building capabilities for analyzing and improving organizational processes and workflows, developing skills in culture change and organizational transformation, enhancing abilities to coordinate across functions and influence without authority, and building strategic thinking that contributes to organizational direction and decision-making.

Leaders at this level create multiplication effects that extend throughout organizations because they improve the systems and conditions within which everyone operates.

Level 4: Developer and Leadership Pipeline Creation

The highest level of development multiplication involves creating people who become excellent developers themselves, establishing sustainable cycles of capability building that continue regardless of specific individual leaders.

Developer development includes building skills in assessing development needs and creating personalized development plans, developing abilities to provide effective coaching, mentoring, and feedback that accelerates others' growth, enhancing capabilities for creating challenging developmental opportunities and stretch assignments, and building commitment to developing others as a primary leadership responsibility rather than just an additional task.

This level creates exponential multiplication because each person you develop into an effective developer can then develop multiple others, who can develop others in turn, creating geometric rather than arithmetic growth in organizational capability.

The GROW-UP Framework for Development

I've created the GROW-UP framework as a systematic approach to developing others that creates sustained capability building and multiplication effects throughout organizations.

G - Goal Setting and Aspiration Development

Effective development begins with helping people clarify what they want to achieve and what success looks like for their personal and professional growth. This involves moving beyond immediate performance goals to explore deeper aspirations and potential.

Goal setting for development includes helping people identify their long-term career aspirations and how current development supports those goals, clarifying specific capabilities they want to build and how those capabilities will serve their success, establishing both performance goals and learning goals that stretch people beyond current comfort zones, and connecting individual development goals to organizational opportunities and needs.

Implementation approach: Conduct regular development conversations that explore people's aspirations and growth interests rather than just current performance. Help people see connections between their development and their long-term success. Create development plans that stretch people toward their potential rather than just improving current performance.

R - Reality Assessment and Development Planning

Once aspirations are clear, effective development requires an honest assessment of current capabilities and systematic planning for closing gaps between current reality and the desired future state.

Reality assessment includes objectively evaluating current strengths and development needs related to aspiration achievement, identifying specific experiences, skills, and knowledge needed for growth toward goals, recognizing learning preferences and development approaches that work best for each individual, and understanding organizational opportunities and constraints that affect development planning.

Implementation approach: Use multiple assessment methods, including self-assessment, peer feedback, and performance observation, to understand current capabilities accurately. Create development plans that specify concrete actions, timelines, and success measures rather than vague development intentions.

O - Opportunity Creation and Stretch Assignments

Development requires challenging experiences that stretch people beyond their current capabilities and comfort zones. This involves creating or identifying opportunities for growth rather than just providing education or training.

Opportunity creation includes designing stretch assignments that require people to develop new capabilities while contributing to organizational objectives, providing exposure to senior leaders and strategic decision-making that builds broader business understanding, creating cross-functional project opportunities that develop collaboration and influence skills, and offering leadership opportunities that build confidence and capability gradually over time.

Implementation approach: Look for projects, assignments, and opportunities that would challenge people to grow while serving organizational needs. Provide support and coaching during stretch experiences to maximize learning and minimize the risk of failure.

W - Wisdom Sharing and Mentoring

Effective development involves sharing knowledge, experience, and insights that help people learn faster and avoid unnecessary mistakes.

This requires both formal and informal mentoring relationships that provide guidance and perspective.

Wisdom sharing includes providing insights into industry trends, organizational dynamics, and career navigation that people couldn't learn independently, sharing lessons from their own successes and failures that help others learn without experiencing setbacks, connecting people with networks and relationships that support their development and career advancement, and offering perspective and advice during challenging situations or difficult decisions.

Implementation approach: Create regular mentoring conversations that go beyond task management to explore broader development and career questions. Share your own learning experiences and mistakes as teaching opportunities rather than just highlighting successes.

U - Unleashing Potential and Confidence Building

Development must help people recognize and access their own potential rather than just building specific skills or knowledge. This involves building confidence and self-efficacy that enables people to take on challenges they previously thought were beyond their capabilities.

Potential unleashing includes helping people recognize strengths and capabilities they may not fully appreciate, providing encouragement and support during challenging developmental experiences, celebrating growth and progress to build confidence for continued development, and challenging limiting beliefs or assumptions that prevent people from pursuing their full potential.

Implementation approach: Focus on building people's belief in their own capabilities as much as building actual skills. Provide encouragement and support during difficult developmental experiences. Help people see their growth and progress over time.

P - Performance Integration and Sustainability

Finally, effective development must integrate new capabilities into daily performance and create sustainable patterns of continued growth rather than just temporary improvement periods.

Performance integration includes helping people apply new capabilities in their regular work rather than just in special development situations, creating support systems and accountability that maintain development momentum over time, establishing measurement and feedback systems that track development progress and impact, and building habits of continuous learning and development that persist regardless of formal development programs.

Implementation approach: Help people integrate new capabilities into their regular work responsibilities rather than treating development as separate from performance. Create ongoing support and accountability for continued growth. Establish development as a continuous process rather than a temporary program.

Advanced Development Strategies for Maximum Multiplication

Strategy 1: Cohort Development and Peer Learning

Individual development is powerful, but group development creates additional learning opportunities through peer interaction, shared challenges, and collaborative problem-solving.

Cohort development includes creating development groups that learn together and support each other's growth, designing group challenges and projects that require collaboration while building individual capabilities, facilitating peer coaching and feedback that accelerates learning for everyone involved, and creating alumni networks that maintain development relationships over time.

Implementation approach: Organize development cohorts that combine individual development with group learning experiences. Create opportunities for teaching and learning within development programs. Establish ongoing communities of practice that support continued development.

Strategy 2: Reverse Mentoring and Multi-Directional Learning

Traditional mentoring assumes that senior people always have more to teach junior people, but effective development recognizes that learning can flow in multiple directions.

Reverse mentoring includes creating opportunities for junior people to teach senior leaders about new technologies, market trends, or customer perspectives, establishing cross-generational learning partnerships that benefit both parties, encouraging diverse perspectives that challenge conventional thinking and approaches, and building cultures where learning is valued regardless of hierarchical position.

Implementation approach: Create mentoring relationships where both parties have something to teach and learn from each other. Encourage senior leaders to learn from junior colleagues about areas where they have expertise or fresh perspectives.

Strategy 3: Development Through Teaching and Knowledge Transfer

One of the most effective ways to accelerate development is to have people teach others what they're learning, which deepens their own understanding while creating multiplication effects.

Teaching-based development includes having people present their learning to others as part of their development process, creating opportunities for people to train or coach others in areas where they're developing expertise, establishing knowledge transfer responsibilities that require people to document and share their learning, and using teaching assignments as development opportunities that build communication and leadership skills.

Implementation approach: Include teaching and knowledge transfer in all development plans. Have people share their learning with others as a way of reinforcing their own development while helping others learn.

Your Development Leadership Plan

Becoming an effective developer of others requires systematic capability building over extended time periods. Here's my recommended approach based on helping leaders become exceptional developers:

Months 1-2: Development Philosophy and Assessment involves clarifying your approach to developing others and assessing your current development capabilities. Define your philosophy about development and your role in developing others, assess your current skills in coaching, mentoring, and development planning, evaluate the development needs and potential of people you currently lead, and identify development opportunities and resources available within your organization.

Months 3-4: Development Planning and Goal Setting Skills focuses on building your capability to help others clarify their development goals and create effective development plans. Learn to facilitate development conversations that explore aspirations and potential rather than just current performance, develop skills in assessing development needs and creating personalized development plans, practice connecting individual development goals to organizational opportunities and needs, and create systems for tracking and supporting development progress over time.

Months 5-6: Opportunity Creation and Stretch Assignment Design builds your ability to create developmental experiences that challenge people to grow while contributing to organizational objectives. Identify and create stretch assignments that build capabilities while serving business needs, develop skills in providing support and coaching during challenging developmental experiences, learn to balance challenge and support to maximize learning while minimizing risk of failure, and create networks and relationships that provide developmental opportunities for others.

Months 7-8: Coaching and Mentoring Excellence develops your capabilities for providing ongoing guidance and support that accelerates others' development. Build skills in effective coaching conversations that promote learning and insight rather than just advice-giving, develop abilities to provide feedback that promotes growth rather than just performance evaluation, learn to share wisdom and experience in ways that accelerate others' learning, and create mentoring relationships that provide sustained support for long-term development.

Months 9-12: Development Culture and System Building expands your focus from individual development relationships to creating organizational cultures and systems that support development throughout your sphere of influence. Implement development systems and processes that support systematic capability building, train other leaders on development principles and practices so they become developers too, create organizational expectations and rewards that prioritize developing others as a core leadership responsibility, and establish development as a sustainable organizational capability rather than just individual leader activity.

Remember that developing others is one of the most rewarding and impactful responsibilities of leadership. Every person you develop successfully multiplies your impact and creates capabilities that continue producing value long after your direct involvement ends. Organizations that develop systematic development capabilities create sustainable competitive advantages through their people and build leadership pipelines that enable continued growth and adaptation to changing market conditions.

CHAPTER 28

Building Leadership Systems - Your Approach to Scale

Addressing The Leadership Scalability Crisis

Leadership scalability is another failure I've identified: the inability to scale leadership effectiveness beyond their individual capacity and direct span of control. Most leaders excel at creating results through personal effort and direct supervision, but struggle when organizational success requires leadership that extends far beyond what any individual can personally manage. The result is leadership bottlenecks that limit organizational growth, inconsistent leadership quality across different areas, and leadership capabilities that diminish rather than multiply as organizations become larger and more complex.

I regularly encounter successful entrepreneurs who have built thriving businesses through personal leadership but struggle when their companies outgrow their ability to personally direct every important decision. I see senior executives in large organizations who create excellent results in their immediate areas but fail to develop leadership systems that produce similar results throughout their divisions. I work with organizations that have outstanding individual leaders but inconsistent leadership quality across functions, locations, and levels.

This leadership scalability crisis isn't just about delegation or organizational structure, but it's about fundamental failure to understand that sustainable organizational success requires building leadership systems that work regardless of specific individuals, that produce consistent results across diverse circumstances, and that continue improving over time through systematic learning and adaptation. True leadership scaling involves creating organizational capabilities that multiply leadership effectiveness rather than just adding more leaders to handle increased complexity.

The latest research by Harvard Business School, McKinsey, and leading organizational effectiveness consultancies reveals that organizations with scalable leadership systems achieve 45% better performance consistency across functions and locations, develop leadership capabilities 60% faster than those relying on individual leader excellence, and demonstrate significantly greater resilience during leadership transitions. Yet studies consistently show that fewer than 20% of organizations have systematic approaches to building leadership systems, and most scaling efforts focus on adding people rather than building capabilities.

The cost of poor leadership scaling extends far beyond immediate performance limitations. Organizations that can't scale leadership effectively become vulnerable to competitive disruption because they can't respond consistently to market changes. They experience talent flight because high-potential people don't see clear development paths. They miss growth opportunities because they lack the leadership infrastructure needed to expand successfully into new markets or business areas.

Leadership Systems That Scale

When I talk about building leadership systems, I am not referring to organizational charts, reporting structures, or leadership development programs that operate independently of daily business operations. I am talking about integrated systems of processes, practices, and capabilities that consistently produce effective leadership throughout organizations, regardless of specific individuals, circumstances, or challenges. These systems create leadership results that persist through personnel changes and improve continuously through systematic learning and adaptation.

Leadership systems are fundamentally about creating organizational muscle memory that guides effective leadership behavior even when formal leaders aren't present or when situations arise that haven't been encountered before. They involve embedding leadership principles, practices, and capabilities so deeply into organizational DNA that effective leadership becomes the natural and expected way of operating rather than something that depends on exceptional individuals.

True leadership systems have several essential characteristics that distinguish them from traditional leadership development or organizational design approaches. They're integrated rather than fragmented, connecting leadership practices across all organizational functions and levels rather than treating different leadership roles as separate and unrelated. They're systematic rather than random, following consistent principles and practices that produce predictable results rather than relying on individual leadership styles or personalities.

Leadership systems are also adaptive rather than rigid, evolving and improving based on experience and changing circumstances, rather than following fixed procedures regardless of effectiveness. They're scalable rather than position-dependent, working equally well across different organizational sizes, complexities, and contexts rather than being limited to specific situations. Most importantly, leadership systems are sustainable rather than personality-dependent, continuing to produce excellent leadership results regardless of individual leader changes or transitions.

I've learned that building effective leadership systems requires both systematic thinking about how leadership capabilities can be embedded in organizational operations and practical experience in implementing leadership practices that work across diverse circumstances and personalities. The most effective leadership system builders combine analytical rigor with practical wisdom, systematic planning with adaptive implementation, and individual leadership excellence with organizational capability development.

The Five Elements of Scalable Leadership Systems

I've identified five interconnected elements that must work together to create leadership systems that produce consistent results across diverse circumstances and personnel changes.

Element 1: Leadership Philosophy and Principles

Scalable leadership systems begin with a clear, shared understanding of what leadership means within the organization and what principles should guide leadership behavior across all situations and levels. This provides the conceptual foundation that enables consistent leadership approaches regardless of individual personalities or specific circumstances.

Leadership philosophy development includes articulating core beliefs about leadership's purpose and value creation within your organizational context, defining specific leadership principles that should guide behavior and decision-making across all situations, creating shared language and frameworks that enable consistent leadership communication and development, and establishing leadership values that align with organizational mission and culture while providing practical guidance for difficult decisions.

Without clear philosophy and principles, leadership systems become collections of disconnected practices that produce inconsistent results because different leaders interpret expectations differently and make decisions based on personal preferences rather than shared organizational standards.

Element 2: Leadership Development Architecture

Effective leadership systems require systematic approaches to developing leadership capabilities throughout the organization rather than relying on random experience or individual initiative. This involves creating development architectures that build leadership competence progressively and consistently.

Development architecture includes establishing clear leadership competency models that define capabilities needed at different organizational levels, creating systematic development processes that build leadership skills progressively from entry level through senior executive roles, implementing assessment and feedback systems that provide accurate information about leadership development needs and progress, and designing development experiences that combine formal learning with practical application in increasingly challenging leadership situations.

Development architecture ensures that leadership capability building happens systematically throughout the organization rather than depending on individual leaders' commitment to developing others or people's personal initiative in seeking development opportunities.

Element 3: Leadership Process and Practice Integration

Leadership systems must integrate leadership practices into daily organizational operations rather than treating leadership as separate from operational excellence. This involves embedding leadership behaviors, decision-making processes, and accountability mechanisms into routine business practices.

Process integration includes incorporating leadership responsibilities and behaviors into standard operating procedures and workflow designs, establishing decision-making processes that develop leadership capabilities while achieving business objectives, creating accountability systems that measure and reward leadership effectiveness as well as operational results, and designing communication processes that reinforce leadership expectations and provide ongoing feedback about leadership performance.

When leadership practices are integrated into operational processes, effective leadership becomes the natural way of accomplishing work rather than an additional responsibility that competes with operational demands.

Element 4: Leadership Decision-Making and Governance Systems

Scalable leadership requires systematic approaches to decision-making that produce consistent quality regardless of who is making decisions and that develop decision-making capabilities throughout the organization. This involves creating governance systems that balance autonomy with coordination and individual initiative with organizational alignment.

Decision-making systems include establishing clear decision-making authorities and accountability at different organizational levels, creating decision-making frameworks that ensure consistent quality and organizational alignment, implementing governance processes that coordinate decisions across functions and levels without micromanaging, and developing decision-making capabilities that enable people to make effective choices independently while supporting organizational objectives.

Effective decision-making systems enable organizations to operate effectively at scale because people understand their decision-making authority and have frameworks for making choices that serve both their immediate responsibilities and broader organizational success.

Element 5: Leadership Learning and Adaptation Systems

Finally, scalable leadership systems must include mechanisms for continuous learning and improvement that enable leadership practices to evolve and improve based on experience, changing circumstances, and emerging best practices. This involves creating organizational learning capabilities that capture and share leadership insights throughout the organization.

Learning systems include establishing systematic approaches to capturing and analyzing leadership successes and failures across the organization, creating knowledge management processes that preserve and share leadership insights and best practices, implementing innovation processes that encourage experimentation with new leadership approaches and adaptation to changing circumstances, and developing organizational memory systems that prevent repetition of leadership mistakes while building on proven leadership successes.

Learning and adaptation systems ensure that leadership capabilities continue improving over time rather than becoming stagnant or outdated as circumstances change and new challenges emerge.

The SYSTEMS Framework for Leadership Scaling

Use the SYSTEMS framework as a comprehensive approach to creating leadership systems that produce consistent excellence regardless of organizational size, complexity, or personnel changes.

S - Standardize Leadership Excellence

Building scalable leadership begins with defining what excellent leadership looks like within your organizational context and creating standards that guide leadership behavior and development across all levels and functions.

Leadership standardization includes defining specific leadership behaviors and practices that produce excellent results within your organizational culture and context, creating leadership competency models that specify capabilities needed at different organizational levels and roles, establishing leadership performance standards that provide clear expectations for leadership effectiveness, and developing leadership assessment criteria that enable consistent evaluation of leadership performance across different situations and evaluators.

Implementation approach: Document examples of excellent leadership from within your organization and analyze what makes them effective. Create competency models that specify observable behaviors rather than abstract concepts. Establish assessment processes that provide consistent feedback about leadership effectiveness.

Y - Yield Systematic Development Processes

Once leadership excellence is defined, scalable systems require systematic processes for developing leadership capabilities throughout the organization rather than relying on individual initiative or random experience.

Systematic development includes creating structured development pathways that build leadership capabilities progressively from entry level through senior leadership roles, establishing mentoring and coaching systems that provide ongoing guidance and support for leadership development, implementing stretch assignment and project rotation programs that provide diverse leadership experiences, and developing assessment and feedback systems that track leadership development progress and identify continued development needs.

Implementation approach: Map leadership development journeys that show how people can progress from individual contributor roles through increasing levels of leadership responsibility. Create formal and informal development relationships that support ongoing learning. Design challenging experiences that build leadership confidence and capability.

S - Structure Decision-Making and Accountability

Scalable leadership requires clear structures for decision-making and accountability that enable consistent leadership quality while empowering people to act independently within appropriate boundaries.

Decision-making structure includes establishing clear decision-making authorities and accountability at different organizational levels, creating decision-making frameworks that ensure quality and consistency without micromanaging, implementing governance processes that coordinate decisions across functions while maintaining autonomy, and developing escalation procedures that enable complex decisions to be handled appropriately.

Implementation approach: Map decision-making authority throughout your organization and identify areas where clarity is needed. Create decision-making frameworks that help people make consistent choices. Establish governance processes that provide coordination without controlling every decision.

T - Transfer Knowledge and Best Practices

Leadership systems must include mechanisms for capturing and sharing leadership knowledge throughout the organization so that insights from one area can benefit leadership effectiveness everywhere.

Knowledge transfer includes creating documentation systems that capture leadership best practices and lessons learned from various experiences, establishing communication processes that share leadership insights across functions and locations, implementing training and development programs that transfer proven leadership approaches to new leaders, and developing organizational memory systems that preserve leadership knowledge through personnel changes.

Implementation approach: Create systematic processes for documenting and sharing leadership successes and failures. Establish communities of practice where leaders can share experiences and insights. Develop training programs that transfer proven leadership approaches rather than generic leadership concepts.

E - Embed Leadership in Operations

Sustainable leadership systems integrate leadership practices into daily operational activities rather than treating leadership as separate from business execution.

Operational embedding includes incorporating leadership behaviors and responsibilities into standard operating procedures and workflow designs, establishing performance management systems that measure and reward leadership effectiveness alongside operational results, creating communication processes that reinforce leadership expectations during routine business activities, and designing organizational structures that support leadership development through regular business operations.

Implementation approach: Review operational processes to identify opportunities for embedding leadership development and practice. Modify performance management systems to include leadership effectiveness measures. Create organizational structures that provide leadership opportunities as part of regular work.

M - Measure and Monitor Leadership Effectiveness

Finally, scalable leadership systems require systematic measurement and monitoring of leadership effectiveness that provides feedback for continuous improvement and early warning of leadership challenges.

Leadership measurement includes establishing leadership effectiveness metrics that track both individual leadership performance and overall leadership system health, creating assessment processes that provide regular feedback about leadership development and impact, implementing monitoring systems that identify leadership challenges before they become critical problems, and developing reporting processes that inform leadership system improvements and investments.

Implementation approach: Define specific measures of leadership effectiveness that can be tracked consistently across the organization. Create regular assessment and feedback processes. Establish monitoring systems that identify leadership trends and issues early.

S - Sustain Through Continuous Improvement

The final element involves creating continuous improvement capabilities that enable leadership systems to evolve and improve based on experience, changing circumstances, and emerging best practices.

Sustainability includes establishing regular review processes that assess leadership system effectiveness and identify improvement opportunities, creating innovation and experimentation processes that test new leadership approaches and practices, implementing change management capabilities that enable leadership system evolution without disrupting operational effectiveness, and developing resilience capabilities that maintain leadership effectiveness during challenging periods and organizational transitions.

Implementation approach: Create regular review cycles that assess leadership system effectiveness and identify areas for improvement. Encourage experimentation with new leadership approaches while maintaining successful practices. Build change management capabilities that enable leadership system evolution.

Your Leadership Systems Development Plan

Building scalable leadership systems requires sustained effort over multiple years rather than quick implementation projects. Here's my recommended approach for helping organizations create scalable leadership capabilities:

Year 1, Quarters 1-2: Foundation Assessment and Design involves evaluating your current leadership capabilities and designing systematic approaches to leadership scaling. Complete a comprehensive assessment of current leadership effectiveness and scalability across your organization, analyze leadership challenges and opportunities that affect organizational success, design leadership philosophy, principles, and standards that provide a foundation for system building, and create leadership system blueprints that specify development priorities and implementation approaches.

Year 1, Quarters 3-4: Core System Implementation focuses on implementing the fundamental elements of scalable leadership systems. Implement leadership development architecture that provides systematic capability building throughout the organization, establish decision-making and accountability structures that enable consistent leadership quality, create knowledge transfer and best practice sharing systems that multiply leadership effectiveness, and begin embedding leadership practices into operational processes and performance management systems.

Year 2, Quarters 1-2: System Integration and Coordination expands leadership systems to work across all organizational functions and levels rather than just in individual areas. Integrate leadership systems across different functions, locations, and organizational levels, establish governance and coordination processes that maintain system consistency while enabling local adaptation, implement measurement and monitoring systems that track leadership system effectiveness, and create feedback loops that enable continuous system improvement based on experience and results.

Year 2, Quarters 3-4: Advanced Capability and Innovation develops sophisticated leadership system capabilities that provide competitive advantages and support continued organizational growth. Implement advanced leadership development capabilities that create leadership pipeline depth throughout the organization, establish innovation and experimentation processes that continuously improve leadership effectiveness, create leadership system resilience that maintains effectiveness during challenging periods and major changes, and develop leadership system replication capabilities that support organizational expansion and scaling.

Year 3 and Beyond: Continuous Evolution and Optimization makes leadership systems a permanent organizational capability that continues improving and adapting to changing circumstances and opportunities. Establish ongoing leadership system review and improvement processes that maintain effectiveness over time, create leadership system knowledge management that preserves organizational learning and prevents repetition of mistakes, implement leadership system adaptation capabilities that enable evolution based on changing business conditions and requirements, and develop leadership system teaching and transfer capabilities that enable sharing with partners, acquisitions, and new business areas.

Remember that building scalable leadership systems is one of the most valuable and sustainable investments organizations can make. While individual leaders come and go, leadership systems create organizational capabilities that persist and improve over time, providing competitive advantages that are difficult for competitors to replicate and enabling growth and adaptation that would be impossible through individual leadership excellence alone.

CHAPTER 29

Leadership Legacy - The Story You Want to Leave

In thinking about my own leadership journey, I faced the same questions that so many people encounter: What am I leaving behind? Has my life and knowledge mattered? Is there anything left unfinished? The motivation for writing this book stemmed from reflecting on these ideas. Your life journey, your leadership quest, will likely encounter similar reflections. So I offer these final parting thoughts:

The Legacy Question That Changes Everything

There's a certain amount of humility that exemplifies really good leaders. I've learned that the most effective leaders are those who think beyond their immediate responsibilities and current challenges to consider the lasting impact they want to create through their leadership. Leadership isn't about fame, recognition, or personal achievement. The most memorable leaders are people who do the work as much as they talk the talk. So, the fundamental question that should guide every leadership decision:

"After I'm gone, what story do I want people to tell about my leadership?"

The most important question isn't "Am I successful?". Rather, we need to ask, "Am I building something that will continue creating value long after I'm no longer leading?"

Often I encounter leaders who are so focused on quarterly results, immediate crises, and short-term pressures that they never pause to consider whether their daily leadership choices are building toward something meaningful and lasting. They manage their careers efficiently, but never design their legacy intentionally. They solve problems skillfully, but never ask whether they're creating the conditions for sustainable success that will persist after their tenure ends.

Research on leadership effectiveness reveals that leaders who think systematically about their legacy achieve 45% better long-term results, create 60% more sustainable organizational improvements, and develop significantly more leaders who go on to create positive impact themselves. Yet, studies consistently show fewer than 25% of leaders have clear visions for the legacy they want to create, and most leadership development focuses on immediate effectiveness rather than lasting impact.

This "legacy neglect" isn't just about missed opportunities for personal fulfillment, but about a fundamental failure to understand the ultimate purpose of leadership: Creating a positive impact that extends far beyond an individual's presence and contribution.

Leadership Legacy That Matters

When I talk about leadership legacy, I am not referring to monuments, recognition programs, or buildings named in honorarium. I am talking about the systematic creation of positive impact that persists and multiplies long after direct leadership involvement ends. True legacy is measured not by what was personally accomplished, but by what continues to happen because of the foundations you built, the people you developed, and the changes you initiated after you left.

Several essential characteristics distinguish leadership legacy from personal achievement and temporary success. Leadership legacy is:

1. multiplicative rather than additive.
2. values-based rather than metrics-based.
3. sustainable rather than temporary.
4. developmental rather than transactional.
5. systematic rather than accidental.
6. others-focused rather than self-focused.

Thought of another way, a leadership legacy:

1. creates an impact that grows over time rather than just accumulates accomplishments.
2. establishes patterns and capabilities that persist through changing circumstances and leadership transitions.
3. builds others' capabilities rather than merely achieving immediate results.
4. advances principles and purposes that matter beyond just organizational performance indicators.
5. results from intentional choices and sustained effort rather than just good intentions or random positive outcomes.
6. measures the impact on people, organizations, and communities rather than just personal recognition or career advancement.

You aren't seeking to showcase your own capabilities. The likelihood of seeing your "'dividends" likely won't occur until after you've moved into another role. To achieve a meaningful leadership legacy requires:

- both long-term thinking and daily discipline.
- making decisions that may not provide immediate benefits.
- investing in people and capabilities.
- choosing approaches that develop others.

You are building towards having a lasting, positive impact.

The A-E-I-O-U Legacy Framework

Your leadership legacy could ultimately be determined by how effectively you apply the A-E-I-O-U framework, not just to achieve immediate results, but to create lasting positive change that continues long after your direct involvement ends.

A - Application Legacy: Teaching Others to Bridge Knowing and Doing

Legacy question: "How many people will be more effective at turning insights into action because of my leadership influence?"

Your application legacy is about building the capability in others which enables them to create change throughout their careers. While your own ability to apply leadership principles is important for exhibiting the qualities of a good leader, application is also measured by how many people you've taught to translate insights into action, concepts into behaviors, and intentions into results.

When thinking about application legacy, we need to consider:

- developing others' ability to take leadership concepts and make them practical and actionable in their specific contexts,
- teaching systematic approaches to behavior change that people can use to continuously improve their effectiveness,
- modeling application discipline that shows others how to turn learning into lasting capability building, and
- creating organizational cultures where application is valued and rewarded rather than just knowledge acquisition.

E - Execution Legacy: Building Organizational Discipline

Legacy question: "Will this organization be more disciplined about completing important initiatives because of my leadership influence?"

Your execution legacy is determined by the organizational discipline and completion capabilities you build that enable sustained achievement long after your direct involvement. This involves creating systems, processes, and cultural norms that ensure important initiatives get completed successfully regardless of who is leading them.

Execution legacy includes:

- establishing organizational systems that support disciplined follow-through on important commitments,
- developing others' capabilities for managing complex initiatives from inception through successful completion,
- creating cultural expectations that completion and follow-through are fundamental leadership responsibilities, and
- building organizational muscle memory that maintains execution discipline through leadership transitions and changing circumstances.

I - Implementation Legacy: Creating Systems That Outlast You

Legacy question: "What systems and capabilities will continue creating value long after I'm no longer involved?"

Your implementation legacy involves the systems, processes, and capabilities you create that continue producing value independent of individual leaders. Leaders build organizational infrastructure that enables sustainable performance and continuous improvement over time.

Implementation legacy requires:

- designing systems and processes that capture and institutionalize best practices rather than relying on individual knowledge,
- creating organizational capabilities that enable continuous improvement and adaptation to changing circumstances,

- building knowledge management and transfer systems that preserve organizational learning through personnel changes, and
- establishing governance and decision-making processes that maintain effectiveness while enabling evolution and growth.

O - Ownership Legacy: Developing Accountable Leaders

Legacy question: "How many people will lead with greater ownership and accountability because of my influence?"

Your ownership legacy is measured by how many people you've influenced to take full responsibility for outcomes, to lead with integrity and courage, and to hold themselves and others accountable for commitments and results. This involves developing others' willingness and ability to own challenges and drive solutions.

Ownership legacy involves:

- developing others' commitment to taking responsibility for outcomes rather than just activities,
- teaching courage and integrity that enables people to address difficult situations and make principled decisions,
- modeling accountability that shows others how to own mistakes and drive solutions, and
- creating organizational cultures where ownership is expected and supported rather than just hoped for.

U - Unity Legacy: Building Collaborative Cultures

Legacy question: "Will people work together more effectively because of the collaborative culture I helped create?"

Your unity legacy embraces the collaborative capabilities and cultural norms you create that enable people to work together effectively toward shared objectives long after your direct leadership involvement.

You are building an organizational DNA that values and enables effective teamwork and stakeholder coordination.

Unity legacy encompasses:

- developing others' abilities to create alignment among diverse stakeholders with different interests and priorities,
- establishing cultural norms that value collaboration and coordination over individual achievement,
- creating processes and systems that enable effective teamwork and cross-functional coordination, and
- building organizational capabilities for managing conflicts constructively and finding solutions that serve multiple stakeholder interests.

The Legacy Development Process

As you set out to create a leadership legacy, be meaningful in both the intent and approach. Instead of hoping to have a positive impact or expecting that your good intentions will naturally translate into good leadership, sit with - and have a systematic approach to the enactment of - your goals.

Phase 1: Legacy Vision Creation

Begin with a clear vision - how do you "see" the lasting impact of your leadership? What would it "look like" if you walked into your legacy as an outsider?

Legacy vision creation includes:

1. reflecting on your deepest values and how you want them to be expressed through your leadership impact,
2. identifying the problems or opportunities where your leadership could create lasting positive change,
3. clarifying what success would look like if measured years or decades after your direct involvement ends, and

4. connecting your leadership activities to purposes that extend beyond immediate organizational responsibilities.

The process of envisioning what the future contains involves thinking beyond immediate goals and career objectives. Consider what difference you want to make in 1) people's lives, 2) organizational capabilities, and 3) community conditions.

Development exercise: Write your leadership legacy statement by completing this sentence: "Twenty years from now, I want people to say that because of my leadership influence..." Focus on impact on others rather than recognition for yourself.

Phase 2: Legacy Gap Analysis

Once your legacy vision is clear, assess the delta. What is the gap between your current leadership approach and your desired legacy impact? Once the difference is determined, then identify the changes needed to get from the current, to the future, state.

Legacy gap analysis includes:

1. evaluating whether your current leadership activities are building toward your desired legacy or just achieving immediate results,
2. identifying specific changes needed in your leadership approach to create lasting positive impact,
3. recognizing capabilities you need to develop to influence others in ways that create multiplicative rather than just additive impact, and
4. understanding what support, resources, or partnerships you need to achieve your legacy objectives.

Development exercise: Create a legacy dashboard that identifies and tracks the changes you are implementing. What key information would help you assess the progress of your weekly leadership activities? What data identifies if the "needle is moving" your organizational culture toward your long-term legacy vision? Are there superficial drivers that clutter your perspective or just address the immediate pressures and opportunities?

Phase 3: Legacy Building Implementation

Legacy creation requires integrating legacy considerations into daily leadership decisions and activities rather than treating legacy as something you'll focus on later in your career.

Legacy building requires:

1. making leadership decisions based on both immediate effectiveness and long-term legacy impact,
2. investing time and energy in developing others even when it doesn't provide immediate personal benefits,
3. creating systems and processes that will continue producing value after your direct involvement ends, and
4. measuring success based on others' growth and organizational capability building as well as immediate results.

Development exercise: Identify three current leadership responsibilities. What can you modify in your approach to those responsibilities that would help you build a legacy? Is there a different way you could execute those responsibilities and maintain immediate effectiveness? From the list of items you create, rank in terms of effort and ripple effect. Which one could be implemented immediately, and which one(s) could be systematically rolled out over the next quarter? Choose ONE to put into effect and measure how that "moves the needle". Once you have collected data of the effectiveness, then choose another one to implement. This systematic process enables you to not only see the effects of what you are doing, but also guard against too many "cooks in the kitchen." If you put too many items into effect at the same time, you won't know what is actually working.

Phase 4: Legacy Monitoring and Adjustment

Legacy development requires ongoing assessment and adjustment because legacy impact often becomes apparent only over extended time periods.

Legacy monitoring includes:

1. tracking whether your leadership influence is developing others' capabilities in ways that create lasting positive impact,
2. assessing whether organizational changes you're implementing are sustainable and likely to persist through transitions,
3. gathering feedback about whether your leadership is creating the kind of culture and capabilities you want to be remembered for, and
4. adjusting your approach based on evidence about what's creating lasting, positive change.

Development exercise: Create annual legacy reviews where you assess progress toward your legacy vision and identify adjustments needed in your leadership approach to better align with your desired lasting impact. Use the data compiled in Phase 3 to track performance and make data-driven decisions. Creating a meaningful leadership legacy requires systematic action rather than just thoughtful reflection.

Your Legacy Action Plan

Here's my recommended approach for building legacy through daily leadership practice:

Immediate Actions (Next 30 Days)

- Write your personal leadership legacy statement that clarifies the lasting impact you want to create.
- Identify three people you could develop who would multiply your leadership impact.

- Assess one organizational system or process you could improve to create lasting value.
- Begin a collaborative initiative that would continue creating benefits after your involvement.

Short-term Initiatives (Next 90 Days)

- Implement a systematic approach to developing others' A-E-I-O-U capabilities.
- Create or improve organizational processes that capture and share your leadership insights.
- Establish measurement systems that track legacy indicators as well as immediate results.
- Begin building the relationships and coalitions needed to achieve your legacy objectives.

Medium-term Projects (Next Year)

- Design and implement leadership development initiatives that multiply your impact through others.
- Create organizational changes that embed your leadership principles into standard practices.
- Build systems that preserve and transfer your leadership knowledge and approaches.
- Establish collaborative partnerships that extend your influence beyond your direct authority.

Long-term Commitments (Throughout Your Career)

- Continuously develop leaders who will create a positive impact in other organizations.
- Build organizational cultures and capabilities that serve stakeholders long after your tenure.
- Create industry or community contributions that improve leadership effectiveness broadly.
- Maintain focus on legacy impact even as immediate pressures and opportunities compete for attention.

As you finish this book and begin applying the A-E-I-O-U framework more systematically in your leadership practice, I challenge you to think beyond immediate effectiveness to consider the lasting impact you want to create through your leadership influence and legacy.

The Legacy Leadership Challenge

Your leadership legacy is being created through every decision you make, every person you influence, and every change you implement. The question isn't whether you'll leave a legacy. The question is whether that legacy will be one you're proud of and one that creates the kind of positive impact you want to be remembered for.

Your leadership legacy starts now - with the choices you make today. How you choose to apply the AEIOU principles in your current leadership challenges and opportunities will have lasting effects. Make YOUR choices count. Create a positive impact that will persist long after your direct leadership involvement ends. Make your choices worthy of a leadership story that you would be proud to hear people talk about. I've given you the framework that can generate a legacy story.

The A-E-I-O-U framework provides tools for creating leadership, a legacy that matters:

- The **APPLICATION** helps you turn insights into lasting behavior change in yourself and others.
- **EXECUTION** generates organizational discipline that enables sustained achievement.
- **IMPLEMENTATION** creates systems that continue producing value independent of individual leaders.
- **OWNERSHIP** develops accountability and integrity that enable others to take responsibility for positive change.
- **UNITY** builds collaborative capabilities that enable people to work together effectively toward shared objectives.

The world needs leaders who think beyond their current roles and responsibilities, who consider how their leadership could create positive change that persists and multiplies over time. Organizations need leaders who build capabilities and cultures for lasting impact on stakeholders long after individual leaders move on to other opportunities. Communities need leaders who address challenges and create opportunities that benefit future generations and current constituents.

The world is waiting for leaders who will use their influence to create positive change that lasts. Now it's time to use it to build the legacy you want to leave and be a leadership practitioner, not a poser!

APPENDICES

Appendix A
Overall A-E-I-O-U
Leadership Assessment

Instructions: Rate yourself on each statement using a 1-10 scale, where 1 = never true, 5 = sometimes true, and 10 = always true. Be honest in your self-assessment, because development requires an accurate understanding of current capabilities.

APPLICATION ASSESSMENT

Behavioral Translation Capability

- I consistently translate leadership concepts I learn into specific behavioral changes (1-10)
- I can take abstract leadership principles and make them practical for my specific context (1-10)
- Others would say I "walk the talk" when it comes to leadership principles (1-10)
- I create specific action plans when I learn new leadership concepts (1-10)

Practice Implementation

- I create deliberate practice opportunities for developing new leadership skills (1-10)
- I follow through on behavioral commitments I make during leadership development (1-10)
- I practice new leadership approaches even when they feel uncomfortable initially (1-10)
- I seek feedback on my application of new leadership behaviors (1-10)

Progress Tracking

- I systematically track my progress in applying new leadership behaviors (1-10)
- I can measure whether my attempts to apply new concepts are working (1-10)
- I adjust my approach when initial application attempts aren't successful (1-10)
- I maintain application discipline even when other priorities compete for attention (1-10)

Teaching and Sharing

- I teach others how to apply leadership concepts they're learning (1-10)
- I share my application experiences, including failures and adjustments (1-10)
- I help others create specific plans for applying leadership insights (1-10)
- I model application discipline that others can observe and learn from (1-10)

Application Total Score: ___/160

EXECUTION ASSESSMENT

Goal Clarity and Planning

- I consistently complete important initiatives on time and within budget (1-10)
- I create crystal-clear objectives that specify what success looks like (1-10)
- I break large projects into manageable milestones with clear deadlines (1-10)
- I create realistic timelines that account for potential obstacles and delays (1-10)

Obstacle Management

- I proactively identify and address obstacles before they derail projects (1-10)
- I develop contingency plans for potential problems before they occur (1-10)
- I maintain momentum and focus even when projects become difficult or tedious (1-10)
- I solve problems quickly rather than hoping they'll resolve themselves (1-10)

Progress Monitoring

- I track progress systematically throughout project lifecycles (1-10)
- I identify problems early while they can still be addressed effectively (1-10)
- I adjust strategies and tactics based on progress data and changing circumstances (1-10)
- I maintain awareness of both leading and lagging indicators of project success (1-10)

Accountability and Follow-through

- I hold myself and others accountable for commitments and deadlines (1-10)
- I address performance problems quickly when execution is suffering (1-10)
- I celebrate completion milestones to maintain motivation and momentum (1-10)
- I conduct post-project reviews to improve future execution capability (1-10)

Execution Total Score: ___/160

IMPLEMENTATION ASSESSMENT

Systems Thinking

- I create systems and processes that prevent problems from recurring (1-10)
- I think systematically about how to scale successful approaches (1-10)
- I design solutions that work regardless of who's implementing them (1-10)
- I understand how different parts of my organization interact with each other (1-10)

Capability Building

- I build capabilities in others rather than solving everything myself (1-10)
- I invest time in creating sustainable solutions rather than quick fixes (1-10)
- I develop others' ability to handle challenges independently (1-10)
- I create learning opportunities that build organizational knowledge (1-10)

Process Documentation

- I document important processes so others can replicate successful approaches (1-10)
- I capture tribal knowledge and make it accessible to others (1-10)
- I create checklists and guidelines that ensure consistent execution (1-10)
- I establish standard operating procedures for critical activities (1-10)

Culture Integration

- I embed successful practices into organizational culture and norms (1-10)
- I create conditions where good practices become "how I do things here" (1-10)
- I influence organizational systems to support rather than hinder effectiveness (1-10)
- I build organizational muscle memory that persists through personnel changes (1-10)

Implementation Total Score: ___/160

OWNERSHIP ASSESSMENT

Responsibility Taking

- I take full responsibility for outcomes in my area of leadership (1-10)
- I focus on solutions rather than excuses when problems occur (1-10)
- I take the initiative to address problems even when they're not technically my responsibility (1-10)
- I own both successes and failures rather than shifting blame or credit (1-10)

Accountability Culture

- I hold myself and others accountable for commitments and results (1-10)
- I address performance problems directly rather than hoping they'll improve (1-10)
- I admit mistakes quickly and focus on learning from them (1-10)
- I create cultures where people feel safe to take ownership and initiative (1-10)

Decision Making

- I make decisions based on what's best for the organization, not what's comfortable for me (1-10)
- I take calculated risks when they're needed for organizational success (1-10)
- I stand behind my decisions even when they're unpopular or difficult (1-10)
- I involve others in decisions while maintaining clear accountability for outcomes (1-10)

Results Focus

- I measure success based on outcomes achieved, not just activities completed (1-10)
- I maintain focus on what matters most rather than getting distracted by urgent but unimportant tasks (1-10)
- I persist through challenges and setbacks to achieve important objectives (1-10)
- I help others understand how their work contributes to larger organizational outcomes (1-10)

Ownership Total Score: ___/160

UNITY ASSESSMENT

Stakeholder Alignment

- I effectively align diverse stakeholders around shared objectives (1-10)
- I understand different stakeholder perspectives and interests (1-10)
- I build consensus while respecting different viewpoints and approaches (1-10)
- I create a shared understanding of priorities and expectations (1-10)

Collaboration Facilitation

- I help groups work through disagreements constructively (1-10)
- I facilitate productive discussions that lead to better decisions (1-10)
- I bring out the best thinking from diverse group members (1-10)
- I create psychological safety that enables open dialogue and debate (1-10)

Communication Excellence

- I create clear communication and coordination across different functions (1-10)
- I adapt my communication style to different audiences and situations (1-10)
- I ensure important information flows effectively throughout my area of responsibility (1-10)
- I listen actively and seek to understand before seeking to be understood (1-10)

Conflict Resolution

- I address conflicts directly rather than hoping they'll resolve themselves (1-10)
- I help people find common ground even when they disagree on approaches (1-10)
- I manage my own emotions effectively during difficult conversations (1-10)
- I create win-win solutions that address multiple stakeholder interests (1-10)

Unity Total Score: ___/160

LEADERSHIP IMPACT ASSESSMENT

Individual Development

- People who work with me grow in their capabilities and confidence (1-10)
- I spend significant time coaching and developing others (1-10)
- Others seek my advice and guidance on leadership challenges (1-10)
- People I've led have gone on to successful leadership roles themselves (1-10)

Team Performance

- Teams I lead consistently achieve or exceed their objectives (1-10)
- Team members are engaged and motivated to do their best work (1-10)
- My teams collaborate effectively and support each other's success (1-10)
- Team performance improves over time under my leadership (1-10)

Organizational Contribution

- I make positive contributions to organizational culture and effectiveness (1-10)
- I help solve problems that extend beyond my immediate responsibilities (1-10)
- I contribute to organizational learning and improvement (1-10)
- Others throughout the organization value my leadership contribution (1-10)

External Impact

- I build effective relationships with external stakeholders (1-10)
- I represent my organization professionally and effectively (1-10)
- I contribute to my industry or community beyond my immediate job responsibilities (1-10)
- I help create value for customers and other external stakeholders (1-10)

Leadership Impact Total Score: ___/160

SCORING INTERPRETATION

Score Ranges and Development Priorities:

140-160 (Excellent): This area represents a significant strength. Focus on using this capability to multiply your impact by developing others and creating organizational systems that leverage your excellence.

120-139 (Good): This area shows solid capability with room for enhancement. Identify 2-3 specific behaviors that could move you toward excellence.

100-119 (Developing): This area needs focused development attention. Create systematic development plans with specific practice opportunities and feedback mechanisms.

80-99 (Significant Gap): This area represents a critical development need. Consider seeking coaching, mentoring, or training support to build these capabilities.

Below 80 (Critical): This area requires immediate and intensive development attention. Consider whether this gap limits your overall leadership effectiveness.

Development Planning Template

Based on your assessment scores, complete the following development planning process:

My Strongest A-E-I-O-U Area: _____ **How I will leverage this strength to help others:** _____

My Priority Development Area: _____ **Specific behaviors I will focus on improving:**

1. _____
2. _____
3. _____

Development Action Plan:

- **Learning resources, I will use:** _____
- **Practice opportunities I will create:** _____
- **Feedback sources I will utilize:** _____
- **Progress measures I will track:** _____
- **Timeline for improvement:** _____

Accountability Partner: _____ **Check-in Schedule:** _____

Appendix B
My 90-Day
Implementation Guide

Overview: Systematic Leadership Development in 90 Days

This guide provides a structured approach to implementing the A-E-I-O-U framework over 90 days. Rather than trying to develop all areas simultaneously, this guide uses a focused, sequential approach that builds capabilities systematically while maintaining your current leadership responsibilities.

Implementation Principles:

- Focus on one primary A-E-I-O-U element every 30 days
- Practice new behaviors in low-risk situations before applying them to critical challenges
- Seek feedback regularly to accelerate learning and adjustment
- Track progress systematically to maintain motivation and identify what's working
- Build on successes while learning from setbacks

Days 1-30: APPLICATION FOCUS

"Turning Insights Into Action"

Week 1: Foundation Building

Day 1-2: Assessment and Planning

- Complete the Application Assessment from Appendix A
- Identify your strongest and weakest application areas
- Select 2-3 specific application behaviors to develop
- Create your application development plan

Daily Practice: Choose one leadership concept you've learned recently but haven't fully applied. Create a specific action plan for implementing this concept in your daily leadership practice.

Day 3-7: Behavioral Specificity Development

- **Daily Action**: Each day, take one abstract leadership principle and translate it into three specific, observable behaviors you could demonstrate
- **Practice Exercise**: When you catch yourself using vague leadership language ("I need to be more strategic"), immediately reframe it into specific actions ("I will spend 30 minutes each morning reviewing industry trends and their implications for my team priorities")
- **Reflection Questions**:
  - What leadership concepts do I understand intellectually but struggle to apply practically?
  - How can I make my leadership commitments more specific and actionable?

Week 2: Practice Planning

Day 8-14: Systematic Practice Development

- **Daily Action**: Identify one new leadership behavior you want to develop and create a specific practice plan for that behavior
- **Practice Structure**:
  o Monday: Choose the behavior and define success criteria
  o Tuesday-Thursday: Practice the behavior in low-stakes situations
  o Friday: Seek feedback and adjust approach
  o Weekend: Reflect on progress and plan next week's practice

Implementation Exercise: Create "if-then" plans for your target behaviors (e.g., "If I find myself getting defensive in meetings, then I will take a deep breath, ask a clarifying question, and listen to the full response")

Week 3: Progress Tracking

Day 15-21: Measurement and Adjustment

- **Daily Action**: Track your application of target behaviors using a simple scoring system (1-5 scale)
- **Weekly Review**: Assess what's working, what isn't, and what adjustments are needed
- **Feedback Collection**: Ask trusted colleagues to observe and provide feedback on your application efforts

Tools: Use a leadership journal, mobile app, or simple tracking sheet to record daily application scores and observations

Week 4: Teaching and Sharing

Day 22-30: Multiplication Through Others

- **Daily Action**: Share one application insight or experience with a colleague who could benefit from your learning
- **Teaching Opportunity**: Lead a discussion or presentation about application principles with your team
- **Mentoring Practice**: Help someone else create specific application plans for their leadership development

Month 1 Assessment: Complete the Application Assessment again and compare to your baseline scores. Identify improvements and continued development needs.

Days 31-60: EXECUTION FOCUS

"Getting Things Done Consistently"

Week 5: Execution Assessment and Planning

Day 31-35: Execution Foundation

- Complete the Execution Assessment from Appendix A
- Analyze your current execution patterns and challenges
- Identify 2-3 specific execution capabilities to develop
- Select a current project or initiative to use for execution practice

Daily Practice: Apply systematic execution principles to one ongoing project, including milestone creation, obstacle anticipation, and progress tracking

Week 6: Goal Clarity and Milestone Management

Day 36-42: Systematic Project Management

- **Daily Action**: Practice creating crystal-clear objectives for tasks and projects, specifying outcomes, timelines, and success criteria
- **Milestone Practice**: Break one large project into smaller, manageable milestones with specific deadlines and deliverables
- **Communication Exercise**: Practice communicating project objectives and milestones clearly to stakeholders

Execution Tools: Implement project tracking systems (digital tools, dashboards, or simple checklists) that provide regular visibility into progress

Week 7: Obstacle Management and Problem Solving

Day 43-49: Proactive Problem Management

- **Daily Action**: For each project you're managing, identify potential obstacles and develop contingency plans
- **Problem-Solving Practice**: When obstacles arise, practice systematic problem-solving rather than reactive responses
- **Momentum Maintenance**: Implement strategies for maintaining progress even when projects become difficult or tedious

Skills Development: Practice rapid problem diagnosis, solution generation, and decision-making under time pressure

Week 8: Accountability and Follow-Through

Day 50-60: Results Achievement

- **Daily Action**: Hold accountability conversations with team members about project commitments and results
- **Completion Celebration**: Systematically recognize and celebrate project milestones and completions
- **Process Improvement**: Conduct post-project reviews to capture lessons learned and improve future execution

Month 2 Assessment: Complete the Execution Assessment again and measure improvement in your ability to complete important initiatives successfully.

Days 61-90: OWNERSHIP FOCUS

"Taking Full Responsibility for Results"

Week 9: Ownership Assessment and Development

Day 61-67: Ownership Foundation

- Complete the Ownership Assessment from Appendix A
- Identify areas where you avoid or delay taking full ownership
- Practice taking responsibility for outcomes, both positive and negative
- Address one situation where you've been avoiding ownership

Daily Practice: In every meeting or interaction, look for opportunities to take initiative and responsibility rather than waiting for others to act

Week 10: Accountability Culture Building

Day 68-74: Creating Accountability

- **Daily Action**: Have direct conversations about performance and results with team members who need accountability
- **Culture Practice**: Model taking responsibility for mistakes and failures while sharing credit for successes
- **Problem Ownership**: Take initiative to address organizational problems even when they're not technically your responsibility

Skills Development: Practice difficult conversations, performance management, and creating psychological safety for ownership

Week 11: Decision-Making and Risk-Taking

Day 75-81: Courageous Leadership

- **Daily Action**: Make at least one decision that requires courage or carries personal risk
- **Values Practice**: Align decisions with your values even when it's difficult or unpopular
- **Strategic Focus**: Practice maintaining focus on what matters most rather than getting distracted by urgent but unimportant tasks

Ownership Exercises: Practice owning strategic decisions, admitting when you don't know something, and taking calculated risks for organizational benefit

Week 12: Results Focus and Legacy Building

Day 82-90: Sustainable Ownership

- **Daily Action**: Help others understand how their work contributes to larger organizational outcomes
- **Results Measurement**: Focus on outcomes achieved rather than just activities completed
- **Legacy Practice**: Make decisions based on long-term organizational benefit rather than short-term convenience

Month 3 Assessment: Complete the Ownership Assessment again and evaluate your progress in taking full responsibility for results.

90-Day Integration and Planning Forward

Day 90: Comprehensive Assessment and Future Planning

Complete Assessment Process:

1. Retake all A-E-I-O-U assessments
2. Compare 90-day results to baseline scores
3. Identify areas of greatest improvement
4. Recognize continued development needs

Integration Reflection:

- How have the three focus areas (Application, Execution, Ownership) affected each other?
- Which changes have been most sustainable?
- What leadership challenges do you now handle more effectively?
- How have others responded to changes in your leadership approach?

Next 90-Day Planning:

- Select your next 1-2 A-E-I-O-U focus areas (Implementation and/or Unity)
- Create development plans based on lessons learned from your first 90 days
- Identify support systems and accountability mechanisms for continued development
- Establish measurement systems for tracking ongoing leadership improvement

Implementation Support Tools

Daily Leadership Journal Template

Date: _____

A-E-I-O-U Focus Today: _____

Specific Behaviors I Practiced:

1. _____
2. _____
3. _____

Results/Outcomes Observed:

- _____

Feedback Received:

- _____

Adjustments for Tomorrow:

- _____

Progress Rating (1-5): _____

Weekly Review Questions

1. **Application**: What insights did I successfully turn into action this week?
2. **Execution**: What did I complete successfully? What got stalled and why?
3. **Implementation**: What systems or processes did I improve to create lasting value?
4. **Ownership**: Where did I take full responsibility for outcomes, both positive and negative?
5. **Unity**: How effectively did I create alignment and collaboration among stakeholders?

Monthly Assessment Template

Month: _____ **A-E-I-O-U Focus**: _____

Quantitative Progress:

- Assessment scores: Start _____ End _____
- Specific metrics tracked: _____

Qualitative Changes:

- Leadership behaviors that improved: _____
- Feedback from others: _____
- Personal confidence/satisfaction changes: _____

Lessons Learned:

- What worked best: _____
- What was most challenging: _____
- What I would do differently: _____

Next Month Focus:

- Primary development area: _____
- Specific behaviors to practice: _____
- Support/resources needed: _____

Appendix C
Resources I Recommend

Essential Reading by A-E-I-O-U Focus Area

APPLICATION - Turning Knowledge Into Action

Core Books:

- *"The Knowing-Doing Gap"* by Jeffrey Pfeffer and Robert Sutton - The definitive work on why organizations struggle to implement what they know
- *"Switch: How to Change Things When Change Is Hard"* by Chip Heath and Dan Heath - Practical framework for creating behavior change
- *"Atomic Habits"* by James Clear - Systematic approach to building new behaviors and breaking old ones
- *"The Power of Moments"* by Chip Heath and Dan Heath - Creating breakthrough experiences that drive lasting change

Research Articles:

- "Implementation Intentions: Strong Effects of Simple Plans" by Peter Gollwitzer (1999) - Research foundation for if-then planning

- "The Case for Behavioral Strategy" by McKinsey Quarterly - Business application of behavioral insights

EXECUTION - Getting Things Done Consistently

Core Books:

- *"Execution: The Discipline of Getting Things Done"* by Larry Bossidy and Ram Charan - Classic framework for organizational execution
- *"The 4 Disciplines of Execution"* by Chris McChesney, Sean Covey, and Jim Huling - Systematic approach to achieving important goals
- *"Getting Things Done"* by David Allen - Personal productivity system that scales to organizational application
- *"Grit: The Power of Passion and Perseverance"* by Angela Duckworth - Research on sustained effort and completion

Tools and Systems:

- Project management software: Asana, Monday.com, Microsoft Project
- Execution tracking: OKR software (Lattice, 15Five)
- Personal productivity: Todoist, Things, Notion

IMPLEMENTATION - Building Systems That Scale

Core Books:

- *"The E-Myth Revisited"* by Michael Gerber - Building systems that work without dependence on individuals
- *"Built to Last"* by Jim Collins and Jerry Porras - Creating enduring organizational systems
- *"The Toyota Way"* by Jeffrey Liker - Implementation excellence in manufacturing and operations
- *"Scaling Up"* by Verne Harnish - Systematic approach to growing organizations

Systems Thinking:

- *"The Fifth Discipline"* by Peter Senge - Foundation for systems thinking in organizations
- *"Thinking in Systems"* by Donella Meadows - Practical guide to understanding complex systems

OWNERSHIP - Taking Full Responsibility

Core Books:

- *"Extreme Ownership"* by Jocko Willink and Leif Babin - Military leadership principles for business application
- *"The Oz Principle"* by Roger Connors, Tom Smith, and Craig Hickman - Creating cultures of accountability
- *"Integrity: The Courage to Meet the Demands of Reality"* by Henry Cloud - Personal and organizational integrity
- *"The Hard Thing About Hard Things"* by Ben Horowitz - Ownership and decision-making under pressure

Accountability Tools:

- Performance management: 15Five, Lattice, BambooHR
- 360-degree feedback: Zenger Folkman, Center for Creative Leadership tools
- Personal accountability: StickK, Beeminder, Coach.me

UNITY - Creating Alignment and Collaboration

Core Books:

- *"Getting to Yes"* by Roger Fisher and William Ury - Principled negotiation and conflict resolution
- *"Crucial Conversations"* by Kerry Patterson, Joseph Grenny, Ron McMillan, and Al Switzler - Managing difficult dialogues
- *"The Five Dysfunctions of a Team"* by Patrick Lencioni - Building team cohesion and trust

- *"Nonviolent Communication"* by Marshall Rosenberg - Communication that builds understanding and cooperation

Collaboration Tools:

- Communication: Slack, Microsoft Teams, Zoom
- Collaboration: Miro, Mural, Figma
- Decision-making: Luma Workplace, AJ&Smart decision-making frameworks

Leadership Development Resources

Assessment Tools

- **Clifton Strengths**: Individual strengths identification and development
- **EQi 2.0**: Emotional intelligence assessment and development
- **Hogan Assessments**: Personality, values, and derailment factors
- **360-degree feedback**: Zenger Folkman Leadership Versatility Index
- **Team assessments**: Team Diagnostic Survey, Everything DiSC Team Dimensions

Coaching and Development

- **Center for Creative Leadership**: Research-based leadership development programs
- **Harvard Business School Executive Education**: Advanced leadership programs
- **Stanford Graduate School of Business**: Executive development
- **International Coach Federation**: Directory of certified executive coaches
- **Leadership Circle**: Integral leadership assessment and development

Learning Platforms

- **LinkedIn Learning**: Extensive library of leadership development courses
- **Coursera Business**: University-level leadership programs
- **MasterClass**: Leadership lessons from world-class leaders
- **Harvard Business Review**: Case studies, articles, and research
- **MIT Sloan Management Review**: Cutting-edge management research

Industry-Specific Resources

Technology Leadership

- *"The Innovator's Dilemma"* by Clayton Christensen
- *"Crossing the Chasm"* by Geoffrey Moore
- *"Lean Startup"* by Eric Ries
- **Resources**: First Round Review, a16z blog, Y Combinator Startup School

Healthcare Leadership

- *"Leading Change"* by John Kotter (healthcare applications)
- *"The Checklist Manifesto"* by Atul Gawande
- **Organizations**: American Organization for Nursing Leadership, Healthcare Financial Management Association

Manufacturing Leadership

- *"The Goal"* by Eliyahu Goldratt
- *"Lean Thinking"* by James Womack and Daniel Jones
- **Resources**: Lean Enterprise Institute, Society of Manufacturing Engineers

Non-Profit Leadership

- *"Good to Great and the Social Sectors"* by Jim Collins
- *"The Nonprofit Sector"* by Burton Weisbrod
- **Resources**: BoardSource, Independent Sector, Chronicle of Philanthropy

Research and Academic Resources

Leadership Research Centers

- **Center for Creative Leadership**: Ongoing leadership effectiveness research
- **Harvard Business School**: Leadership case studies and research
- **Wharton School**: Leadership and team effectiveness studies
- **Stanford Leadership Development Center**: Research on leadership development
- **MIT Sloan**: Systems thinking and organizational learning research

Key Research Journals

- *Academy of Management Journal*
- *Harvard Business Review*
- *MIT Sloan Management Review*
- *Administrative Science Quarterly*
- *Journal of Applied Psychology*

Research Databases

- **Google Scholar**: Academic research across all leadership topics
- **JSTOR**: Academic journal access
- **Harvard Business Review Database**: Case studies and articles
- **Gallup Research**: Employee engagement and leadership effectiveness studies

Development Communities and Networks

Professional Organizations

- **Society for Human Resource Management (SHRM)**: Leadership development resources
- **Association for Talent Development (ATD)**: Learning and development community
- **International Leadership Association**: Academic and practitioner network
- **Young Presidents' Organization (YPO)**: Peer learning for executives

Online Communities

- **LinkedIn Groups**: Various leadership development communities
- **Reddit**: r/Leadership, r/Management subreddits
- **Facebook Groups**: Leadership development and coaching communities
- **Slack Communities**: Leadership-focused professional networks

Crisis and Change Leadership Resources

Crisis Leadership

- *"The Crisis Manager"* by Otto Lerbinger
- *"Crisis Leadership Now"* by Laurence Barton
- **Resources**: Crisis & Emergency Management, International Association of Emergency Managers

Change Management

- *"Leading Change"* by John Kotter
- *"The Change Leader's Roadmap"* by Linda Ackerman Anderson and Dean Anderson
- **Certification**: Prosci Change Management, ACMP (Association of Change Management Professionals)

Technology Tools for Leadership Development

Learning Management Systems

- **Cornerstone OnDemand**: Enterprise learning platform
- **Degreed**: Skill development and tracking
- **Pluralsight**: Technology and business skills
- **Udemy for Business**: Corporate learning platform

Performance and Development Tracking

- **Lattice**: Performance management and development
- **15Five**: Continuous performance management
- **Culture Amp**: Employee feedback and development
- **Glint**: Employee engagement and development insights

Communication and Collaboration

- **Slack**: Team communication and collaboration
- **Microsoft Teams**: Integrated communication platform
- **Zoom**: Video conferencing and webinars
- **Miro**: Visual collaboration and brainstorming

Measurement and Analytics Tools

Leadership Effectiveness Measurement

- **Zenger Folkman**: Leadership effectiveness assessment
- **Development Dimensions International (DDI)**: Leadership assessment and development
- **Lominger Leadership Architect**: Competency-based assessment
- **Hogan Assessment Suite**: Personality and leadership assessment

Organizational Health Measurement

- **Gallup Q12**: Employee engagement measurement
- **Culture Amp**: Cultural assessment and improvement
- **Glint**: Employee satisfaction and engagement
- **TINYpulse**: Regular employee feedback and pulse surveys

Business Impact Measurement

- **Balanced Scorecard**: Strategic performance measurement
- **OKR Software**: Objectives and key results tracking
- **Tableau**: Data visualization and analysis
- **Power BI**: Business intelligence and analytics

Recommended Development Sequence

For New Leaders (0-2 years leadership experience)

1. Start with **Application** and **Execution** focus
2. Read: "The First 90 Days," "The Coaching Habit," "Crucial Conversations"
3. Seek: Mentor relationship, formal leadership training, 360-degree feedback
4. Practice: Basic delegation, feedback conversations, project management

for Experienced Leaders (3-10 years experience)

1. Focus on **Implementation** and **Unity** development
2. Read: "The Fifth Discipline," "Getting to Yes," "The Hard Thing About Hard Things"
3. Seek: Executive coaching, peer learning groups, stretch assignments
4. Practice: Systems building, cross-functional collaboration, strategic thinking

For Senior Executives (10+ years experience)

1. Emphasize **Ownership** and **Legacy** building
2. Read: "Good to Great," "Built to Last," "The Infinite Game"
3. Seek: Board involvement, industry leadership roles, teaching opportunities
4. Practice: Organizational transformation, succession planning, industry influence

Continuous Learning Plan

Daily (15-30 minutes)

- Read leadership articles (Harvard Business Review, MIT Sloan Management Review)
- Listen to leadership podcasts during commute
- Practice one specific leadership behavior
- Reflect on leadership challenges and lessons learned

Weekly (1-2 hours)

- Read leadership book chapters
- Participate in leadership discussion forums
- Seek feedback from colleagues or team members
- Plan the upcoming week's leadership development focus

Monthly (4-6 hours)

- Complete leadership assessment or 360-degree feedback
- Attend a leadership development workshop or webinar
- Review and adjust the leadership development plan
- Connect with a mentor, a coach, or a peer learning partner

Quarterly (8-12 hours)

- Attend a leadership conference or an intensive program
- Conduct a comprehensive review of leadership progress
- Set new development goals and priorities
- Participate in a leadership development retreat or intensive

Annually (40-60 hours)

- Complete comprehensive leadership development program
- Participate in a leadership assessment center or intensive coaching
- Lead leadership development initiative for others
- Review and revise the long-term leadership development strategy

About the Author

James "Jim" DeLung, Ph.D.

Dr. DeLung's leadership expertise spans the full spectrum addressed in *The A-E-I-O-U of Leadership and Y It Matters*. He has successfully developed intrapersonal development as a training director, managed interpersonal dynamics in high-stress public safety environments, built high-performing teams across multiple public and private organizations, guided organizational change in complex corporate and bureaucratic systems, and navigated external stakeholder relationships in politically sensitive roles. His current position as the Police Administrator for the Prescott (AZ) Police Department, serving as the Director of the Prescott Regional Communications Center, exemplifies the systems thinking and stakeholder management principles detailed in this book. In this role, he directs 16 partner agencies across 5,000+ square miles while maintaining operational excellence with the greatest team members in the world!

His academic credentials include a Ph.D. in Business Administration with emphasis on Organizational Leadership from National University (formerly Northcentral University), along with a Master of Education and a Bachelor of Science degree from Northern Arizona University. It is his combination of scholarly research with hands-on leadership experience and consulting that makes his approach in this book uniquely effective. After honorably retiring from the Phoenix Police Department in 2014, where he concluded his service developing leaders for the Arizona Peace Officer Standards and Training Board, Dr. DeLung has continued applying and refining the leadership principles that form the foundation of this book.

Dr. DeLung's previous publications include *Police Personalities: Why Cops Act the Way They Do* and his doctoral dissertation on *Examination of Factors for Workplace Satisfaction of Millennial-aged Police Officers*, demonstrating his commitment to understanding what motivates people and drives organizational effectiveness. These themes run throughout *The A-E-I-O-U of Leadership and Y It Matters*.

Currently residing in Prescott, Arizona, with his wife Erin, Dr. DeLung maintains an active lifestyle and continuous learning mindset that he advocates for all leaders. When not developing organizational capabilities or speaking to leadership audiences, he can be found horseback riding with his wife or kayak fishing with his friends. These activities reinforce his belief that effective leaders must maintain a mental and physical health synthesis while pursuing excellence.

The A-E-I-O-U of Leadership and Y It Matters represents the culmination of Dr. DeLung's decades of experience leading diverse organizations, developing leaders, and researching what works in the complex reality of modern organizational life. His practical, no-nonsense approach to leadership development reflects a simple truth he's learned through experience: the best leadership development combines rigorous thinking with practical application, academic insight with real-world testing, and proven principles with personal adaptation.

"Leadership is not rocket science; it's people science!"
-Jim DeLung, Ph.D.

References

Academic Research and Theory

Avolio, B. J., Reichard, R. J., Hannah, S. T., Walumbwa, F. O., & Chan, A. (2009). A meta-analytic review of leadership impact research: Experimental and quasi-experimental studies. *The Leadership Quarterly*, 20(5), 764-784.

Bennis, W., & Thomas, R. J. (2002). *Geeks and Geezers: How Era, Values, and Defining Moments Shape Leaders*. Harvard Business Review Press.

Duhigg, C. (2012). *The Power of Habit: Why I Do What I Do in Life and Business*. Random House.

Edmondson, A. (1999). Psychological safety and learning behavior in work teams. *Administrative Science Quarterly*, 44(2), 350-383.

Ericsson, K. A., Krampe, R. T., & Tesch-Römer, C. (1993). The role of deliberate practice in the acquisition of expert performance. *Psychological Review*, 100(3), 363-406.

Ericsson, A., & Pool, R. (2016). *Peak: Secrets from the New Science of Expertise*. Houghton Mifflin Harcourt.

Eurich, T. (2017). *Insight: The Surprising Truth About How Others See Us, How I See Ourselves, and Why the Answers Matter More Than I Think*. Crown Business.

Gioia, D. A., & Thomas, J. B. (1996). Identity, image, and issue interpretation: Sensemaking during strategic change in academia. *Administrative Science Quarterly*, 41(3), 370-403.

Goldsmith, M. (2007). *What Got You Here Won't Get You There: How Successful People Become Even More Successful*. Hyperion.

Gollwitzer, P. M. (1999). Implementation intentions: Strong effects of simple plans. *American Psychologist*, 54(7), 493-503.

Herzberg, F. (1959). *The Motivation to Work*. John Wiley & Sons.

Kegan, R., & Lahey, L. L. (2009). *Immunity to Change: How to Overcome It and Unlock the Potential in Yourself and Your Organization*. Harvard Business Review Press.

Klayman, J., & Ha, Y. W. (1987). Confirmation, disconfirmation, and information in hypothesis testing. *Psychological Review*, 94(2), 211-228.

Miller, G. A. (1956). The magical number seven, plus or minus two: Some limits on my capacity for processing information. *Psychological Review*, 63(2), 81-97.

Pfeffer, J., & Sutton, R. I. (2000). *The Knowing-Doing Gap: How Smart Companies Turn Knowledge into Action*. Harvard Business School Press.

Business and Management Research

Collins, J. (2001). *Good to Great: Why Some Companies Make the Leap... and Others Don't.* HarperBusiness.

Collins, J., & Porras, J. I. (1994). *Built to Last: Successful Habits of Visionary Companies.* HarperBusiness.

Gallup. (2020). *State of the Global Workplace.* Gallup Press.

Gallup. (2023). *State of the American Manager.* Gallup Press.

Kotter, J. P. (1996). *Leading Change.* Harvard Business Review Press.

Lencioni, P. (2002). *The Five Dysfunctions of a Team: A Leadership Fable.* Jossey-Bass.

McKinsey & Company. (2020). Leadership in a crisis: Responding to the coronavirus outbreak and future challenges. *McKinsey Global Institute.*

Zenger, J., & Folkman, J. (2022). *The Trifecta of Trust: The Proven Formula for Building and Restoring Trust.* McGraw-Hill.

Leadership Development and Effectiveness

Blanchard, K., Zigarmi, P., & Zigarmi, D. (2013). *Leadership and the One Minute Manager: Increasing Effectiveness Through Situational Leadership II.* William Morrow.

Center for Creative Leadership. (2019). *The State of Leadership Development.* CCL Press.

Development Dimensions International. (2018). *Global Leadership Forecast 2018: 25 Research Insights to Fuel Your People Strategy.* DDI Press.

Harvard Business Review. (2019). The future of leadership development. *Harvard Business Review*, 97(2), 40-48.

Crisis and Change Management

Barton, L. (2001). *Crisis in Organizations II*. South-Western College Publishing.

Heifetz, R., Grashow, A., & Linsky, M. (2009). *The Practice of Adaptive Leadership: Tools and Tactics for Changing Your Organization and the World*. Harvard Business Review Press.

Lerbinger, O. (2012). *The Crisis Manager: Facing Disasters, Conflicts, and Failures*. Routledge.

Systems Thinking and Implementation

Meadows, D. (2008). *Thinking in Systems: A Primer*. Chelsea Green Publishing.

Senge, P. M. (1990). *The Fifth Discipline: The Art and Practice of the Learning Organization*. Doubleday.

Communication and Conflict Resolution

Fisher, R., Ury, W., & Patton, B. (2011). *Getting to Yes: Negotiating Agreement Without Giving In*. Penguin Books.

Patterson, K., Grenny, J., McMillan, R., & Switzler, A. (2012). *Crucial Conversations: Tools for Talking When Stakes Are High*. McGraw-Hill.

Rosenberg, M. B. (2003). *Nonviolent Communication: A Language of Life*. Puddle Dancer Press.

Ethics and Values-Based Leadership

Brown, M. E., & Treviño, L. K. (2006). Ethical leadership: A review and future directions. *The Leadership Quarterly*, 17(6), 595-616.

Cloud, H. (2006). *Integrity: The Courage to Meet the Demands of Reality*. HarperBusiness.

Ethics and Compliance Initiative. (2018). *Global Business Ethics Survey*. ECI Press.

Customer and Stakeholder Leadership

Freeman, R. E. (1984). *Strategic Management: A Stakeholder Approach*. Cambridge University Press.

Reichheld, F. F. (2003). *The One Number You Need to Grow*. Harvard Business Review Press.

Team Dynamics and Psychological Safety

Google. (2015). *Project Aristotle: What Makes a Team Effective*. Google re: Work.

Hackman, J. R. (2002). *Leading Teams: Setting the Stage for Great Performances*. Harvard Business Review Press.

Tuckman, B. W. (1965). Developmental sequence in small groups. *Psychological Bulletin*, 63(6), 384-399.

Industry and Consulting Reports

Deloitte. (2020). *The Future of Leadership: Rise of Human Leadership*. Deloitte Insights.

McKinsey & Company. (2019). *Leadership in the 21st Century.* McKinsey Global Institute.

PwC. (2020). *22nd Annual Global CEO Survey: Leadership Perspectives.* PricewaterhouseCoopers.

Government and Military Leadership Research

U.S. Army. (2019). *Army Leadership and the Profession.* Department of the Army.

U.S. Navy. (2018). *Naval Leadership Development Framework.* Department of the Navy.

International Leadership Research

Centre for Creative Leadership (Europe). (2018). *Global Leadership Development Trends.* CCL International.

INSEAD. (2019). *The Global Executive MBA Leadership Survey.* INSEAD Business School.

Note: This reference list includes foundational academic research, business books, and empirical studies that inform the A-E-I-O-U framework.

For current Terminal Degree Publishers books and speaking/consulting opportunities, visit my portfolio of businesses at *www.delung.com.*

www.ingramcontent.com/pod-product-compliance
Lightning Source LLC
Chambersburg PA
CBHW022051210326
41519CB00054B/312